Lecture Notes in Computer Science 11759

More information about this series at http://www.springer.com/series/7410

Robert Krimmer · Melanie Volkamer ·
Veronique Cortier · Bernhard Beckert ·
Ralf Küsters · Uwe Serdült ·
David Duenas-Cid (Eds.)

Electronic Voting

4th International Joint Conference, E-Vote-ID 2019
Bregenz, Austria, October 1–4, 2019
Proceedings

 Springer

Editors
Robert Krimmer ⓘ
Department of Innovation and Governance
Tallinn University of Technology
Tallinn, Estonia

Veronique Cortier
Equipe Cassis, Bat A
LORIA
Vandoeuvre-lès-Nancy, France

Ralf Küsters
University of Stuttgart
Stuttgart, Baden-Württemberg, Germany

David Duenas-Cid ⓘ
Tallinn University of Technology
Tallinn, Estonia

Melanie Volkamer ⓘ
Karlsruhe Institute of Technology
Karlsruhe, Baden-Württemberg, Germany

Bernhard Beckert ⓘ
Karlsruhe Institute of Technology (KIT)
Karlsruhe, Baden-Württemberg, Germany

Uwe Serdült ⓘ
Zentrum für Demokratie Aarau ZDA
Aarau, Switzerland

ISSN 0302-9743   ISSN 1611-3349   (electronic)
Lecture Notes in Computer Science
ISBN 978-3-030-30624-3   ISBN 978-3-030-30625-0   (eBook)
https://doi.org/10.1007/978-3-030-30625-0

LNCS Sublibrary: SL4 – Security and Cryptology

This Springer imprint is published by the registered company Springer Nature Switzerland AG
The registered company address is: Gewerbestrasse 11, 6330 Cham, Switzerland

Preface

This volume contains papers presented at E-Vote-ID 2019, the 4th International Joint Conference on Electronic Voting, held during October 1–4, 2019, in Bregenz, Austria. It resulted from the merging of EVOTE and Vote-ID and counting up to 15 years since the first E-Vote conference in Austria. Since the first conference in 2004, over 1,000 experts have attended the venue, including scholars, practitioners, authorities, electoral managers, vendors, and PhD Students. The conference collected the most relevant debates on the development of Electronic Voting, from aspects relating to security and usability through to practical experiences and applications of voting systems, also including legal, social, or political aspects, amongst others; turning out to be an important global referent in relation to this issue.

Also, this year, the conference consisted of:

- Security, Usability, and Technical Issues Track
- Administrative, Legal, Political, and Social Issues Track
- Election and Practical Experiences Track
- PhD Colloquium, Poster, and Demo Session on the day before the conference

E-VOTE-ID 2019 received 45 submissions, being, each of them, reviewed by 3 to 5 Program Committee members, using a double-blind review process. As a result, 13 papers were accepted for this volume, representing 29% of the submitted proposals. The selected papers cover a wide range of topics connected with electronic voting, including experiences and revisions of the real uses of E-voting systems and corresponding processes in elections.

We would also like to thank the German Informatics Society (Gesellschaft für Informatik) with its ECOM working group for their partnership over many years. Further we would like to thank the Swiss Federal Chancellery for their kind support. Special thanks go to the members of the international Program Committee for their hard work in reviewing, discussing, and shepherding papers. They ensured the high quality of these proceedings with their knowledge and experience.

October 2019

Robert Krimmer
Melanie Volkamer
Véronique Cortier
Bernhard Beckert
Ralf Küsters
Uwe Serdült
David Duenas-Cid

Preface

Organization

Program Committee

Marta Aranyossy	Corvinus University of Budapest, Hungary
Myrto Arapinis	The University of Edinburgh, UK
Jordi Barrat i Esteve	eVoting Legal Lab, Spain
Bernhard Beckert	Karlsruhe Institute of Technology, Germany
Josh Benaloh	Microsoft, USA
David Bismark	Votato, Sweden
Nadja Braun-Binder	University of Zurich, Switzerland
Christian Bull	The Norwegian Ministry of Local Government and Regional Development, Norway
Susanne Caarls	Election Consultant, The Netherlands
Gianpiero Catozzi	UNDP, USA
Veronique Cortier	CNRS, Loria, France
Ardita Driza Maurer	Zentrum für Demokratie Aarau, Zurich University, Switzerland
David Duenas-Cid	Tallinn University of Technology, Estonia, and Kozminski University, Poland
Noella Edelmann	Danube University Krems, Austria
Ulle Endriss	University of Amsterdam, The Netherlands
Aleksander Essex	University of Western Ontario, Canada
Joshua Franklin	National Institute of Standards and Technology, USA
David Galindo	University of Birmingham, UK
Micha Germann	University of Bath, UK
J. Paul Gibson	Mines Télécom, France
Kristian Gjøsteen	Norwegian University of Science and Technology, Norway
Nicole Goodman	University of Toronto, Canada
Rajeev Gore	The Australian National University, Australia
Ruediger Grimm	University of Koblenz, Germany
Rolf Haenni	Bern University of Applied Sciences, Switzerland
Thomas Haines	Queensland University of Technology, Australia
Thad Hall	MPR, USA
Jörg Helbach	Rheinische Fachhochschule Köln, Germany
Toby James	University of East Anglia, UK
Tarmo Kalvet	Tallinn University of Technology, Estonia
Reto Koenig	Berne University of Applied Sciences, Switzerland
Robert Krimmer	Tallinn University of Technology, Estonia
Ralf Kuesters	University of Stuttgart, Germany
Oksana Kulyk	ITU Copenhagen, Denmark

Contents

E-Voting – An Overview of the Development in the Past 15 Years and Current Discussions

Robert Krimmer[1] [iD], Melanie Volkamer[2] [iD],
and David Duenas-Cid[1,3(✉)] [iD]

[1] Tallinn University of Technology, Akadeemia tee 3, 12618 Tallinn, Estonia
{robert.krimmer,david.duenas}@taltech.ee
[2] Karlsruhe Institute of Technology, Kaiserstr. 89, 76131 Karlsruhe, Germany
melanie.volkamer@kit.edu
[3] Kozminski University, Jagiellonska 57/59, 03-301 Warsaw, Poland

Abstract. This opening article introduces the Fourth International Joint Conference on Electronic Voting and, on the occasion of the 15 years since the first E-Vote conference in Austria, presents an analysis of the network of co-authorships based on the books published by the Electronic Voting Conference Series. The goal of the analysis is to provide an overview of the development of the network of authors involved in the conference and to give some insights on the internal dynamics of collaboration within the field. Its comprehension sheds light on the creation of influence, internal norms and performance of the publications, enlarging the knowledge on the field and highlighting the contribution of the conferences on its development.

Keywords: E-Vote-ID Conference series · Network of co-authorships · Social network analysis

1 Looking Back in Time: A Network Analysis

On the occasion of celebrating the first 15 years since starting the Electronic Voting Conference Series, we introduce an opening chapter to conduct a retrospective analysis of evolution of the Conference with regards to its impact on creating a community of scholars interested in this field. After these years elapsing, the network of scholars working on it has increased, but are no more certain of its extent than the personal perceptions derived from interactions between colleagues. In our humble opinion, one of the main successes of these 15 years of conferences on electronic voting has been the contribution to the consolidation of a field of research and to the creation of a regular meeting point for the researchers interested in the topic. We assume that these meetings helped to create new connections that consolidated in common projects and publications. In order to shed some light on the impact of the conference, we conducted an analysis of the network of scholars created amongst the participants in the conference, based on their collaborative work. As Cugmas et al. [6] cite, there are different ways to collaborate scientifically [25], but most are invisible [26]: collaboration involving a division of labor, service collaboration, providing access to research equipment, the transmission of know-how, mutual stimulation, and trusted assessment. Amongst the "visible" and formal ones, the same authors [5] reference six indicators of collaborative relationships between scientists [12]: co-authorship; shared editing of publications; joint supervision of PhD projects; writing research proposals together; participation in formal research programs; and jointly organizing scientific conferences.

In this analysis we will focus on one particular type of collaboration, the network resulting from the collaboration in common published papers. Networks of co-authorships have been analyzed in diverse fields such as digital libraries [29], organizational studies [2] or healthcare [7], and they normally share a common background sustained by the idea that collaboration is a basic element of academic life as it increases the productivity of the researcher [27] and impact of his/her research [10], helping to increase the citation rate for publications [31] and the overall quality of research [15]. This process helps to weave a wider network of interconnected researchers together, contributes to sharing resources that are relevant in the field, such as information, common understanding and knowledge [28], and serves as a way of introduce new members (PhD students, for example) to the field of research [1].

On the other hand, analyzing social networks helps us describe and understand the underlying processes in social relations. As Fitzhugh and Butts [9] describe, the structural influence of countless social processes rarely occur in isolation, but in relation to the social network in which they are inserted. Networks allow us to understand, for example, how interaction processes are influenced by the homophilic tendency to relate to people whom we are similar to [30], how networks expand and create relational clusters [35] or how weak connections can bring new opportunities for existing relationships [11]. In this case, formalization of informal relations (as a co-authored publication) may be considered a representation of a common set of interests and goals, crystalizing in a common joint project (a research or a publication), fostering the exchange of information and the improving the resulting work. The accumulative process of creating and developing networks of collaboration helps to create internal dynamics and implicit rules in a given environment. Every organizational environment (field) is defined by a non-written set of standards and norms, behavioral patterns and dynamics and certain forms of capital that help us navigate within it, and to understand how the environment works when you are submerged in it [8]. Following this approach, a field must be conceptualized as a configuration of relationships between nodes represented in a network and the positions that those nodes happen to occupy [8]. The use and analysis of networks helps reveal the internal dynamics of a given field, and to understand the different symbolic positions and strategies followed by their components. Assuming that the Electronic Voting Conference Series is a representation of the electronic voting community, and understanding the network of co-authorships as a representation of internal dynamics in this field of research, analyzing the resulting network gives us clues for detecting how this particular field of knowledge works and to celebrate the contribution of the conference series to the creation, development and consolidation of this field.

2 Methodology

We analyze the network of co-authorships on books resulting from the E-Vote, Vote-ID and E-Vote-ID Conference series in this paper. The data regarding publications, co-authorships and citations has been extracted from the profile in Google Scholar which compiles all the information on the Electronic Voting Conference Series[1]. The data was extracted using the Harzing Publish or Perish (version 6)[2] software, a program for looking up scholarly citations and calculating impact metrics. The data was analyzed using Gephi (Version 0.9.2)[3], a program for manipulating and visualizing network graphs.

The data presented here consists of an exploratory analysis of evolution of the network of co-authorships[4] as an indicator for creating a structure of scholars around (and thanks to) the electronic voting conference series and its insights. The relations between nodes (edges) are considered as undirected (two nodes are related, being irrelevant the direction of the relation), and the analysis (Number of nodes connected, Betweenness, PageRank, Detection of hubs) is done taking the cumulative network (2004-2018) as an analytical frame.

3 Analysis

A total of 14 books has been published resulting from the presentations held in the conference [3, 13, 14, 16–24, 32, 33], including a total of 228 articles and 628 collaborators, between authors and editors, since 2004. These publications have been cited up to 2.764 times, an average of 184,3 times per year and 12,1 times per article[5]. Co-authoring articles seems to be the most common practice in the conference series, since just 20% of the articles published are by a single author (Fig. 1).

To create the co-authorship network, we identified every author and publication as a node in the network and every collaboration as an edge connecting the different nodes involved: authors and publications. As a result, we have a network composed of 616 nodes and 1.518 edges[6]. The process creating the network (see Fig. 2) was gradual, up until the current configuration of the network. The nodes are of different sizes depending on their *degree* (the number of nodes they are connected to), highlighting those nodes that are more "popular" in terms of shared publications. The ten most popular nodes are those which had been more active in publishing, co-authoring and involved in co-editing some of the conference proceedings (see Table 1).

---

[1] scholar.google.com/citations?user=KsBkbjkAAAAJ&hl=en (Last Access, 7 May 2019).

[2] Available at: harzing.com/resources/publish-or-perish?source=pop_6.46.6370.7005 (Last Access, 7 May 2019).

[3] Available at: gephi.org/ (Last Access, 7 May 2019).

[4] Co-Editions are included as Co-Authorships.

[5] Last Update of citations, April 2019, Publish or Perish.

[6] Note that the total number of nodes does not correspond to the sum of authors and publications, due to the fact many researchers published more than one text, and, therefore, they are counted just once.

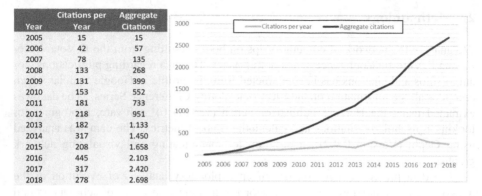

Year	Citations per Year	Aggregate Citations
2005	15	15
2006	42	57
2007	78	135
2008	133	268
2009	131	399
2010	153	552
2011	181	733
2012	218	951
2013	182	1.133
2014	317	1.450
2015	208	1.658
2016	445	2.103
2017	317	2.420
2018	278	2.698

Fig. 1. Evolution in the number of citations

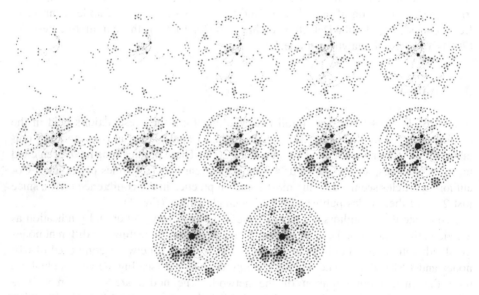

Fig. 2. Cumulative evolution of the network of co-authorships 2004-2018 (Every network corresponds to one Edition of the Electronic Voting Conference Series. The nodes are weighted according to the number of nodes they are connected to, the larger the number, the greater the number of contacts.)

The degree is considered as a measure of centrality, as it allows to identify relevant nodes in a network according to their "popularity". Even so, centrality in a network is not only about being connected to many nodes, but also being connected to relevant nodes. The relevance of connections is analyzed using the *betweenness centrality* measure, which collects information on how often a node appears on the shortest path between different networks or, in other words, which are the nodes that are better placed in a network. The position occupied is directly connected to the amount of information that one node can accumulate in the network and is directly related with

Table 1. Nodes with higher degree in the network

Author	Nodes
M Volkamer	87
R Krimmer	58
V Teague	44
PYA Ryan	41
P Vora	33
C Schürmann	27
S Schneider	25
R Goré	22
A Essex	21
S Popoveniuc	21

holding symbolic power within the field. There is a tendency to correlate between having more nodes and being placed in the center of the network, but there is also a dependency on the nodes to which one is connected. For example, a strategic connection with well-connected nodes gives you a more central position than a large number of poorly connected nodes. In the case we are analyzing, shared publications with relevant nodes can influence the position in the network (see Fig. 3).

Betweenness allows us to determine which is the symbolic center of the network, and it relates to the capacity to influence other nodes in the network. Another estimate of the capacity for influencing is given by the *PageRank* measure, which estimates the relevance of one node in relation with the nodes with whom it is connected, giving a wider approach of the capacity to influence a node and being used, for example, for detecting priorities in networks [34]. Having high values of PageRank in a network represents a combined indicator of the position of a certain node in the network in relation to the capacity of the node to create a hub around it (Table 2).

The measures presented allowed us to detect the most relevant individual nodes within the network. In the case analyzed, the most relevant nodes are researchers who participated in the Conference Series in many times and managed to gather people around them with whom they shared publications. But networks extend beyond the individual position of nodes by including internal dynamics of group behavior. Combining related nodes with dense relationships with themselves create hubs of interrelated nodes, and detecting these hubs is particularly relevant for understanding the internal standards and norms for a network. In the case analyzed here, using the *Modularity* algorithm provided by Gephi, we detected a set of nodes that create hubs or clusters of interrelated nodes due to their greater interconnectedness with themselves than with the rest of the network [4], meaning, in this case, a greater collaboration in co-authoring papers (see Fig. 4). Not all the hubs have been colored to avoid interference in visualizing the network, choosing just those that represented larger numbers of scholars. The singular analysis of each hub provides interesting results but, in order to make the analysis easier, only the most paradigmatic typologies will be presented.

Depending on the internal data of each hub detected, we could find some patterns of similarity in the features and outcomes of different hubs. The main element of

Author	Betweenness
M Volkamer	251.578
R Krimmer	18.892
C Schürmann	9.710
V Teague	8.330
PYA Ryan	8.240
P Vora	6.278
J Benaloh	4.978
R Goré	4.485
J Barrat	4.340
J Helbach	3.516

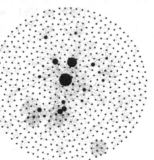

Fig. 3. Betweenness centrality

Table 2. PageRank distribution

Node	PageRank
M Volkamer	0,013
R Krimmer	0,010
C Schürmann	0,007
PYA Ryan	0,005
V Teague	0,005
P Vora	0,004
J Willemson	0,004
RM Alvarez	0,004
L Loeber	0,004
J Puiggalí	0,004

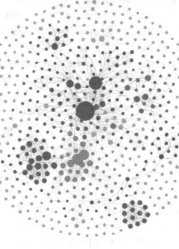

Fig. 4. Division of the network into hubs

similarity and difference relates to the typology of members composing the hub. Two different types of hub are detected in this regard, those which are created based on a diverse group of researchers interacting due to common interests and a second group of hubs that are created based on similarity of the origin of their members. Amongst the first group of hubs, the differences amongst them arise from the position they occupy in the network and the internal patterns of functioning. Amongst the second one, the difference is based on the country/environment of origin of their members. Therefore, four main geographically based groups were detected: An Estonian hub, a Swiss one, an Australian one and one based on their relation with the private vendor Scytl. The first three (Estonian, Swiss and Australian) are composed of scholars who are researching the countries where internet voting systems are deployed, showing the research attractiveness of pioneering examples. The Scytl hub is created around the publications done by researchers link to a private vendor that offers its services worldwide. Their publications, therefore, are generally connected to the places where they deliver their services (Table 3).

A group of three hubs has been defined as central hubs (I, II and III). The reason is that they all share a high degree of betweenness as a common salient feature. They gather a relevant number of researchers who occupy the centrality of the network, but they differ in the internal structure of the hub. While central hubs I and III display a clear priority (Melanie Volkamer and Robert Krimmer for Central hub I -see Fig. 5- and Carsten Schürmann and Jordi Barrat for Central hub III -Fig. 7), Central hub II (Fig. 6) presents a softer and more horizontal distribution, with a higher average interconnectedness (represented by a higher average and median degree). The second central hub also joined the Conference Series, on average, at a later stage, when some internal dynamics had already been created and this might also help create a different relational structure based on commonality of interests[7].

Regarding the other two non-geographically based hubs, named as peripheral and horizontal hubs, these portray a different perception. The peripheral hub (Fig. 8) was more active in the past and now only some of their members still attend the conference and, probably, they will jump across to a different hub in the future if their publishing activity continues with active members of the community. This "lethargy" moved the position of this hub to a non-central space (low betweeness) but with adequate proximity and impact on the overall network. The horizontal hub (Fig. 9) follows the pattern presented for the Central hub II, representing a group of scholars with intense internal dynamics and mutual interconnectedness (higher degree and average number of authors) which might take on more central positions in the future. We would like to remind the reader that networks are live and change, and that this description is just a fixed snapshot in time of a temporary reality that will evolve in years to come.

Finally, the geographically based hubs (Estonia –Fig. 10-, Switzerland -Fig. 11-, Australia -Fig. 12- and Scytl -Fig. 13-) tend to have smaller numbers of researchers and are structured around the link to a certain environment relating to use or research

---

[7] For reading the forthcoming figures: in order to ease the comprehension and comparison of data, average values for all the network have been calculated (Index 1). The data for each hub is presented in comparison with the average value.

Table 3. Main clusters detected in the network

	Central hub I	Central hub II	Horizontal hub	Central hub III	Peripheral hub
Number of members	47	34	28	18	16
Average Degree	8,43	11,09	11,70	6,61	5,63
Median Degree	4	8	12	6	5
Density	0,07	0,14	0,24	0,13	0,16
Average Betweenness	1.114	840	354	862	38
Average Closeness	0,31	0,30	0,25	0,30	0,42
Average Year of first publication	2.010	2.013	2.011	2.012	2.009
Number of Publications	28	19	12	13	12
Average cites per year	1,44	2,32	0,98	0,73	1,76
Average number of authors	3,18	3,89	4,22	2,38	2,50
	Estonian hub	Australian hub	Swiss hub	Scytl hub	Total
Number of members	14	10	9	9	392
Average Degree	6,14	7,30	9,11	6,56	6,24
Median Degree	4	5	7	5	4
Density	0,19	0,34	0,26	0,29	0,01
Average Betweenness	264	449	465	477	342
Average Closeness	0,26	0,23	0,27	0,26	0,35
Average Year of first publication	2.014	2.016	2.012	2.012	2.011
Number of Publications	10	7	12	8	222
Average cites per year	3,86	1,18	1,86	1,99	1,51
Average number of authors	2,80	3,14	2,92	2,88	2,81

Name	Degree	Betweenness	PageRank
M Volkamer	87	25.158	0,013
R Krimmer	58	18.892	0,010
R Grimm	20	908	0,004
S Neumann	19	805	0,003
J Helbach	12	3.516	0,002
K Reinhard	11	1.314	0,003
N Meissner	10	987	0,002
C Feier	9	200	0,001
M Traxl	9	145	0,001
A Prosser	8	4	0,001

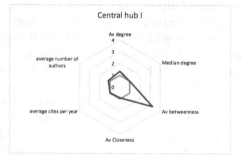

Fig. 5. Values for Central Hub I (Note that the scale for Fig. 5 is different)

Name	Degree	Betweenness	PageRank
V Teague	44	8.330	0,005
PYA Ryan	41	8.240	0,005
S Schneider	25	1.951	0,002
R Wen	19	694	0,002
Z Xia	19	200	0,002
J Heather	17	78	0,002
J Benaloh	16	4.978	0,002
C Culnane	15	257	0,002
JA Halderman	14	1.026	0,002
D Demirel	13	304	0,002

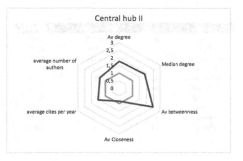

Fig. 6. Values for central hub II

Name	Degree	Betweenness	PageRank
C Schürmann	27	9.710	0,007
J Barrat	17	4.340	0,004
O Pereira	11	1.458	0,003
B Goldsmith	6	0	0,001
D Jandura	6	0	0,001
J Turner	6	0	0,001
M Chevallier	6	0	0,001
N Kersting	6	0	0,001
NB Binder	6	0	0,001
R Sharma	6	0	0,001

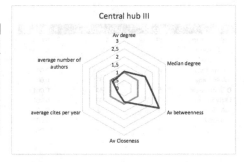

Fig. 7. Values for central hub III

Name	Degree	Betweenness	PageRank
RM Alvarez	13	210	0,004
J Pomares	9	22	0,003
T Hall	8	191	0,003
G Katz	7	11	0,002
L Loeber	7	98	0,004
T Ovejero	6	34	0,002
E Calvo	5	5	0,002
G Lopez	5	3	0,002
I Levin	5	3	0,002
M Escolar	5	5	0,002

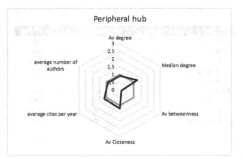

Fig. 8. Values for peripheral hub

on Electronic Voting. In the Estonian, Swiss and Australian cases, the connection is based on implementation of Electronic Voting in their electoral systems, with many publications connected to the observation of use and development, impact, improvements or conditions, amongst others. In the Estonian case, the performance in terms of citations per publication works clearly better than average, showing the general interest of the community by the application of Internet Voting in a real context.

Name	Degree	Betweenness	PageRank
P Vora	33	6.278	0,004
A Essex	21	223	0,003
S Popoveniuc	21	1.658	0,003
R Rivest	20	232	0,003
R Carback	19	56	0,002
D Chaum	18	27	0,002
F Zagorski	18	41	0,002
J Clark	15	640	0,002
A Florescu	14	8	0,002
J Rubio	14	8	0,002

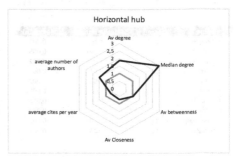

Fig. 9. Values for horizontal hub

Name	Degree	Betweenness	PageRank
J Willemson	19	2.301	0,004
S Heiberg	17	541	0,003
P Vinkel	9	84	0,002
T Martens	6	656	0,002
A Koitmae	5	37	0,001
D Duenas-Cid	5	37	0,001
I Krivonosova	5	37	0,001
A Parsovs	3	0	0,001
I Kubjas	3	0	0,001
K Krips	3	0	0,001

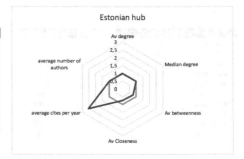

Fig. 10. Values for the Estonian hub

Name	Degree	Betweenness	PageRank
R Haenni	19	718	0,003
RE Koenig	19	2.481	0,003
O Spycher	12	274	0,003
E Dubuis	9	12	0,002
P Locher	7	43	0,001
A Driza-Maurer	6	657	0,002
A Weber	4	0	0,001
G Taglioni	4	0	0,001
M Schlapfer	2	0	0,001

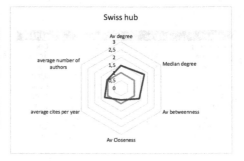

Fig. 11. Values for the Swiss hub

For the other case, the hub relates more to creating a cluster of expertise around their professional practice and the experiences and research carried out using the cases where Scytl offers its services.

Name	Degree	Betweenness	PageRank
R Goré	22	4.485	0,003
D Pattinson	12	4	0,001
M Tiwari	9	2	0,001
MK Ghale	7	1	0,001
LB Moses	5	0	0,001
R Levy	5	0	0,001
T Meumann	5	1	0,001
B Beckert	3	0	0,001
JE Dawson	3	0	0,001
E Lebedeva	2	0	0,001

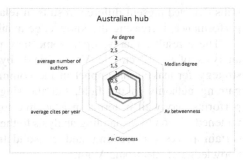

Fig. 12. Values for the Australian hub

Name	Degree	Betweenness	PageRank
J Puiggalí	17	2.750	0,004
S Guasch	11	799	0,002
J Cucurull	7	631	0,002
A Fornós	5	1	0,001
J Lladós	5	1	0,001
JI Toledo	5	1	0,001
D Galindo	3	0	0,001
M Soriano	3	109	0,001
V Morales-Rocha	3	1	0,001

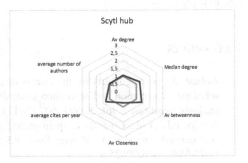

Fig. 13. Values for the Scytl hub

4 Conclusions

This analysis allowed a better understanding of internal patterns of functioning for the field created regarding the Electronic Voting Conference Series. Every field or research creates a set of internal and or written standards and norms, by standardizing behaviors and activities which in turn become accepted in the community. In this case, starting with the assumption that the network of co-authorships represents a formal representation of the real network of relationships in the field, through analyzing it, we were able to detect which are the more central nodes (researchers) in the field and the priorities being created at the same time. A common publication can be understood to be an indicator of social capital and symbolic power, as it means a common interest in publishing together (social capital) and a form of academic respect of the researcher's potentials (symbolic power). The maximization and dispersion of co-authored publications involves a greater centrality in the network and, in practical terms, increasing the authority on the topic in the research field.

Detecting hubs helps visualize the existence of different relational environments and secondary centralities within the same network. The presence of smaller but closely interrelated networks within the network shows the existence of partial priorities and differentiated publishing strategies or patterns of collaboration. Based on the results, the hubs detected present different results in relation with to position, interconnection and performance, increasing the knowledge available on the field and its dynamics.

These results, finally, open some new possibilities for future research on meta-analysis of the Electronic Voting field, by questioning which is the best possible strategy for making an impact in the community. Centrality seems to work well for gaining authority in the field, but the singularity of certain cases and experiences performs very well in terms of academic impact or citations. This research could be widened in soon by expanding analysis to the citation network, deepening the impact of certain pieces for creating and consolidating of the field and, by extension, the knowledge of Electronic Voting.

Acknowledgements. The work of Krimmer and Duenas received support from ETAG personal research grant 1361.

References

1. Abbasi, A., et al.: Identifying the effects of co-authorship networks on the performance of scholars: a correlation and regression analysis of performance measures and social network analysis measures. J. Inf. **5**, 594–607 (2011). https://doi.org/10.1016/j.joi.2011.05.007
2. Acedo, F.J., et al.: Co-authorship in management and organizational studies: an empirical and network analysis. J. Manag. Stud. **43**(5), 957–983 (2006). https://doi.org/10.1111/j.1467-6486.2006.00625.x
3. Alkassar, A., Volkamer, M. (eds.): Vote-ID 2007. LNCS, vol. 4896. Springer, Heidelberg (2007). https://doi.org/10.1007/978-3-540-77493-8
4. Blondel, V.D., et al.: Fast unfolding of communities in large networks. J. Stat. Mech. Theory Exp. (2008). https://doi.org/10.1088/1742-5468/2008/10/P10008
5. Cugmas, M., et al.: Scientific co-authorship networks. In: Doreian, P., et al. (eds.) Advances in Network Clustering and Blockmodeling, p. 460. Wiley-Blackwell, Hoboken (2019)
6. Cugmas, M., et al.: The stability of co-authorship structures. Scientometrics (2016). https://doi.org/10.1007/s11192-015-1790-4
7. E Fonseca, B. de P.F., et al.: Co-authorship network analysis in health research: Method and potential use. Heal Res. Policy. Syst. **14**(34), 1–10 (2016). https://doi.org/10.1186/s12961-016-0104-5
8. Emirbayer, M., Johnson, V.: Bourdieu and organizational analysis. Theory Soc. (2008). https://doi.org/10.1007/s11186-007-9052-y
9. Fitzhugh, S.M., Butts, C.T.: Patterns of co-membership: techniques for identifying subgraph composition. Soc. Networks. **55**, 1–10 (2018). https://doi.org/10.1016/j.socnet.2018.03.006
10. Gazni, A., Didegah, F.: Investigating different types of research collaboration and citation impact: a case study of Harvard University's publications. Scientometrics **87**, 251–265 (2011). https://doi.org/10.1007/s11192-011-0343-8
11. Granovetter, M.: The strength of weak ties: a network theory revisited. Sociol. Theory (2006). https://doi.org/10.2307/202051
12. De Haan, J.: Authorship patterns in Dutch sociology. Scientometrics **39**(2), 197–208 (1997). https://doi.org/10.1007/BF02457448
13. Haenni, R., Koenig, Reto E., Wikström, D. (eds.): VoteID-2015. LNCS, vol. 9269. Springer, Cham (2015). https://doi.org/10.1007/978-3-319-22270-7

14. Heather, J., Schneider, S., Teague, V. (eds.): Vote-ID 2013. LNCS, vol. 7985. Springer, Heidelberg (2013). https://doi.org/10.1007/978-3-642-39185-9
15. Katz, J.S., Martin, B.R.: What is research collaboration? Res. Policy **26**(1), 1–18 (1997). https://doi.org/10.1016/S0048-7333(96)00917-1
16. Kiayias, A., Lipmaa, H. (eds.): Vote-ID 2011. LNCS, vol. 7187. Springer, Heidelberg (2012). https://doi.org/10.1007/978-3-642-32747-6
17. Krimmer, R., et al. (eds.): E-Vote-ID 2018. LNCS, vol. 11143. Springer, Cham (2018). https://doi.org/10.1007/978-3-030-00419-4
18. Krimmer, R.: Electronic Voting 2006 2nd International Workshop. GI Lecture Notes in Informatics, Bregenz (2006)
19. Krimmer, R., et al. (eds.): E-Vote-ID 2016. LNCS, vol. 10141. Springer, Cham (2017). https://doi.org/10.1007/978-3-319-52240-1
20. Krimmer, R., Volkamer, M., Braun Binder, N., Kersting, N., Pereira, O., Schürmann, C. (eds.): E-Vote-ID 2017. LNCS, vol. 10615. Springer, Cham (2017). https://doi.org/10.1007/978-3-319-68687-5
21. Krimmer, R., Grimm, R.: Electronic Voting 2008 (EVOTE 2008) 3rd International Conference. GI Lecture Notes in Informatics, Bregenz (2008)
22. Krimmer, R., Grimm, R.: Electronic Voting 2010 (EVOTE 2010) 4 th International Conference. GI Lecture Notes in Informatics, Bregenz (2010)
23. Krimmer, R., Volkamer, M.: 6th International Conference on Electronic Voting, EVOTE 2014, Lochau/Bregenz, Austria, 28–31 October 2014. TUT Press, Bregenz (2014)
24. Kripp, M., et al. (eds.): 5th International Conference on Electronic Voting 2012. Köllen Druck + Verlag GmbH, Bonn (2012)
25. Laudel, G.: Interdisziplinäre Forschungskooperation: Erfolgsbedingungen der Institution Sonderforschungsbereich. Sigma Ed, Berlin (1999)
26. Laudel, G.: What do we measure by co-authorships? Res. Eval. **11**(1), 3–15 (2002)
27. Lee, S., Bozeman, B.: The impact of research collaboration on scientific productivity. Soc. Stud. Sci. **35**(5), 673–702 (2005). https://doi.org/10.1177/0306312705052359
28. Li, E.Y., et al.: Co-authorship networks and research impact: a social capital perspective. Res. Policy **42**(9), 1515–1530 (2013). https://doi.org/10.1016/j.respol.2013.06.012
29. Liu, X., et al.: Co-authorship networks in the digital library research community. Inf. Process. Manag. **41**, 1462–1480 (2005). https://doi.org/10.1016/j.ipm.2005.03.012
30. McPherson, M., et al.: Birds of a feather: homophily in social networks. Annu. Rev. Sociol. **27**(1), 415–444 (2001). https://doi.org/10.1146/annurev.soc.27.1.415
31. Narin, F., et al.: Scientific co-operation in Europe and the citation of multinationally authored papers. Scientometrics **21**(3), 313–323 (1991). https://doi.org/10.1007/BF02093973
32. Prosser, A., Krimmer, R.: Electronic Voting in Europe – Technology, Law, Politics and Society. GI Lecture Notes in Informatics, Bregenz (2004)
33. Ryan, Peter Y.A., Schoenmakers, B. (eds.): Vote-ID 2009. LNCS, vol. 5767. Springer, Heidelberg (2009). https://doi.org/10.1007/978-3-642-04135-8
34. Wang, R., Zhang, W., Deng, H., Wang, N., Miao, Q., Zhao, X.: Discover community leader in social network with PageRank. In: Tan, Y., Shi, Y., Mo, H. (eds.) ICSI 2013. LNCS, vol. 7929, pp. 154–162. Springer, Heidelberg (2013). https://doi.org/10.1007/978-3-642-38715-9_19
35. Wasserman, S., Faust, K.: Social Network Analysis: Methods and Applications. Cambridge University Press, Cambridge (1994)

UnclearBallot: Automated Ballot Image Manipulation

Matthew Bernhard$^{(\boxtimes)}$, Kartikeya Kandula, Jeremy Wink,
and J. Alex Halderman

Department of Electrical Engineering and Computer Science,
University of Michigan, Ann Arbor, USA
{matber,kartkand,jreremy,jhalderm}@umich.edu

Abstract. As paper ballots and post-election audits gain increased adoption in the United States, election technology vendors are offering products that allow jurisdictions to review ballot images—digital scans produced by optical-scan voting machines—in their post-election audit procedures. Jurisdictions including the state of Maryland rely on such image audits as an alternative to inspecting the physical paper ballots. We show that image audits can be reliably defeated by an attacker who can run malicious code on the voting machines or election management system. Using computer vision techniques, we develop an algorithm that automatically and seamlessly manipulates ballot images, moving voters' marks so that they appear to be votes for the attacker's preferred candidate. Our implementation is compatible with many widely used ballot styles, and we show that it is effective using a large corpus of ballot images from a real election. We also show that the attack can be delivered in the form of a malicious Windows scanner driver, which we test with a scanner that has been certified for use in vote tabulation by the U.S. Election Assistance Commission. These results demonstrate that post-election audits must inspect physical ballots, not merely ballot images, if they are to strongly defend against computer-based attacks on widely used voting systems.

Keywords: Optical scan · Paper ballots · Image manipulation · Drivers · Image processing

1 Introduction

Elections that cannot provide sufficient evidence of their results may fail to adequately gain public confidence in their outcomes. Numerous solutions have been posited to this problem [9], but none has been as elegant, efficient, and immediately practical as post-election audits [21,25,39]. These audits—in particular, ones that seek to limit the risk of confirming an outcome that resulted from undue manipulation—are one of the most important layers of defense for election security [32].

© Springer Nature Switzerland AG 2019
R. Krimmer et al. (Eds.): E-Vote-ID 2019, LNCS 11759, pp. 14–31, 2019.
https://doi.org/10.1007/978-3-030-30625-0_2

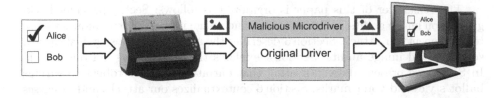

Fig. 1. Attack overview—A voter's paper ballot is scanned by a ballot tabulator, producing a digital image. Malware in the tabulator—in our proof-of-concept, a microdriver that wraps the scanner device driver—alters the ballot image before it is counted or stored. A digital audit shows only the manipulated image.

Risk-limiting audits (RLAs) rely on sampling robust, independent evidence trails created by voter-verified paper ballots. However, other types of post-election audits are gaining popularity in the marketplace. In particular, Clear Ballot, an election technology vendor in the United States, pioneered audit software designed to perform audits of *images* of ballots which have been scanned and tabulated, which we shall refer to as "image audits". Other vendors have adopted support for this kind of audit, and one U.S. state, Maryland, relies on image audits to provide assurances of its election results [33].

While image audits can help detect human error and aid in adjudicating mismarked ballots, we show that they cannot provide the same level of security assurance as audits of physical ballots. Since ballot images are disconnected from the actual source of truth—physical paper ballots—they do not necessarily provide reliable evidence of the outcome of an election under adversarial conditions.

In this paper, we present UnclearBallot, an attack that defeats image audits by automatically manipulating ballot images as they are scanned. Our attack leverages the same computer vision approaches used by ballot scanners to detect voter selections, but adds the ability to move marks from one target area to another. Our method is robust to inconsistent or invalid marks, and can be adapted to many ballot styles.

We validate our attack against a corpus of over 180,000 ballot images from the 2018 election in Clackamas County, Oregon, and find that UnclearBallot can move marks on 34% of the ballots while leaving no visible anomalies. We also test our attack's flexibility using six widely used styles of paper ballots, and its robustness to invalid votes using an established taxonomy of voter marks. As a proof-of-concept, we implement the attack in the form of a malicious Windows scanner driver, which we test using a commercial-off-the-shelf scanner certified for use in elections by the U.S. Election Assistance Commission.

UnclearBallot illustrates that post-election audits in traditional voting systems must involve rigorous examination of *physical ballots*, rather than ballot images, if they are to provide a strong security guarantee. Without an examination of the physical evidence, it will be difficult if not impossible to assure that computer-based tampering has not occurred.

The remainder of this paper is organized as follows: Sect. 2 provides background on image audits, ballot scanners, and image processing techniques we use to implement our attack. Section 3 describes the attack scenarios against optical scanners and image audits. Section 4 explains the methodology of our attack. In Sect. 5 we present data indicating that our attack can be robust to various ballot styles and voter marks. Section 6 contextualizes our attacks and discusses mitigations. We conclude in Sect. 7.

2   Background

Our attack takes advantage of two aspects of optical scanner image audits: the scanning and image processing techniques used by scanners, and the reliance on scanned images by image audits. Here we provide a brief discussion of both.

2.1   Ballot Images

Jones [23] put forth an analysis of the way that ballot scanners work, particularly the mark-sense variety that is most common today. All optical scanners currently sold to jurisdictions, as well as the vast majority of scanners used in practice in the U.S., rely on mark-sense technology [44]. Scanners first create a high-resolution image of a ballot as it is fed past a scan head. Software then analyzes the image to identify dark areas where marks have been made by the voter.[1] Once marks have been detected, systems may use template matching to translate marks into votes for specific candidates, typically relying on a barcode or other identifier on the ballot that specifies a ballot style to match to the scanned image.

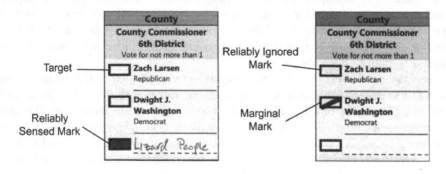

Fig. 2. Terms for parts of a marked ballot, following Jones [23].

Detecting and interpreting voter marks can be a difficult process, as voters exhibit a wide range of marking and non-marking behavior, including not filling

---

[1] The details of how marks are identified vary by hardware and scanning algorithm. See [13] for an example.

in targets all the way, resting their pens inside targets, or marking outside the target. The terms Jones developed to refer to the ballot and marks are illustrated in Fig. 2. Marks that adequately fill the target and are unambiguously interpreted as votes by the scanner are called *reliably sensed* marks, and targets that are unambiguously not filled and therefore not counted are *reliably ignored* marks. Marks of other types are deemed *marginal*, as a scanner may read or ignore them. Moreover, whether a mark should be counted as a vote is frequently governed by local election statute, so some marginal marks may be unambiguously counted or ignored under the law, even if not by the scanner.

Check   Cross   Partial   Light   Overfilled   Empty   Filled

Fig. 3. Taxonomy of voter marks adapted from Bajcsy [2], including the five leftmost marks that may be considered marginal marks.

Bajcsy et al. [2] further develops a systematization of marginal marks and develops some improvements on mark-detection algorithms to better account for them. An illustration of Bajcsy et al.'s taxonomy is shown in Fig. 3. Ji et al. [22] discuss different types of voter marks as applied to write-in votes, as well as developing an automated process for detecting and tabulating write-in selections.

2.2   Image Audits

Risk-limiting post-election audits rely on physical examination of a statistical sample of voter-marked ballots [24,26,39,40]. However, this can create logistical challenges for election officials, which has prompted some to propose relaxations to traditional audit requirements. To reduce workload, canvass audits and recounts in many states rely on retabulation of ballots through optical scanners (see the 2016 Wisconsin recount, for example [31]).

Some election vendors take retabulation audits a step further: rather than physically rescan the ballots, the voting system makes available images of all the ballots for independent evaluation after the election [15,16,42].[2] While the exact properties of these kinds of image audits vary by vendor, they typically rely on automatically retabulating all or some images of cast ballots, as well as electronic adjudication for ballots with marginal marks. These "audits" never examine the physical paper trail of ballots, which our attack exploits.

Several jurisdictions have relied on these image audits, including Cambridge, Ontario, which used Dominion's AuditMark [17], and the U.S. state of Maryland,

---

[2] While the review is made available to the public, the actual images themselves are seldom published in full out of concern for voter anonymity.

which uses Clear Ballot's ClearAudit [28]. Maryland has also codified image audits into its election code, requiring that an image audit be performed after every election [27].

3   Attack Scenarios

Elections in which voters make their selections on a physical ballot are frequently held as the gold standard for conducting a secure election [32]. However, the property that contributes most to their security, software independence [34], only exists if records computed by software are checked against records that cannot be altered by software without detection. Image audits enable election officials to view images of ballots and compare them with the election systems' representation of the particular ballot they are viewing (called a cast vote record or CVR). While these two trails of evidence may be independent from each other (for example, Clear Ballot's ClearAudit [15] technology can be used to audit a tabulation performed by a different election system altogether), they are not software independent. A clever attacker can exploit the reliance on software by both evidence trails to defeat detection.

To surreptitiously change the outcome of the election in the presence of an image audit, the attacker must alter both the tabulation result as well as the ballot images themselves. Researchers have documented numerous vulnerabilities that would allow an attacker to infect voting equipment and change tabulation results (see [10,20,30] among others), so we focus on the feasibility of manipulating ballot images once an attacker has successfully infected a machine where they are stored or processed.

The most straightforward attack scenario occurs when the ballot images are created by the same equipment that produces the CVR. In this case, the attacker can simply infect the scanner or tabulator with malware that corrupts both the CVR and the images at the same time. The attack could change the image before the tabulator processes it to generate the CVR, or directly alter both sets of records.

In some jurisdictions, the ballot images that are audited are collected in a separate process from tabulation—that is, by scanning the ballots again, as in Maryland's use of ClearAudit from 2016 [28]. In this case, the adversary has to separately attack both processes, and has to coordinate the cheating to avoid mismatches between the initial tally and the altered ballot images.

Depending on the timing of the audit, manipulation of ballot images need not be done on the fly. For example, if the ballot images are created during tabulation but the image audit does not occur until well after the election, an attacker could modify the ballot images while they are in storage.

For ease of explication, the discussion that follows assumes that ballot images are created at the time of tabulation, in a single scan. The attack we develop targets a tabulation machine and manipulates each ballot online as it is scanned.

4   Methodology

To automatically modify ballot images, an attacker can take a few approaches. One approach would be to completely replace the ballot images with ballots filled in by the attacker. However, this risks being detected if many ballots have the same handwriting, and requires sneaking these relatively large data files into the election system without being detected. For these reasons, we investigate an alternative approach: automatically and selectively doctoring the ballot scans to change the vote selections they depict.

For the attack to work successfully, we need to move voter marks to other targets without creating visible artifacts or inconsistencies. We must be able to dynamically detect target areas and marks, alter marks in a way that is consistent with the voter's other marks, and do so in a way that is undetectable to the human eye. However, there is a key insight that works in the adversary's favor: an attacker seeking to alter election results does not have to be able to change *all* ballots undetectably, only sufficiently many to swing the result. This means that the attacker's manipulation strategy is not required to be able to change *every* mark—it merely has to reliably detect *which* marks it can safely alter and change enough of them to decide the election result.

4.1   Reading the Ballot

To interpret ballot information, we rely on the same techniques that ballot scanners use to convert paper ballots into digital representations. Attackers have access to the ballot templates, as jurisdictions publish sample ballots well ahead of scheduled elections. Using template matching, an attacker does not have to perform any kind of sophisticated character recognition, they simply have to find target areas and then detect which of the targets are filled.

Our procedure to read a ballot is illustrated in Fig. 4. First, we perform template matching to extract each individual race within a ballot. Next, we use OpenCV's [11] implementation of the Hough transform to detect straight lines that separate candidates and break the race into individual panes for each candidate. Notably, the first candidate in each race may have the race title and extra information in it (see Fig. 4c), which is cropped out based on white space.

Target areas are typically printed on the ballot as either ovals or rectangles. To detect them, we construct a bounding box around the target by scanning horizontally from the left of the race and then vertically from the bottom up, and compute pixel density values. The bounds are set to the coordinates where the density values first increase and last decrease. Once we have detected all the target areas, we compute the average pixel density of the area within the bounding box to determine whether or not a target area is marked. We then use our template to convert marks into votes for candidates.

4.2   Changing Marks

Once we have identified which candidate was marked by the voter, we can move the mark to one of the other target locations we identified. If the vote is for a

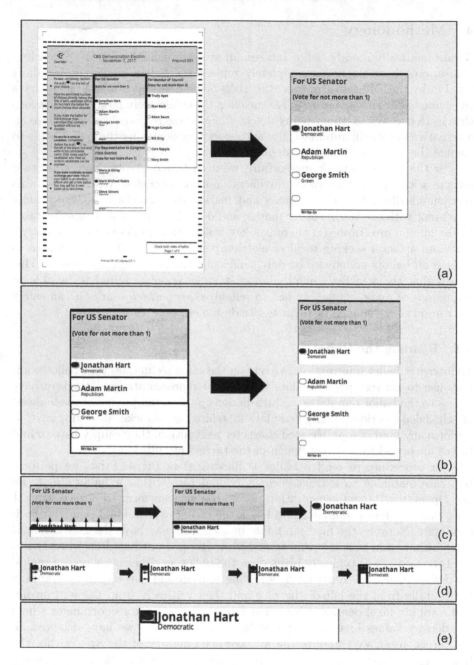

Fig. 4. Ballot manipulation algorithm—First, (a) we apply template matching to extract the race we intend to alter. Then, (b) we use Hough line transforms to separate each candidate. If the first candidate has a race title box, (c) we remove it by computing the pixel intensity differences across a straight line swept vertically from the bottom. For each candidate, (d) we identify the target and mark (if present) by doing four linear sweeps and taking pixel intensity. Finally, (e) we identify and move the mark. At each step we apply tests to detect and skip ballots where the algorithm might leave artifacts.

candidate the attacker would like to receive fewer votes—or if it is not a vote for a candidate they would like to win—the attacker can simply swap the pixels within the bounding boxes of the voter's marked candidate and an unmarked candidate. By moving marks on each ballot separately, we ensure that the voter's particular style of filling in an oval is preserved and consistent across the ballot. Figure 5 shows some marks swapped by our algorithm, and how the voters original mark is completely preserved in the process.

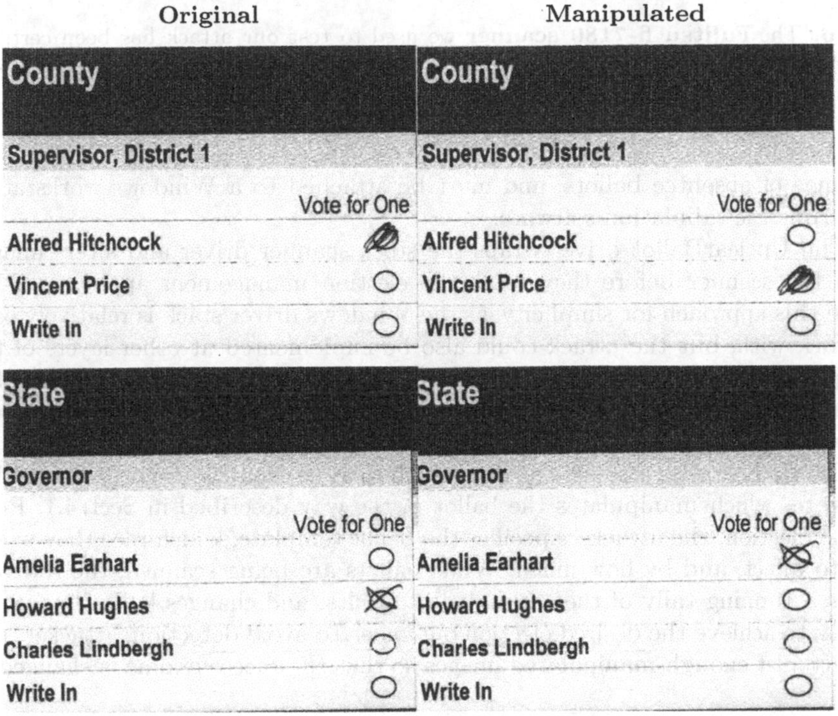

Fig. 5. **Automatically moving voter marks**—UnclearBallot seamlessly moves marks to the attacker's preferred candidate while preserving the voter's marking style. It is effective for a wide variety of marks and ballot designs. In the examples above, original ballot scans are shown on the left and manipulated images on the right.

4.3 UnclearBallot

To illustrate the attack, we created UnclearBallot, a proof-of-concept implementation packaged as a malicious Windows scanner driver, which consists of 398 lines of C++ and Python. We tested it with a Fujistu fi-7180 scanner (shown in Fig. 6), which is federally certified for use in U.S. elections as part of Clear Ballot's ClearVote system [43]. These scanners are typically used to handle small

Fig. 6. The **Fujitsu fi-7180 scanner** we used to test our attack has been certified by the U.S. Election Assistance Commission for use in voting systems. Our proof-of-concept implementation is a malicious scanner driver that alters ballots on the fly.

volumes of absentee ballots, and must be attached to a Windows workstation that runs the tabulation software.

The UnclearBallot driver wraps the stock scanner driver and alters images from the scanner before they reach the election management application. We chose this approach for simplicity, as the Windows driver stack is relatively easy to work with, but the attack could also be implemented at other layers of the computing stack. For instance, it could be even harder to detect if implemented as a malicious change to the scanner's embedded firmware. Alternatively, it could be engineered as a modification to the tabulation software itself.

Once a ballot is scanned, the resulting bitmap is sent to our image processing software, which manipulates the ballot in the way described in Sect. 4.1. Prior to the election, the attacker specifies the ballot template, which race they would like to affect, and by how much. While ballots are being scanned, the software keeps a running tally of the actual ballot results, and changes ballot images on the fly to achieve the desired election outcome. To avoid detection, attackers can specify just enough manipulated images so that the race outcome is changed.

5   Evaluation

We evaluated the performance and effectiveness of UnclearBallot using two sets of experiments. In the first set of experiments, we marked different ballot styles by hand using types of marks taxonomized by Bajcsy et al. [2]. In the second set of experiments, we processed 181,541 ballots from the 2018 election in Clackamas County, Oregon.

5.1   Testing Across Ballot Styles

In order for our application to succeed at its goal (surreptitiously changing enough scanned ballots to achieve a chosen election outcome), it must be able to detect marks that constitute valid votes as well as distinguish marks which would be noticeable if moved. The marks in the latter case represent a larger

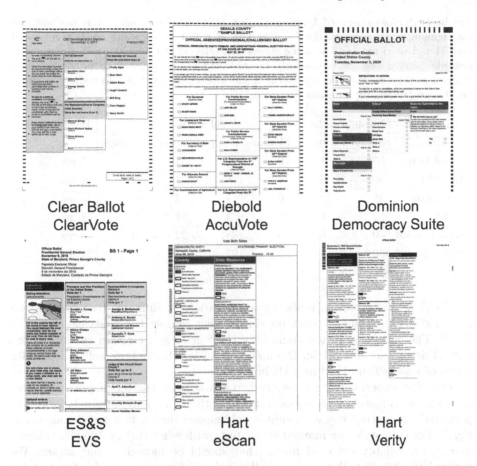

Clear Ballot
ClearVote

Diebold
AccuVote

Dominion
Democracy Suite

ES&S
EVS

Hart
eScan

Hart
Verity

Fig. 7. Ballots Styles—We tested ballot designs from five U.S. voting system vendors: Clear Ballot, Diebold, Dominion, ES&S, and Hart (two styles, eScan and Verity).

set than just marginal marks, as they may indeed be completely valid votes, but considered invalid by our mark-moving algorithm. For example, if we were to swap the targets on a ballot where the user put a check through their target, we may leave a significant percentage of the check around the original target when swapping. The same applies for marked ballots where the filled in area extends into the candidate's name, which could lead our algorithm to swap over parts of the candidate's name when manipulating the image.

To detect anomalies for invalid ballots, we leverage the same intensity checking algorithm that first found the marked areas. The program checks if the width or height is abnormally large, which would indicate an overfilled target, as well as if there are too few or too many areas of high intensity, which would indicate no target or too many targets are filled out. If the program detects an invalid ballot, it will not be modified by the program.

Table 1. Performance of UnclearBallot—We tested how accurately our software could manipulate voter marks for a variety of ballot styles using equal numbers of invalid and valid marks. The table shows how often the system skipped a mark, successfully altered one, or erroneously created artifacts we deemed to be visible upon manual inspection. We also report the mean processing time for successfully manipulated races, excluding template matching.

Ballot style	Invalid marks			Valid marks			Time/Success
	Skipped	Success	Failure	Skipped	Success	Failure	
Clear Ballot	55	5	0	26	34	0	25 ms
Diebold	60	0	0	6	54	0	11 ms
Dominion	38	22	0	7	53	0	30 ms
ES&S	52	8	0	29	31	0	54 ms
Hart (eScan)	60	0	0	38	22	0	46 ms
Hart (Verity)	60	0	0	27	33	0	21 ms

To show our attack is replicable on a variety of different ballot styles, we modified our program to work on six different sample ballot styles, shown in Fig. 7. The ballots we tested come from the four largest election vendors in the U.S. (ES&S, Hart InterCivic, Dominion, and Clear Ballot), as well as two older styles of ballots from Hart and Diebold.

Our first experiment was designed to characterize the technique's effectiveness across a range of ballot styles and with both regular and marginal marks. We prepared 720 marked contests, split evenly among the six ballot styles shown in Fig. 7. For each style, we marked 60 contests with what Bajcsy [2] calls "Filled" marks, i.e. reliably detected marks that should be moved by our attack. We marked another 60 ballots in each ballot style with marginal marks, ten each for the five kinds of marginal marks shown in Fig. 2 and ten empty marks.

Because the runtime of the template matching step of our algorithm is highly dependent on customization for the particular races on a ballot, we opted to skip it for this experiment. Rather than marking full ballots, we marked cropped races from each ballot style and then ran them through our program. We then manually checked to ensure that the races the program moved were not detectable by inspection. Results for these experiments are shown in Table 1.

Despite rejecting some valid ballots, our program is still able to confidently swap a majority of valid votes. In a real attack, only a small percentage of votes would need to actually be modified, a task easily accomplished by our program. Our program also correctly catches all votes that we have deemed invalid for swapping. This would make it unlikely to be detected in an image audit.

Dominion ballots saw a much higher rate of invalid mark moving, and Diebold and Dominion ballots saw a much higher rate of valid mark moving. This is likely due to the placement of targets: on the Dominion ballots, the mark is right justified, separating it significantly from candidate label information, as can be seen in Fig. 7. Similarly, the Diebold ballot provides more space around

Original   Manipulated

Measure 102	Measure 102
Referred to the People by the Legislative Assembly	Referred to the People by the Legislative Assembly
Amends Constitution: Allows local bonds for financing affordable housing with nongovernmental entities. Requires voter approval, annual audits	**Amends Constitution: Allows local bonds for financing affordable housing with nongovernmental entities. Requires voter approval, annual audits**
Result of "Yes" Vote: "Yes" vote allows local governments to issue bonds to finance affordable housing with nongovernmental entities. Requires local voters' approval of bonds, annual audits, public reporting.	**Result of "Yes" Vote:** "Yes" vote allows local governments to issue bonds to finance affordable housing with nongovernmental entities. Requires local voters' approval of bonds, annual audits, public reporting.
Result of "No" Vote: "No" vote retains constitutional prohibition on local governments raising money for/ loaning credit to nongovernmental entities; no exception for bonds to pay for affordable housing.	**Result of "No" Vote:** "No" vote retains constitutional prohibition on local governments raising money for/ loaning credit to nongovernmental entities; no exception for bonds to pay for affordable housing.
☐ Yes	▨ Yes
▨ No	☐ No

Fig. 8. Attacking Real Ballots—Using 181,541 images of voted ballots from Clackamas County, Oregon, we attempted to change voters' selections for the ballot measure shown above. UnclearBallot determined that it could safely alter 34% of the ballots. For reference, Measure 102 passed by a margin of 5%, well within range of manipulation [14]. We inspected 1,000 of them to verify that the manipulation left no obvious artifacts.

the target and less candidate information that can be intercepted by marks, which would cause Unclear Ballot to skip moving the mark.

In an online attack scenario (such as if a human is waiting to see the output from the scanner), the attacker needs to be able to modify ballot scans quickly enough not to be noticed. Factors which might affect how quickly our program can process and manipulate ballots include ballot style, layout, and type of mark. During the accuracy experiment just described, we collected timing data for successfully manipulated ballot, and report the results in Table 1. The results show that after the target race has been extracted, the algorithm completes extremely quickly for all tested ballot styles. We present additional timing data at the end of the following section.

5.2   Testing with Real Voted Ballots

To assess the effectiveness of UnclearBallot in a real election, we used a corpus of scans of 181,541 real ballots from the November 6, 2018, General Election in Clackamas County, Oregon, which were made available by Election Integrity Oregon [18]. Like all of Oregon, Clackamas County uses vote-by-mail as its primary voting method, and votes are centrally counted using optical scanners. All images were Hart Verity-style ballots, as shown in Fig. 7.

We selected a ballot measure that appeared on all the ballots (Fig. 8) and attempted to change each voter's selection. UnclearBallot rejected 20,117 (11%) of the ballots because it could not locate the target contest. We examined a subset of the rejected ballots and found that they contained glitches introduced during scanning (such as vertical lines running the length of the ballot), which interfered with the Hough transform.

To simulate a real attacker, we configured UnclearBallot with conservative parameters, so that it would only modify marks when there was high confidence that the alteration would not be noticeable. As a result, it would only manipulate marks that were nearly perfectly filled in. In most cases, marks that were skipped extended well beyond the target, but the program also skipped undervotes, overvotes, or mislabeled scans. Under these parameters, the program altered the target contest in 62,400 (34%) of the ballot images.

Two authors independently inspected a random sample of 1,000 altered ballots to check whether any contained artifacts that would be noticeable to an attentive observer. Such artifacts might include marks which were unnaturally cut off, visible discontinuities in pixel darkness (i.e. dark lines around moved marks), and so on. If these artifacts were seen during an audit, officials might recheck all of the physical ballots and reverse the effects of the attack. None of the altered ballots we inspected contained noticeable evidence of manipulation.

We also collected timing data while processing Clackamas County ballots. Running on a system with a 4-core Intel E3-1230 CPU running at 3.40 GHz with 64 GB of RAM, UnclearBallot took an average of 279 ms to process each ballot. For reference, Hart's fastest central scanner's maximum scan rate is one ballot per 352 ms [37], well above the time needed to carry out our attack.

These results show that UnclearBallot can successfully and efficiently manipulate ballot images to change real voters' marks. Moreover, the alterations likely would be undetectable to human auditors who examined only the ballot images.

6   Discussion and Mitigations

UnclearBallot demonstrates the need for a software-independent evidence trail against which election results can be checked. It shows that audits based on software which is independent from the rest of the election system is still not software independent. To date, the only robust and secure election technology that is widely used is optical-scan paper ballots with risk-limiting audits based on a robust, well-maintained, *physical* audit trail. However, image audits are not useless, and here we discuss uses for them as well as potential mitigations for our attack.

Uses for Image Audits. So long as image audits are not the sole mechanism for verifying election results, they do provide substantial benefits to election officials. Using an image audit vastly simplifies some functions of election administration, like ballot adjudication in cases where marks cannot be interpreted by scanners or are otherwise ambiguous. Image audits can be used to efficiently identify and document election discrepancies, as has occurred in Maryland where nearly 2,000 ballots were discovered missing from the audit trail in 2016 [28]. Image audits also identified a flaw in the ES&S DS850 high speed scanner, where it was causing some ballots to stick together and feed two at a time [29].

Another way to utilize image audits is a transitive audit. Methods like SOBA [8] seek to construct an audit trail using all available means of election evidence, rooting the audit in some verification of physical record. By using physical records to verify other records, like CVRs or ballot images, confidence in election outcomes can be transitively passed on to non-physical audit trails. The drawback with this kind of audit is that it usually requires the same level of work as an RLA, plus whatever work is needed to validate the other forms of evidence. However, since ballot image audits already require a low amount of effort, they may augment RLAs and provide better transparency into the auditing process.

Image audits are an augmentation and a convenience for election administration, however, and should not be viewed as a security tool. Only physical examination of paper ballots, as in a risk-limiting audit, can provide a necessary level of mitigation to manipulated election results.

End-to-end (E2E) Systems. Voting systems with rigorous integrity properties and tamper resistance such as Scantegrity [12] and Prêt à Voter [35] provide a defense to UnclearBallot. In Scantegrity, when individuals mark their ballots, a confirmation code is revealed that is tied to the selected candidate. This enables a voter to verify that their ballot collected-as-cast and counted-as-collected, as they can look up their ballot on a public bulletin board. Since each mark reveals a unique code, moving the mark would match the code with the wrong candidate, so voters would be unable to verify their ballots. If enough voters complain, this might result in our attack being detected.

Prêt à Voter randomizes the candidate order on each ballot, which creates a slightly higher barrier for our attack, as an additional template matching step would be needed to ascertain candidate order. More importantly, the candidate list is physically separated from the voter's marks upon casting the ballot, so malware which could not keep track of the correct candidate order could not successfully move marks to a predetermined candidate. Since the candidate order is deciphered via a key-sharing scheme, malicious software would have to infect a significant portion of the election system and act in a highly coordinated way to reconstruct candidate ordering. Moreover, as with Scantegrity, votes are published to a public bulletin board, so any voter could discover if their vote had not been correctly recorded.

Other E2E systems which make use of optical scanning and a bulletin board, like STAR-Vote [6], Scratch and Vote [1], and VeriScan [7], are similarly protected from attacks like UnclearBallot.

Other Mitigations. Outside of E2E, there may be other heuristic mitigations that can be easily implemented even in deployed voting systems to make our attack somewhat more difficult. As mentioned above, randomizing candidate order on each ballot increases the computation required to perform our attack. Voters drawing outside the bubbles can also defeat our attack, though this might also result in their votes not counting and may be circumvented by replacing the whole race on the ballot image with a substituted one. Collecting ballot images from a different source than the tabulator makes our attack more difficult, as votes now have to be changed in two places. Other standard computer security technologies, like secure file systems, could be used to force the attacker to alter ballot images in a way that also circumvents protections like encryption and permissions.

Detection. Technologies that detect image manipulation may also provide some mitigation. Techniques like those discussed in [3–5,38], among others, could be adapted to try to automatically detect moved marks on ballots. However, as noted by Farid [19], image manipulation detection is a kind of arms race: given a fixed detection algorithm, adversaries can very likely find a way to defeat it. In our context, an attacker with sufficient access to the voting system to implant a manipulation algorithm would likely also be able to steal the detector code. The attacker could improve the manipulation algorithm or simply use the detector as part of their mark-moving calculus: if moving a mark will trip the detector, an attacker can simply opt not to move the mark.

While a fixed and automatic procedure for detecting manipulation can provide little assurance, it remains possible that an adaptive approach to detection could be a useful part of a post-election forensics investigation. However, staying one step ahead of sophisticated adversaries would require an ongoing research program to advance the state of the art in detection methods.

A less costly and more dependable way to detect ballot manipulation detection would be to use a software independent audit trail to confirm election outcomes. This can be accomplished with risk-limiting audits, and the software independence enabled by RLAs provides other robust security properties to elections, including defending against other potential attacks on tabulation equipment and servers.

Future Work. We have only focused on simple-majority elections here, because those are the kinds of elections used by jurisdictions that do image audits. Audits of more complex election methods, like instant-runoff voting or D'Hondt, have been examined to some extent [36,41], but future work is needed into audits of these kinds of elections altogether. Because the marks made in these elections are different than the kind we've discussed here, manipulating these ballot images may not be able to employ the same image processing techniques we have used. Additionally it may be difficult for malware to know how many marks it needs to move, since margins in complex elections are difficult to compute. We leave exploration of image manipulation of these elections to future work.

7 Conclusion

In this paper, we demonstrated an attack that defeats ballot image audits of the type performed in some jurisdictions. We presented an implementation using a real scanner, and evaluated our implementation against a set of real ballots and a set of systematically marked ballots from a variety of ballot styles. Our attack shows that image audits cannot be relied upon to verify that elections are free from computer-based interference. Indeed, the only currently known way to verify an election outcome is with direct examination of physical ballots.

Acknowledgements. The authors thank Vaibhav Bafna and Jonathan Yan for assisting in the initial version of this project. They also thank Josh Franklin, Joe Hall, Maurice Turner, Kevin Skoglund, Jared Marcotte, and Tony Adams for their invaluable feedback. We also thank our anonymous reviewers and our shepherd, Roland Wen. This material is based upon work supported by the National Science Foundation under grant CNS-1518888.

References

1. Adida, B., Rivest, R.L.: Scratch and Vote: self-contained paper-based cryptographic voting. In: ACM Workshop on Privacy in the Electronic Society, pp. 29–40 (2006)
2. Bajcsy, A., Li-Baboud, Y.S., Brady, M.: Systematic measurement of marginal mark types on voting ballots. Technical report, National Institute for Standards and Technology (2015)
3. Bayar, B., Stamm, M.C.: A deep learning approach to universal image manipulation detection using a new convolutional layer. In: Proceedings of the 4th ACM Workshop on Information Hiding and Multimedia Security, pp. 5–10. ACM (2016)
4. Bayram, S., Avcıbaş, İ., Sankur, B., Memon, N.: Image manipulation detection with binary similarity measures. In: 2005 13th European Signal Processing Conference, pp. 1–4. IEEE (2005)
5. Bayram, S., Avcibas, I., Sankur, B., Memon, N.D.: Image manipulation detection. J. Electron. Imaging **15**(4), 041102 (2006)
6. Bell, S., et al.: STAR-vote: a secure, transparent, auditable, and reliable voting system. USENIX J. Election Technol. Syst. **1**(1) (2013)
7. Benaloh, J.: Administrative and public verifiability: can we have both? In: USENIX/ACCURATE Electronic Voting Technology Workshop, EVT 2008, August 2008
8. Benaloh, J., Jones, D., Lazarus, E., Lindeman, M., Stark, P.B.: SOBA: secrecy-preserving observable ballot-level audit. In: Proceedings of USENIX Accurate Electronic Voting Technology Workshop (2011)

9. Bernhard, M., et al.: Public evidence from secret ballots. In: Krimmer, R., Volkamer, M., Braun Binder, N., Kersting, N., Pereira, O., Schürmann, C. (eds.) E-Vote-ID 2017. LNCS, vol. 10615, pp. 84–109. Springer, Cham (2017). https://doi.org/10.1007/978-3-319-68687-5_6

10. Bowen, D.: Top-to-Bottom Review of voting machines certified for use in California. Technical report, California Secretary of State (2007). https://www.sos.ca.gov/elections/voting-systems/oversight/top-bottom-review/

11. Bradski, G.: The OpenCV Library. Dr. Dobb's J. Softw. Tools **120**, 122–125 (2000)

12. Carback, R., et al.: Scantegrity II municipal election at Takoma Park: the first E2E binding governmental election with ballot privacy. In: 18th USENIX Security Symposium, August 2010

13. Chung, K.K.T., Dong, V.J., Shi, X.: Electronic voting method for optically scanned ballot, US Patent 7,077,313, 18 July 2006

14. November 6, 2018 general election. https://dochub.clackamas.us/documents/drupal/f4e7f0fb-250a-4992-918d-26c5f726de3c

15. Clear Ballot: ClearAudit. https://clearballot.com/products/clear-audit

16. Dominion Voting: Auditmark. https://www.dominionvoting.com/pdf/DD

17. Dominion Voting: Cambridge Case Study. https://www.dominionvoting.com/field/cambridge

18. Election Integrity Oregon. https://www.electionintegrityoregon.org

19. Farid, H.: Digital forensics in a post-truth age. Forensic Sci. Int. **289**, 268–269 (2018)

20. Feldman, A.J., Halderman, J.A., Felten, E.W.: Security analysis of the Diebold AccuVote-TS voting machine. In: USENIX/ACCURATE Electronic Voting Technology Workshop, EVT 2007, August 2007

21. Hall, J., et al.: Implementing risk-limiting post-election audits in California. In: 2009 Workshop on Electronic Voting Technology/Workshop on Trustworthy Elections, p. 19. USENIX Association (2009)

22. Ji, T., Kim, E., Srikantan, R., Tsai, A., Cordero, A., Wagner, D.A.: An analysis of write-in marks on optical scan ballots. In: EVT/WOTE (2011)

23. Jones, D.W.: On optical mark-sense scanning. In: Chaum, D., et al. (eds.) Towards Trustworthy Elections. LNCS, vol. 6000, pp. 175–190. Springer, Heidelberg (2010). https://doi.org/10.1007/978-3-642-12980-3_10

24. Lindeman, M., Halvorson, M., Smith, P., Garland, L., Addona, V., McCrea, D.: Principles and best practices for post-election audits, September 2008. http://electionaudits.org/files/bestpracticesfinal_0.pdf

25. Lindeman, M., Stark, P.: A gentle introduction to risk-limiting audits. IEEE Secur. Priv. **10**, 42–49 (2012)

26. Lindeman, M., Stark, P., Yates, V.: BRAVO: ballot-polling risk-limiting audits to verify outcomes. In: 2011 Electronic Voting Technology Workshop/Workshop on Trustworthy Elections (EVT/WOTE 2012). USENIX (2012)

27. Maryland House of Delegates: House Bill 1278: An act concerning election law - postelection tabulation audit. http://mgaleg.maryland.gov/2018RS/bills/hb/hb1278E.pdf

28. Maryland State Board of Elections: 2016 post-election audit report, December 2016. http://dlslibrary.state.md.us/publications/JCR/2016/2016_22-23.pdf

29. Maryland State Board of Elections: December 15, 2016 meeting minutes, December 2016. https://elections.maryland.gov/pdf/minutes/2016_12.pdf

30. McDaniel, P., Blaze, M., Vigna, G.: EVEREST: evaluation and validation of election-related equipment, standards and testing. Technical report, Ohio Secretary of State (2007). http://siis.cse.psu.edu/everest.html

31. Mebane Jr., W.R.M., Bernhard, M.: Voting technologies, recount methods and votes in Wisconsin and Michigan in 2016. In: Zohar, A., et al. (eds.) FC 2018. LNCS, vol. 10958, pp. 196–209. Springer, Heidelberg (2019). https://doi.org/10.1007/978-3-662-58820-8_14

32. National Academies of Sciences, Engineering, and Medicine: Securing the Vote: Protecting American Democracy. The National Academies Press, Washington, DC (2018). https://www.nap.edu/catalog/25120/securing-the-vote-protecting-american-democracy

33. National Conference of State Legislatures: Post-election audits, January 2019. http://www.ncsl.org/research/elections-and-campaigns/post-election-audits635926066.aspx

34. Rivest, R.: On the notion of 'software independence' in voting systems. Phil. Trans. R. Soc. A **366**(1881), 3759–3767 (2008)

35. Ryan, P.Y.A., Bismark, D., Heather, J., Schneider, S., Xia, Z.: Prêt à Voter: a voter-verifiable voting system. IEEE Trans. Inf. Forensics Secur. **4**(4), 662–673 (2009)

36. Sarwate, A.D., Checkoway, S., Shacham, H.: Risk-limiting audits and the margin of victory in nonplurality elections. Stat. Polit. Policy **4**(1), 29–64 (2013)

37. ScannerOne: Kodak i5600. http://www.scannerone.com/product/KOD-i5600.html

38. Stamm, M.C., Liu, K.R.: Forensic detection of image manipulation using statistical intrinsic fingerprints. IEEE Trans. Inf. Forensics Secur. **5**(3), 492–506 (2010)

39. Stark, P.: Conservative statistical post-election audits. Ann. Appl. Stat. **2**(2), 550–581 (2008)

40. Stark, P.: Super-simple simultaneous single-ballot risk-limiting audits. In: 2010 Electronic Voting Technology Workshop/Workshop on Trustworthy Elections (EVT/WOTE 2010). USENIX (2010)

41. Stark, P.B., Teague, V., Essex, A.: Verifiable European elections: risk-limiting audits for D'Hondt and its relatives. {USENIX} J. Election Technol. Syst. ({JETS}) **1**, 18–39 (2014)

42. Unisyn Voting Solutions: OpenElect OCS Auditor. https://unisynvoting.com/openelect-ocs/

43. U.S. Election Assistance Commission: Certificate of conformance: ClearVote 1.5, March 2019. https://www.eac.gov/file.aspx?A=zgte4IhsHz

44. Verified Voting Foundation: The Verifier: Polling place equipment (2019). https://www.verifiedvoting.org/verifier/

Election Manipulation with Partial Information

Michelle Blom[1](✉), Peter J. Stuckey[2], and Vanessa J. Teague[1]

[1] School of Computing and Information Systems, The University of Melbourne,
Melbourne, Australia
{michelle.blom,vjteague}@unimelb.edu.au
[2] Faculty of Information Technology, Monash University, Melbourne, Australia
peter.stuckey@monash.edu

Abstract. We consider the case of manipulating the results of Instant Runoff Voting (IRV) elections. Previous work in this area looked at *posthoc* manipulation with complete information, where the manipulator may alter ballots after reading the whole election profile. In this paper we examine the much more realistic, but challenging, problem of manipulating ballots during the election process, having observed only some ballots. The aim of the manipulator is to modify as few ballots as possible to ensure their candidate's victory with high probability. We show that this it quite feasible in practice to generate efficient manipulations with a high probability of success. We also add some extra conditions on the manipulations so it is less likely they will be detected by naive methods.

1 Introduction

Instant Runoff Voting (IRV), also known as Alternative Vote (AV), is a system of preferential voting in which voters rank candidates in order of preference. Tallying proceeds by eliminating the least popular candidate and redistributing their votes to the next-preferred candidate—see Sect. 2 for a precise algorithm. It is used in presidential, parliamentary and local government elections in countries such as Australia, Fiji, Papua New Guinea, Ireland, Bosnia/Herzogovinia, the UK and United States [6].

IRV elections can be complicated—an early alteration in the elimination order can cascade into an entirely different election result. It is NP-hard even to compute the true margin of victory [7]. But the hard examples are somewhat contrived, and real elections follow patterns which make it relatively easy in practice to compute both margins [3,5] and successful manipulations [2]. However, prior work has required complete information about all the votes cast in the election. In contrast, the related problem of manipulating ones own vote to increase the likelihood of a desired outcome has been studied in the context of both full and partial knowledge of the preferences of other voters [4] .

In this work, we examine for the first time whether an attacker with only partial information can devise a successful manipulation with a high probability

© Springer Nature Switzerland AG 2019
R. Krimmer et al. (Eds.): E-Vote-ID 2019, LNCS 11759, pp. 32–49, 2019.
https://doi.org/10.1007/978-3-030-30625-0_3

of success. This models a realistic attacker (such as a corrupt scanner or voting machine) who must generate manipulated electronic records on the fly after reading only a few of them. The problem we consider is known as 'election control by replacing voters' in the computational social choice literature. We find that it remains easy to generate successful manipulations, though of course success is not guaranteed. Our emphasis is on practical attacks in a realistic setting. We do not prove optimality nor a bound on the probability of success, but we demonstrate successful practical attacks by simulating the algorithm on state election data from Australia. We also examine a number of ways the attacker could refine the manipulation to be less likely to raise suspicion.

We assume the adversary has sufficient access to the election system to read ballots as they are received, and to modify each ballot before it is recorded. Unlike in prior work [2], our adversary cannot modify ballot recordings once made, but must perform manipulations based on the partial sample seen so far. This models a man-in-the-middle attack where ballots are intercepted between the voter and the final counting, and altered by the adversary. It is precisely the attacker model of a corrupted scanning process in which scanned ballots must be immediately output, but may be misrecorded on the fly. It is also appropriate for an e-voting process with immutable logs, in which the manipulated votes must be written immediately onto the log and cannot later be altered.

We look at an adversary that computes some manipulation rules to apply at periodic intervals, after they have seen some ballots scanned through. The attacker succeeds if their desired candidate wins. We compare a number of ways of generating the rules, and how effective they are at actually achieving a desired winner change. We find that if the adversary sees the first quarter or half of the votes then, with a few seconds of computation, it can compute a manipulation close to the optimal, and then apply it to the next 3/4 or half of the votes with a success probability usually higher than 90%.

Avoiding suspicion. The last round margin (LRM) of an IRV election – the difference in tallies of the final two remaining candidates, divided by two and rounded up – is commonly used as an indicator of how close the election was. Blom *et al.* [3] have shown that the true margin of victory (MOV) of the election – the smallest number of votes one would have to alter to change who won the election – is generally equal to the last round margin, but not always. In some cases, the MOV can be much smaller than the last round margin. The Australian Electoral Commission (AEC) use the "margin between the two leading candidates" after all remaining candidates have been eliminated, and their preferences distributed, to determine whether an automatic recount of cast votes should be automatically performed.[1] In practice, the LRM plays a major role in determining whether further scrutiny of the outcome is performed.

---

[1] https://www.aec.gov.au/Elections/candidates/files/hor-recount-policy.pdf.
The AEC definition of a "margin" is the difference in tallies of two candidates (not divided by two).

Our first suspicion-avoiding extension is for the adversary to generate manipulations that result in a large last-round margin. The adversary wants to alter the smallest number of electronic records so that their desire of changing the outcome is realised, while at the same time ensuring that the last round margin of the manipulated election is larger than a given threshold. Another important way of avoiding suspicion is to minimize changes in first preferences. This is significant because, in preferential elections, first-preference tallies are often manually counted in a polling place independently of the scanning process. Modifying first preferences is therefore much more likely to be detected than other alterations. We find, surprisingly, that this constraint usually makes an insignificant difference to the number of ballots that need to be changed. A clever surreptitious manipulation is almost as easy as an obvious one. These attacks would be defeated if a rigorous risk-limiting audit was applied. The trick with LRMs would be defeated by a careful computation of the true MOV [3]. The purpose of this paper is to demonstrate that these rigorous methods are necessary, because an active adversary can defeat heuristic methods of assessing when to re-examine an election result.

Our contributions. Using the Australian New South Wales (NSW) 2015 Legislative Assembly election as a case study, we simulate the attack by randomly determining the order in which ballots arrive at the scanner, computing a best-guess manipulation at periodic intervals, and then applying that manipulation to later ballots as they are scanned. We then compare the outcome of the modified election to that of the unmodified election to see whether the manipulation succeeded.

We report the number of ballots that this adversary needs to modify, and the number of first preferences on ballots they need to modify, in order to have a high chance of altering the election outcome, assuming that the proportion of the ballots they saw before computing the manipulation were a random sample of all ballots.

2   Preliminaries and Prior Work

Votes are tallied in an IRV election in a series of rounds (see Fig. 1). In each round, the candidate with the smallest number of votes (their tally) is eliminated, with the last remaining candidate declared the winner. All votes in an eliminated candidate's tally are distributed to the next most-preferred (remaining) candidate in their ranking.

We denote an IRV election, with a set of candidates $\mathcal{C}$, as $\mathcal{B}$. A sequence of candidates π is represented in list notation (e.g., $\pi = [c_1, c_2, c_3, c_4]$, which means that c_1 is the highest preference, c_2 the next-preferred, and so on). Such sequences represent both votes and the order in which candidates are eliminated. An election $\mathcal{B}$ is defined as a multiset[2] of votes, each vote $b \in \mathcal{B}$ a sequence of candidates in $\mathcal{C}$, with no duplicates, listed in order of preference (most preferred

---

[2] A multiset allows for the inclusion of duplicate items.

> Initially, all candidates remain standing (are not eliminated)
> **While** there is *more than one* candidate standing
> **For** every candidate c standing
> Tally (count) the votes in which c is the highest-ranked
> candidate of those standing
> Eliminate the candidate with the smallest tally
> The winner is the one candidate not eliminated

Fig. 1. The IRV vote tallying process: the candidate with the smallest tally is repeatedly eliminated, with the ballots in their tally redistributed according to their next preference.

to least). The first candidate appearing in a sequence π is denoted $first(\pi)$ (e.g., $first([c_2, c_3]) = c_2$). In each round of vote counting, there are a current set of eliminated candidates $\mathcal{E}$ and a current set of candidates still standing $\mathcal{S} = \mathcal{C} \setminus \mathcal{E}$. The winner c_w of the election is the last standing candidate.

Our definitions for a candidate's tally, the margin of victory (MOV), and last round margin (LRM) of an IRV election are replicated from [2].

Definition 1. Tally $t_{\mathcal{S}}(c)$ *Given candidates $\mathcal{S} \subseteq \mathcal{C}$ are still standing in an election $\mathcal{B}$, the tally for candidate $c \in \mathcal{C}$, denoted $t_{\mathcal{S}}(c)$, is defined as the number of votes $b \in \mathcal{B}$ for which c is the most-preferred candidate of those remaining.[3] Let $p_{\mathcal{S}}(b)$ denote the sequence of candidates mentioned in b that are also in $\mathcal{S}$.*

$$t_{\mathcal{S}}(c) = \mid [b \in \mathcal{B} \mid c = first(p_{\mathcal{S}}(b))] \mid \tag{1}$$

Definition 2. Margin of Victory (MOV) *The MOV in an election $\mathcal{B}$ with candidates $\mathcal{C}$ and winner $c_w \in \mathcal{C}$, is the smallest number of votes in $\mathcal{B}$ whose ranking must be modified (by an adversary) so that a candidate $c' \in \mathcal{C} \setminus \{c_w\}$ is elected.*

Definition 3. Last Round Margin (LRM) *The LRM of an election $\mathcal{B}$, in which two candidates $\mathcal{S} = \{c, c'\}$ remain with $t_{\mathcal{S}}(c)$ and $t_{\mathcal{S}}(c')$ votes in their tallies, is equal to half the difference between the tallies of c and c' rounded up.*

$$LRM = \left\lceil \frac{|t_{\mathcal{S}}(c) - t_{\mathcal{S}}(c')|}{2} \right\rceil \tag{2}$$

In the design of our adversary, we consider the concept of an elimination margin (EM) – the margin by which a candidate is eliminated in a given round. We find that a manipulator can be much more effective when controlling the elimination margin of the two runner-ups (the candidate eliminated just prior to the runner-up, and the runner-up themselves) rather than just the LRM of the runner-up and winner. In settings where there is a genuine three candidate race for winner, successful manipulations typically require the elimination of a specific candidate in third

---

[3] Square brackets have been used to denote a multiset.

place whose preferences will mostly flow to the desired winner. Consider a manipulation designed to elect a candidate a with a certain margin, but where tallies of the candidates up for elimination in that crucial third place position are similar. Given uncertainty in what types of ballots a manipulator will see as it is changing votes on the fly, it is likely to be more successful it aims to eliminate the required candidate in third place with a larger elimination margin.

Definition 4. Elimination Margin (EM) *The EM in a round of counting* i, *in which candidate* c_i *is eliminated and candidates* $S \setminus \{c_i\}$ *are still standing, is equal to half the smallest difference in tallies between* $t_S(c_i)$ *and* $t_S(c')$ *for* $c' \in S \setminus \{c_i\}$ *rounded up.*

$$EM_i = \min_{c' \in S \setminus \{c_i\}} \left\lceil \frac{t_S(c') - t_S(c_i)}{2} \right\rceil \tag{3}$$

Example 1. Consider the election with ballots shown in Table 1(a). The true election result is shown in Table 1(b), with c the winner with a last round margin of 13. The margin of victory is actually only 5. Changing five ballots from $[c, a]$ to $[b, c]$ results the totals shown in Table 1(e). In this election a wins as shown in Table 1(f). In the true election, b is eliminated with an EM of $\lceil 9/2 \rceil = 5$ votes, and a with an EM of 13. $\square$

Table 1. IRV example, with (a) the number of votes cast with each listed ranking over candidates a, b, c, and (b) tallies after each round of vote counting (c) the ballot count 25% into the election and the estimated complete election (d) the tallies of each round of vote counting in the estimated election (e) the number of votes recorded after manipulation, and (f) the tallies after each round of vote counting in the manipulated election

Ranking	Count B
[a]	55
[c, a]	30
[b, c]	36
[c]	15

(a)

Candidate	Round 1	Round 2
a	55	55
b	36	—
c	45	81

(b)

Ranking	Partial Count B_T	Estimated Completion $\tilde{B}$
[a]	11	44
[c, a]	9	36
[b, c]	10	40
[c]	4	16

(c)

Candidate	Round 1	Round 2
a	44	44
b	36	—
c	52	88

(d)

Ranking	Manipulated Count
[a]	55
[c, a]	25
[b, c]	41
[c]	15

(e)

Candidate	Round 1	Round 2
a	55	80
b	41	41
c	40	—

(f)

2.1 Modifying an Election Outcome

In this paper we make use of algorithms for determining minimal manipulations of IRV elections in order to change their outcome, developed by Blom *et al.* [2]. They consider the case where all recorded ballots can be manipulated *after* they have all been scanned. This is clearly a necessary starting point for determining a more restricted manipulation.

These algorithms are based on the *margin-irv* algorithm for computing the true MOV of an IRV election. A description of *margin-irv* can be found in Blom *et al.* [3]. We summarise the algorithm in this section, and explain how it can be modified to compute the smallest number of vote changes required to: (i) bring about a change in the outcome of the election; (ii) produce a manipulated election with certain properties, modelled as side constraints; and (iii) produce a manipulated election that minimises discrepancies between a manual hand count of first preference tallies (based on non-manipulated paper ballots) and the first preference tallies of the manipulated election.

The *margin-irv* Algorithm. Consider an IRV election $\mathcal{B}$ with candidates $\mathcal{C}$ and winner $w \in \mathcal{C}$. The *margin-irv* algorithm starts by adding $|\mathcal{C}| - 1$ partial elimination sequences to a search tree, one for each of alternate or desired winner $c \in \mathcal{C} \setminus \{w\}$. These partial sequences form a frontier F, with each sequence containing a single candidate – an alternate winner. Note that a partial sequence $[a, b, c]$ represents an election outcome in which a and b are the last two candidates eliminated, and c the winner. All other candidates are assumed to have been eliminated in some prior round.

An adversary is likely to to have a desired winner $a \neq w$. We can modify *margin-irv* by initializing the frontier F with the single sequence $[a]$. Then it only considers election sequences where a wins. The same idea is used by Blom *et al.* [1].

For each partial sequence $\pi \in F$, we compute a lower bound on the number of vote changes required to realise an elimination sequence that *ends* in π. These lower bounds are used to guide construction of the search tree, and are computed by both solving an Integer Linear Program (ILP), and applying several rules for lower bound computation. These rules are described in Blom *et al.* [3]. The ILP, denoted DISTANCETO, computes a lower bound on the smallest number of vote changes required to transform the election $\mathcal{B}$, with an elimination sequence π', to one with an elimination sequence that ends in π. When applied to a complete order π, containing all candidates, DISTANCETO exactly computes the smallest number of votes changes required to realise the outcome π. The largest of the lower bounds computed by the rules of Blom *et al.* [3] and the DISTANCETO ILP is assigned to each partial sequence π as it is added to F. The DISTANCETO ILP is defined in Sect. 2.2. To enforce additional constraints on the nature of any manipulated election, we add these constraints to each ILP solved.

The partial sequence $\pi \in F$ with the smallest assigned lower bound is selected and *expanded*. For each $c \in \mathcal{C}$ that is not already present in π, we create a new sequence with c appended to the front. For example, given a set of candidates e,

f, and g, with winning candidate g, the partial sequence $\pi = [f]$ will be expanded to create two new sequences $[e, f]$ and $[g, f]$. We evaluate each new sequence π' by assigning it a lower bound on the number of votes required to realise any elimination order ending in π'.

While exploring and building elimination sequences, *margin-irv* maintains a running *upper bound* on the value of the true margin. Without any side constraints designed to inject desirable properties into a manipulated election, this upper bound is initialised to the last round margin of the original election. To enforce additional constraints on the properties of any manipulated election, we need to manipulate at least as many, and often more, votes than required to simply change the original outcome. Consequently, we must set the upper bound maintained by *margin-irv* to a higher value. In this context, we set the initial upper bound to the total number of votes cast in the election. This is clearly always a correct upper bound on any manipulation.

When a sequence π containing all candidates is constructed, the DISTANCETO ILP computes the exact number of vote manipulations required to realise it, while satisfying all desired side constraints. If this number is lower than our current upper bound, the upper bound is revised, and all orders in F with a lower bound greater than or equal to it are pruned from consideration (removed from F). This process continues until F is empty (we have considered or pruned all possible alternate elimination sequences). The final value of the running upper bound is the true electoral MOV (with side constraints).

2.2 DISTANCETO with Side Constraints

We now present the DISTANCETO Integer Linear Program (ILP) used to compute lower bounds on the degree of manipulation required to realise an election outcome ending in a given candidate sequence, and the (exact) smallest number of vote changes required to realise a given (complete) alternate elimination sequence. This ILP, without added side constraints, was originally presented by Magrino *et al.* [5].

We consider additional side constraints to inject desirable properties into any manipulated election, and describe how we can minimise both the total number of vote changes required to elect a desired winner, and the total changes made to first preference tallies between the true and manipulated election profiles.

Let $\mathbf{R}$ denote the set of possible (partial and total) rankings R of candidates $\mathcal{C}$ that could appear on a vote, N_R the number of votes cast with ranking $R \in \mathbf{R}$, and N the total number of votes cast. Let $\mathcal{R}_{j,i}$ denote the subset of rankings $(\mathcal{R}_{j,i} \subset \mathbf{R})$ in which c_j is the most preferred candidate still standing (i.e., that will count toward c_j's tally) at the start of round i (in which c_i is eliminated). For each $R \in \mathbf{R}$, we define variables:

q_R integer number of votes to be changed into R;

m_R integer number of votes with ranking R in the unmodified
        election to be changed into something other than R; and

y_R number of votes in the modified election with ranking R.

Given a partial or complete order π, the DISTANCETO ILP is:

$$\min \sum_{R \in \mathbf{R}} q_R \tag{4}$$

$$N_R + q_R - m_R = y_R \qquad\qquad \forall R \in \mathbf{R} \tag{5}$$

$$\sum_{R \in \mathbf{R}} q_R = \sum_{R \in \mathbf{R}} m_R \tag{6}$$

$$\sum_{R \in \mathcal{R}_{i,i}} y_R \leq \sum_{R \in \mathcal{R}_{j,i}} y_R \qquad\qquad \forall c_i, c_j \in \pi \,.\, i < j \tag{7}$$

$$n \geq y_R \geq 0, \ N_R \geq m_R \geq 0, \ q_R \geq 0 \qquad\qquad \forall R \in \mathbf{R} \tag{8}$$

Constraint (5) states that the number of votes with ranking $R \in \mathbf{R}$ in the new election is equal to the sum of those with this ranking in the unmodified election and those whose ranking has *changed to* R, minus the number of votes whose ranking has been *changed from* R. Constraint (7) defines a set of *special elimination constraints* which force the candidates in π to be eliminated in the stated order. Constraint (6) ensures that the total number of votes cast in the election does not change as a result of the manipulation. The objective minimises the total number of ballot changes required to manipulate the election and enforce a desired elimination sequence.

The above ILP does not include any additional side constraints – properties that we want the manipulated election to satisfy besides resulting in a different winner to that of the original election. Manipulated elections found by *margin-irv* in this setting are almost always evidently close, with a last round margin of 0 or 1 vote. This makes sense as the algorithm is trying to manipulate as few votes as possible, breaking any ties in favour of an alternate outcome. An adversary with the ability to modify electronic records of cast votes, however, will want to create a manipulated election that is not evidently close. An election with a tie in the final round of counting, or a difference of several votes in the tallies of the final two remaining candidates, is likely to be closely scrutinised. Australian IRV elections in which the final tallies of the last two candidates differ by less than 100 votes, for example, trigger an automatic recount.

Given the widespread use of the last round margin as the indicator of how close an IRV election is, rather than the true MOV of the election, our adversary can use this to their advantage. Consider a candidate elimination sequence π, containing at least n candidates from a set $\mathcal{C}$. Let the last n candidates in the sequence π be denoted by $c_k, c_{k+1}, \ldots, c_{k+n}$, with c_{k+n} denoting the winning candidate according to π. Adding the following side constraint to DISTANCETO ensures that margin by which each candidate c_i for $k \leq i \leq k+n-1$ is eliminated (the EM, Definition 4) is at least Δ votes. This allows us to ensure that both the last round margin of the manipulated election, and the elimination margin of any number of prior rounds, is at least a certain size.

$$\sum_{R \in \mathcal{R}_{i,i}} y_R \leq \sum_{R \in \mathcal{R}_{j,i}} y_R + 2\Delta \qquad\qquad \forall i \in \{k, \ldots, k+n-1\} \tag{9}$$

An important side constraint we will make use in the design of our manipulators is *limiting the manipulation*. Since in our scenario the attacker will modify ballots in the middle of the election its important that we calculate manipulations that do not remove ballots already recorded. Suppose C_R is the number of ballots already recorded for ranking R. We must ensure that the modified election has at least C_R ballots with ranking R, since they cannot be changed. Adding the following constraint ensures this.

$$y_R \geq C_R \qquad \forall R \in \mathbf{R} \tag{10}$$

2.3   Minimising Change to First Preference Counts

To both minimise discrepancies between any manual count of first preference tallies, and that computed by counting software applied to a manipulated election, we solve the DISTANCETO ILP of Sect. 2.2 twice for each complete elimination sequence π.

For every such π that *margin-irv* encounters (these are the leaves of the generated search tree), we first solve the ILP with an objective to minimise first preference tally discrepancies. Let $t_C(c)$ denote the first preference tallies of each candidate $c \in C$. The first preference tally for candidate $c \in C$ in any solution of our ILP, $t'_C(c)$, is given by:

$$t'_C(c) = \sum_{R \in \mathbf{R}.c=first(R)} y_R \tag{11}$$

Let FPD denote the total number of first preference tally discrepancies between any manipulated profile found by DISTANCETO ILP, and the true election profile of the original election (Eq. 12). For each complete candidate elimination sequence π, containing all candidates, we first solve the DISTANCETO ILP with the objective shown in Eq. 13. Let fpd denote the value of FPD in the optimal solution found when solving DISTANCETO with this objective. We then constrain the ILP to ensure that any subsequently found solutions must satisfy the constraint in Eq. 14.

$$FPD = \sum_{c \in C} |t_C(c) - t'_C(c)| \tag{12}$$

$$\min FPD \tag{13}$$

$$FPD \leq fpd \tag{14}$$

We re-solve our DISTANCETO ILP with the objective shown in Eq. 4 – to minimise total ballot changes given the constraint limiting permitted change to first preference counts. The result is a manipulated election profile that first aims to minimise the total number of discrepancies between the true and manipulated elections, as a first priority, and the total number of ballot changes as a second.

3   Manipulation Algorithms

We consider a setting in which all ballots are assumed to be scanned at a central location, and the resulting electronic records passed into counting software that computes the result of the election. We assume the scanner has been compromised, and the attacker is able to manipulate (change) the ranking on the electronic record of ballots at the moment they are scanned. Alternatively, we can also consider a setting where votes are scanned at disparate locations, but the attacker is able to intercept and modify the scanned record before it is passed to the counting software. In both cases the attacker manipulates the record of ballots before they are used for counting. In either case, first preference counts may have been completed manually at polling booths and/or at the central scanning location. We assume the attacker has some reasonable estimate of the total number of ballots E expected in the election. Note that in places like Australia with compulsory voting the expected number of ballots E is known with high confidence, in other jurisdictions there will be more variance. Across all experiments in which we simulate our manipulators, we use $E = |\mathcal{B}|$ where $\mathcal{B}$ is the historical set of ballots.

The algorithm applied by our manipulators is as follows. The parameter α, determining how often the attacker computes a set of manipulation rules, and k, the number of rounds on which to apply an elimination margin constraint, are given as input.

1. Let E be the expected number of ballots for the election. Let $n = \lceil \alpha E \rceil$ be a proportion α of this expected number of votes.
2. Collect the first n ballots $\mathcal{B}_T$, passing them on to the counting software unmanipulated. Let $\mathcal{B}_\mathcal{M} = \mathcal{B}_T$, the current profile of the manipulated election.
3. Compute an approximate complete election profile $\hat{\mathcal{B}}$ by extending the (manipulated) ballots $\mathcal{B}_\mathcal{M}$ processed so far with ballots uniformly drawn from the set of true (unmanipulated) ballots seen so far $\mathcal{B}_T$.
4. Use the methods of [2] to determine a minimal manipulation $\mathcal{M}$ of $\hat{\mathcal{B}}$ in order to achieve the desired winner with an EM of Δ applied to the last k rounds. Note that this manipulation may be null if the desired winner already wins in $\hat{\mathcal{B}}$ by Δ.
5. Examining the minimal manipulation made in $\mathcal{M}$ and the assumed unseen ballots $\mathcal{U} = \hat{\mathcal{B}} - \mathcal{B}_\mathcal{M}$, determine a set of manipulation rules $\mathcal{R}$ which will ensure that applying $\mathcal{R}$ to $\mathcal{U}$ will result in manipulation $\mathcal{M}$.
6. Intercept the next n ballots. If an incoming ballot b matches one of the manipulation rules, $r \in \mathcal{R}$, replace b by $r(b)$ before passing it on to the counting software.
7. Let $\mathcal{B}_T$ be the true ballots seen so far. Let $\mathcal{B}_\mathcal{M}$ be the manipulated ballots processed so far – the current state of the manipulated election profile. If all ballots have been processed, the algorithm is complete, otherwise we return to step 3.

We now examine the individual steps in the approach in detail.

Completing an Election. At any given point during the scanning of ballots, our adversary has seen a proportion δ of the total number of expected ballots, E. The manipulated election profile at this point contains δE ballots. Some of these ballots have been manipulated (altered from their true state), and others have been left unchanged. To compute a set of manipulation rules to apply to future ballots, the adversary needs to estimate what a complete election profile could look like (i.e., a profile containing the current set of manipulated ballots, and an estimate of future ballots). Let $\hat{B}$ denote this estimated profile. To compute $\hat{B}$, we start with the current set of ballots in $B_{\mathcal{M}}$ and add $E - |B_{\mathcal{M}}|$ further ballots. These additional ballots are drawn uniformly at random (with replacement) from $B_{\mathcal{T}}$ – the set of ballots, unmodified, that have been seen so far. Each sampled ballot is added to $\hat{B}$.

Example 2. Suppose the first quarter of ballots of the election in Table 1(a), $B_{\mathcal{T}}$, is as shown in Table 1(c). Then an estimation of the complete election $\hat{B}$ might be determined as shown in the same table. The result of the estimated election is shown in Table 1(d). Candidate c remains the winner with a LRM of 22.   □

Computing a Manipulation. We consider two methods of computing a set of manipulation rules to apply to future scanned ballots, given an estimate of what the eventual election profile could look like, $\hat{B}$, assuming the adversary makes no further changes. Each method first simulates the outcome of $\hat{B}$ to determine whether any further manipulation is needed. If the desired candidate wins, no manipulation rules are generated. Otherwise, a set of rules indicating what kind of ballots to look for during the scanning process, and what to replace them with when they are seen, are formed. When a rule is followed by either of our manipulators, that rule is removed from their rule set.

Our first method for generating such rules uses *margin-irv*, as described in Sect. 2.1, to determine a minimal manipulation $\mathcal{M}$ of the election $\hat{B}$ so that the candidate selected by the attacker wins. Note that we add the side constraints of Eq (10) where $C_R = |\{r \mid r \in B_{\mathcal{M}}, r = R\}|$ is the current count of ballots of the form R.

We then translate this minimal manipulation into a set of rules for the attacker to follow. Our second method does not compute a minimal manipulation of $\hat{B}$, but simply computes the difference between final tallies of the eventual winner w, and the desired winner w', $\Delta_{w,w'}$. The adversary will seek to remove $\lceil \Delta_{w,w'}/2 \rceil$ votes in which w is preferred first, and replace them with a vote in which w' is preferred first.

Example 3. Imagine the attacker wants candidate a to win with a last round margin of 20. One such manipulation (certainly not the minimal one) is to change the ballots to sum to the counts in Table 1(e) which results in election shown in Table 1(f).

The manipulation needs to remove one $[c]$ vote and 11 $[c, a]$ votes and add one $[b, c]$ vote and 11 $[a]$ votes, to end with these tallies from the estimated completion $\hat{\mathcal{B}}$.   □

MOV-Based Manipulator. A minimal manipulation $\mathcal{M}$ found by *margin-irv* specifies, for each type of ballot $R \in \mathbf{R}$, the number of ballots of that type that should be *added to* or *removed from* the election profile to achieve a desired elimination sequence π. The manipulation $\mathcal{M}$ simply records for each ranking R of candidates: how many ballots are modified q_R to take on the new ranking R, and how many ballots with ranking R are modified m_R to show a different ranking. Its not possible that both q_R and m_R are non-zero for the same R, otherwise there is a smaller manipulation with the same effect.

In order for such a manipulation to be found in a reasonable time frame, the ILP of Sect. 2.2 operates over *equivalence classes* of ballot rankings, $\tilde{\mathbf{R}}$, rather than all possible rankings over a set of candidates $\mathcal{C}$, $\mathbf{R}$. Given an elimination sequence to achieve, π, each ranking in $\mathbf{R}$ is reduced to a ballot class in $\tilde{\mathbf{R}}$. The original ranking is reduced by removing all candidates that would be eliminated by the time that ballot could possibly be placed in their tally. All ballots in the same class will move between the tally piles of the same set of candidates, at the same times. For example, consider an election with candidates a, b, c, and d, and a desired elimination sequence $\pi = [a,c,d,b]$. Ballots with rankings $[c,a,b,d]$, $[c,b,a]$, and $[c,a,b]$, are reduced to the equivalent class $[c,b]$.

The minimal manipulation $\mathcal{M}$ found by *margin-irv* defines: a candidate elimination sequence to be achieved, π, in which the desired winner is victorious; a set of ballots D, in equivalence class form, to remove from $\hat{\mathcal{B}}$; and a set of ballots A, in equivalence class form, to add to $\hat{\mathcal{B}}$. For each ballot to add to the profile, there is a ballot to remove – leaving the total number of cast ballots unchanged (i.e., $|A| = |D|$).

Our MOV-based manipulator creates a manipulation rule for every ballot in D. For the ith ballot in D, d_i, a rule of the form:

$$reduce_\pi(b) = d_i \rightarrow a_i$$

is formed, stating that if the manipulator sees a ballot b with a ranking that could be reduced to the equivalence class d_i (assuming the eventual elimination sequence will be π), this ballot should be replaced with the ith ballot in A, a_i.

Example 4. The elimination order desired by the attacker is $\pi = [c, b, a]$. The equivalence classes of the seen ballot types are $[a]$, $[c, a]$, $[b]$ and $[c]$ respectively. The manipulation in terms of these equivalence classes is $+11[a]$, $-11[c, a]$, $+1[b]$ and $-1[c]$. We end up with 12 rules: 11 copies of $[c, a] \rightarrow [a]$ and 1 copy of $[c] \rightarrow [b]$.

If we perform the manipulation on the *actual* remaining ballots we will find enough ballots to change resulting in a final manipulated count $B_\mathcal{M}$ of $[a] : 66$, $[c, a] : 19$, $[b, c] : 37$ and $[c] : 14$. The election will first eliminate c and then b with a winning with an LRM of 24. Because the initial ballots were less favorable to the attackers candidate than in the full election the manipulation is larger than required.   □

First Preference Manipulator. Recall that our first preference manipulator seeks to take $\Delta_{w,w'}$ ballots (divided by two and rounded up) in which a candidate w is preferenced first, and replace them with a ballot in which candidate w' is preferenced first. This manipulator creates $\lceil \Delta_{w,w'}/2 \rceil$ rules of the form:

$$[w, \ldots] \rightarrow [w']$$

The pattern on the left hand side of this rule matches all ballots in which candidate w is preferenced first. Such ballots are replaced by the ballot $[w']$ containing a single preference for w'. If the manipulator is seeking to achieve a last round margin of a given size, Δ, it creates $\lceil \Delta_{w,w'}/2 \rceil + \Delta$ rules of the above form. Note that this naive manipulator is able to influence the last round margin of an election, but not the elimination margin of losing candidates in prior rounds. The manipulation is also heuristic – there is no guarantee that it will result in a desired winner, as it does not consider how preferences might flow between candidates. For example, robbing the original winner of some of their primary vote may result in their early elimination, distributing enough votes to cause an alternate candidate $c \neq w'$ to win. The MOV-based manipulator has more control over potential outcomes as it can alter the later preferences on each ballot.

Example 5. The difference in tallies between the actual winner c of the estimated election $\hat{\mathcal{B}}$ and the desired winner a is 44. The first preference manipulator then requires moving $22 + 20$ votes from c to a in order to attain a LRM of 20 for a. The manipulation is then 42 copies of $[c, \ldots] \rightarrow [a]$.

When we apply this manipulation to the actual ballots we find there are only 21 $[c, a]$ and 11 $[c]$ votes arriving in the remainder of the election which are all converted to $[a]$ votes. The final manipulated count is $[a] : 87$, $[c, a] : 9$, $[b, c] : 36$, $[c] : 4$. The winner is a with a LRM of 30 over b. These rather gross manipulations may bring the election result into question, since the final tallies are far from the actual tallies.   □

4   Results and Conclusions

We take the cast ballot data available for 5 seats of the Australian New South Wales (NSW) 2015 Legislative Assembly election, and simulate the use of our first preference and more intelligent MOV-based manipulators. The goal of each manipulator is to bring about the election of a specific candidate. For each type of manipulator, we simulate its application in each seat over 100 trials. In each trial, the order which the cast ballots arrive at the scanner is randomised. We compute, over the 100 trials: the average number of ballot changes made by the manipulator; the average total change in first preference tallies resulting from the manipulations; the number of simulations in which the manipulator achieved its desired winner, and achieved its desired winner with a last round margin sufficient to avoid an automatic recount; and the average number of manipulation rules generated by the manipulator after the processing of each αE batch of ballots. The latter statistic corresponds to the average number of *intended* manipulations the adversary still expects to need at each stage of processing.

All experiments have been conducted on a machine with an Intel Xeon Platinum 8176 chip (2.1 GHz), and 1 TB of RAM. We have used $\alpha = 25\%$ across each batch of 100 simulations. Each batch of 100 simulations have been initialised with the same random seed controlling the order in which ballots arrive at the scanner.

We first consider the relative performance of our first preference manipulator, and a MOV-based manipulator that does not attempt to minimise change across first preference tallies in the true and altered election. We then consider the effectiveness of a MOV-based manipulation that attempts to minimise such discrepancies. The computational requirements of each of our manipulators varies. The first preference manipulator is able to compute a set of manipulation rules in less than a second, the MOV-based manipulators (without first preference tally change minimisation) several seconds, while minimising first preference tally changes extends rule generation time by up to a minute.

Table 2 reports the performance of our first preference and MOV-based manipulators on the IRV elections held across our 5 case study seats: Ballina; Balmain; Campbelltown; Heffron; and Lismore. We report the true MOV, LRM, and number of ballots cast in each election alongside the effectiveness of each manipulator across 100 simulated trials. We have found that the MOV-based manipulator is more effective in achieving a change in winner when it seeks to enforce a reasonably sized elimination margin (EM) on the last two rounds of counting, rather than a margin on just the last round. In all our reported results, the MOV-based manipulators enforce an EM of Δ between the runner-up and winner, and the runner-up and their runner-up. The two settings – enforcing an LRM vs an EM on the last two rounds – are similarly effective in certain seats (Campbelltown, Heffron, and Lismore), with the latter more effective in Ballina. Note that the detailed results of this comparison have been omitted for brevity.

Ballina is a seat where the identity of the candidate coming in third significantly influenced which of the remaining two candidates won. The manipulator needed the Greens candidate to place third so that their preferences flowed to the manipulator's desired candidate from the Country Labor Party. Simply enforcing a certain LRM in this instance resulted in manipulated elections in which the tallies of the two runner-ups were similar when determining third place. When forming a manipulation, there is no guarantee that all generated manipulation rules will be applied, and no guarantee that these rules will bring about the desired change in winner. The rules are computed based on hypothetical completions of partially known election profiles. Forming manipulation rules designed to ensure the Greens candidate was eliminated in this third-last position, with a reasonably sized elimination margin, more reliably achieved the desired result.

Table 2 shows that in general, our MOV-based manipulator requires less ballot changes on average to reliably (more than 90% of the time) bring about a desired change in winner. The first preference manipulator is often more successful, as more of its manipulation rules are likely to be applied in practice. A rule that is looking for a ballot with a certain candidate ranked first is more likely to be applied than one that looking for a ballot with a specific ranking of candidates. While a manipulation based on first preferences may, in some circumstances, underestimate the number of ballot changes required to alter an election outcome, it generally overestimates the degree of manipulation required. By focusing on preference flow in Lismore, the MOV-based manipulator reliably achieves a desired outcome by changing orders of magnitude less ballots, on average. In Balmain and Campbelltown, the first preference manipulator generates a slightly smaller 'intended manipulation', forming less manipulation rules, on average, after seeing the first 25% batch of ballots. The MOV-based manipulator applies fewer of its generated rules, in these two contests, leading to fewer ballot changes on average.

It may be the case that ballots are manually examined to compute first preference tallies for each candidate, while the full count is performed by a computer. In this setting, a large discrepancy between the first preference tallies reported by the software, and that of the manual count, is likely to arouse suspicion. Table 3 compares the average discrepancy in first preference counts (between the true, unmanipulated elections, and those altered by our manipulators) when using a MOV-based manipulator that *does not* focus on minimising these discrepancies, and one that *does*. Note that if a number of ballots N is shifted from the first preference tally of one candidate to another, this is viewed as a discrepancy of $2N$ votes. The discrepancy minimising manipulator was able to reduce change in first preference counts by 2.5 times, on average, between a factor of 1.1 and 9, while requiring only a small increase in total ballot changes. In Ballina, we are able to reliably realise a desired winner change while producing a first preference count discrepancy that is significantly lower than the MOV or LRM of the election. Heffron and Campbelltown, with their large margins of victory, are more challenging to manipulate in a non-obvious manner.

Irrespective of whether first preference count changes are being minimised or not, our MOV-based manipulator can successfully alter the outcomes of elections, while avoiding an automatically triggered recount.

Minimising first preference count changes requires a more subtle manipulation, with the later preferences on ballots being altered more often. The result is that the manipulator must aim to achieve larger elimination margins in the last two eliminations to reliably achieve a desired winner change. The manipulator can be too ambitious however, and try to achieve elimination margins that are not realistically achievable. A limitation of the MOV-based manipulators is that if they cannot find a manipulation of a given hypothetical complete election profile that satisfies all desired side constraints, they give up and fail to generate a set of manipulation rules. A more effective strategy would relax these constraints – with smaller requirements on elimination margins – until the algorithm of Sect. 2.1 is able to find a manipulation.

Table 2. Performance of the first preference manipulator (aiming to enforce a LRM of at least Δ) and MOV-based manipulator (enforcing an elimination margin of Δ over the last 2 rounds of counting). The MOV-based manipulator is not using first preference discrepancy minimisation. We report the number of simulations (/100) in which the manipulators are successful, the average number of ballot manipulations performed, the average resulting change to first preference counts, and the number of manipulation rules (int. ballot changes) generated after each 25% proportion of ballots has been seen.

	First Preference Manipulator				MOV-based Manipulator			
2Δ	100	300	500	1000	100	300	500	1000
Ballina: MOV of 1,130; LRM of 1,267; 47,865 ballots cast								
Desired winner achieved	**100**	**100**	**100**	**100**	76	98	91	95
Avg ballot changes	3198	3198	3198	3198	**1171**	**1265**	**1328**	**1407**
Avg FP count changes	6397	6397	6397	6397	**2059**	**2283**	**2408**	**2591**
Avg int. ballot changes (1)	4699	4799	4899	5149	1218	1310	1396	1629
(2)	0	0	0	0	670	774	754	824
(3)	0	0	0	0	272	310	291	145
Balmain: MOV of 1,731; LRM of 1,731; 46,952 ballots cast								
Desired winner achieved	**84**	**94**	**98**	**100**	71	**94**	93	97
Avg ballot changes	1860	1935	2004	2203	**1779**	**1865**	**1907**	**2023**
Avg FP count changes	3720	3871	4008	4405	**3215**	**3443**	**3556**	**3875**
Avg int. ballot changes (1)	1747	1847	1947	2197	1776	1891	1968	2223
(2)	66	54	34	0	313	304	287	146
(3)	47	34	22	5	111	87	50	29
Campbelltown: MOV of 3,096; LRM of 3,096; 45,124 ballots cast								
Desired winner achieved	**90**	**98**	**99**	**100**	72	92	93	**100**
Avg ballot changes	3232	3313	3392	3590	**3161**	**3237**	**3294**	**3512**
Avg FP count changes	6464	6627	6784	7181	**6166**	**6319**	**6452**	**6903**
Avg int. ballot changes (1)	3130	3230	3330	3580	3151	3272	3357	3586
(2)	75	63	41	5	615	673	770	1023
(3)	27	20	21	5	130	91	61	12
Heffron: MOV of 5,824; LRM of 5,835; 46,367 ballots cast								
Desired winner achieved	**85**	**96**	**97**	**100**	71	95	99	**100**
Avg ballot changes	5928	6006	6087	6327	**5878**	**5973**	**6068**	**6255**
Avg FP count changes	11856	12013	12175	12656	**11357**	**11450**	**11744**	**12346**
Avg int. ballot changes (1)	5862	5962	6062	6312	5883	5979	6047	6320
(2)	744	844	944	1194	2680	2820	2746	3028
(3)	50	29	10	0	589	566	601	747
Lismore: MOV of 209; LRM of 1,173; 47,208 ballots cast								
Desired winner achieved	**100**	99	98	**100**	81	91	90	95
Avg ballot changes	4651	4696	4727	4742	**339**	**396**	**434**	**510**
Avg FP count changes	9304	9392	9455	9486	**601**	**716**	**796**	**974**
Avg int. ballot changes (1)	4371	4475	4572	4814	294	242	514	730
(2)	192	195	151	110	150	150	150	117
(3)	89	44	44	0	52	52	51	23

Table 3. Number of trials (/100) in which two MOV-based manipulators achieve a desired winner change. The first does not minimise first preference count discrepancies, while the second does. We report the number of successful manipulations in which the resulting election avoided an automatic recount (LRM $\geq 100/2 = 50$ votes).

	MOV-based Manipulator No FP change minimisation				MOV-based Manipulator Minimise FP count changes			
2Δ	100	300	500	1000	100	300	500	1000
Ballina: MOV of 1,130; LRM of 1,267; 47,865 ballots cast								
Desired winner achieved	**76**	98	91	**95**	72	**99**	**100**	88
Avoid auto recount	**76**	98	91	**95**	72	**99**	**100**	88
Avg ballot changes	**1171**	**1265**	**1328**	**1407**	1185	1296	1463	1735
Avg FP count changes	2059	2283	2408	2591	**230**	**324**	**512**	**714**
Avg int. ballot changes (1)	1218	1310	1396	1629	1216	1368	1457	2042
(2)	670	774	754	824	789	870	998	1235
(3)	272	310	291	145	398	434	502	403
Balmain: MOV of 1,731; LRM of 1,731; 46,952 ballots cast								
Desired winner achieved	**71**	**94**	93	**97**	50	93	**100**	92
Avoid auto recount	**48**	**82**	83	**94**	26	75	**100**	87
Avg ballot changes	**1779**	**1865**	**1907**	**2023**	1784	1958	2147	2502
Avg FP count changes	3216	3443	3556	3875	**849**	**970**	**1079**	**1136**
Avg int. ballot changes (1)	1776	1891	1968	2223	1783	1954	2130	2585
(2)	313	304	287	146	1173	1241	1316	1429
(3)	112	87	50	29	577	612	637	545
Campbelltown: MOV of 3,096; LRM of 3,096; 45,124 ballots cast								
Desired winner achieved	**72**	92	93	**100**	59	**93**	**100**	95
Avoid auto recount	**57**	**85**	89	**100**	31	79	**100**	92
Avg ballot changes	**3161**	**3237**	**3294**	**3512**	4034	4115	4245	4366
Avg FP count changes	6166	6319	6452	6903	**3051**	**3122**	**3329**	**3654**
Avg int. ballot changes (1)	3151	3272	3357	3586	4213	4325	4380	4661
(2)	615	673	770	1023	2134	2108	2173	2116
(3)	130	91	61	12	875	901	906	758
Heffron: MOV of 5,824; LRM of 5,835; 46,367 ballots cast								
Desired winner achieved	**71**	**95**	99	**100**	45	93	**100**	**100**
Avoid auto recount	**49**	**89**	96	**100**	31	83	**100**	**100**
Avg ballot changes	**5878**	**5973**	**6068**	**6255**	6595	6719	6897	7651
Avg FP count changes	11357	11450	11744	12346	**10607**	**10910**	**11414**	**12029**
Avg int. ballot changes (1)	5883	5979	6047	6320	6635	6748	6904	7611
(2)	2680	2820	2746	3028	2976	3164	3291	3392
(3)	589	566	601	747	1402	1466	1568	1697
Lismore: MOV of 209; LRM of 1,173; 47,208 ballots cast								
Desired winner achieved	**81**	**91**	90	95	72	**91**	**96**	**95**
Avoid auto recount	**77**	83	86	87	67	**91**	**96**	**95**
Avg ballot changes	**339**	**396**	**434**	**510**	339	438	521	621
Avg FP count changes	601	716	796	974	**215**	**283**	**368**	**542**
Avg int. ballot changes (1)	294	242	514	730	384	535	719	1140
(2)	150	150	150	117	206	293	354	240
(3)	52	52	51	23	97	86	64	77

Conclusions. The experiments show that it is quite feasible for an attacker to manipulate an election to change the winner with high confidence in the scenario we examine. Using MOV-based manipulation and minimising first preference changes the attacker can avoid an automatic recount, and often significantly reduce the number of first preference changes. Hence we can conclude that rigorous risk limiting audits of elections is warranted, since simple counting based approaches to auditing can be defeated.

References

1. Blom, M., Stuckey, P.J., Teague, V.J.: Computing the margin of victory in preferential parliamentary elections. In: Krimmer, R., et al. (eds.) E-Vote-ID 2018. LNCS, vol. 11143, pp. 1–16. Springer, Cham (2018). https://doi.org/10.1007/978-3-030-00419-4_1
2. Blom, M., Stuckey, P.J., Teague, V.. Election manipulation 100. In: Proceedings of the Fourth Workshop on Advances in Secure Electronic Voting (Voting 2019) (2019)
3. Blom, M., Teague, V., Stuckey, P.J., Tidhar, R.: Efficient computation of exact IRV margins. In: Proceedings of the 22nd European Conference on Artificial Intelligence (2016)
4. Conitzer, V., Walsh, T., Xia, L.: Dominating manipulations in voting with partial information. In: AAAI Conference on Artificial Intelligence (2011)
5. Magrino, T.R., Rivest, R.L., Shen, E., Wagner, D.A.: Computing the margin of victory in IRV elections. Workshop on Trustworthy Elections, USENIX Association Berkeley, CA, USA, In: USENIX Accurate Electronic Voting Technology Workshop (2011)
6. Richie, R.: Instant runoff voting: what mexico (and others) could learn. Election Law J. **3**, 501–512 (2004)
7. Xia, L.: Computing the margin of victory for various voting rules. In: Proceedings of the 13th ACM Conference on Electronic Commerce, EC 2012, pp. 982–999. ACM, New York (2012)

Online Voting in a First Nation in Canada: Implications for Participation and Governance

Brian Budd[1] (ID), Chelsea Gabel[2] (ID), and Nicole Goodman[3](✉) (ID)

[1] Department of Political Science, University of Guelph, Guelph, Canada
buddb@uguelph.ca
[2] Department of Health, Aging and Society and Indigenous Studies Program,
McMaster University, Hamilton, Canada
gabelc@mcmaster.ca
[3] Department of Political Science, Brock University, St. Catharines, Canada
Nicole.goodman@brocku.ca

Abstract. Indigenous communities are increasingly adopting technology to create digital opportunities for members and enhance engagement and governance. One recent trend in the adoption of online services is the use of online voting. To date, more than 90 Indigenous communities in Canada and the United States have deployed online voting with many more considering implementation. This article draws upon interviews with local government officials and voter exit surveys as part of community-engaged research with Wasauksing First Nation in Ontario, Canada to explore the specific opportunities and challenges online voting presents for governance and engagement in Indigenous communities and implications for future adoption. Specifically, we examine a 2017 Land Code vote where online voting was introduced to achieve a participation threshold required to pass the framework. Our findings point to online voting as a key tool to modernize Indigenous governance and enhance participatory capacity by making voting more accessible for members. We argue that online voting is an engine that can advance self-determination and support communities seeking an iterative path to self-government.

Keywords: Online voting · Indigenous governance · First Nations · Self-determination · Canada · Community-Engaged Research

1 Introduction

To date online voting has been used by a growing number of Indigenous communities across Canada and the United States for elections or other types of community votes. Online voting is appealing to Indigenous communities as a tool to improve voter accessibility and engagement, especially for communities where large segments of the membership live off of reserve lands [14]. While the engagement of off-reserve members is important to ensure balanced representation of community voice, in the Canadian context it is crucially important since many communities are subject to federal legislation that has required them to meet participation thresholds in order to pass community laws and gain back autonomy. In this regard, online voting use among

© Springer Nature Switzerland AG 2019
R. Krimmer et al. (Eds.): E-Vote-ID 2019, LNCS 11759, pp. 50–66, 2019.
https://doi.org/10.1007/978-3-030-30625-0_4

First Nations in Canada represents a tool for communities to not only bridge participatory gaps with off-reserve members, but also to increase their capacity to ratify their own legislation and move away from federal control over decision-making and governance processes. Despite optimism about online voting's potential to enhance participation and governance, questions persist about the ability of the technology to do so. There are also important considerations around the cultural appropriateness of online voting and whether its adoption is consistent with Indigenous culture, community visions of self-determination, and local decision-making.

This article examines the opportunities and challenges online voting presents for participation and governance for Indigenous communities through a case study of Wasauksing First Nation in Ontario, Canada. Building upon previous research focused on understanding First Nations' satisfaction with online voting, online voter characteristics and the potential for online voting to improve voter engagement in a First Nation context [14], we draw upon semi-structured interviews with local government officials, participant observation data, and exit survey data from online and paper voters as part of a land code ratification vote in February 2017 to examine how online voting affects perceptions of participation and governance. Specifically, we assess the degree to which online voting contributed to the community's capacity to ratify the land code legislation and its potential to enhance, or limit community capacity and self-determination in the future. The original contribution of this work is its focus on the implications online voting presents for governance and the enhancement of self-determination in First Nations. Findings suggest that online voting is a tool to modernize Indigenous institutions and governance, improve community connectedness, particularly by better connecting off-reserve members in policy discussions, and as an engine to support meeting quorums for critical votes that, if successful, can advance community capacity and enhance self-determination as part of an iterative path to self-government.

This article proceeds as follows. First, we present some brief background about the colonial context in Canada and how online voting can contribute to First Nations gaining back their political power. This is followed by a literature review that explores understandings of Indigenous self-determination and self-government to guide our assessment of the impact of digital technology in Wasauksing First Nation and reviews what studies have found about First Nations' use of online voting. Next, we present an overview of Wasauksing and explain the rationale for, and steps taken to, implement online voting for the ratification vote. In the fourth and fifth sections, we present our methodological approach and analysis. Finally, we discuss what our findings mean for future adoption of online voting in First Nations and Indigenous communities more broadly, notably implications for self-determination, community engagement, and governance.

2 Background

Indigenous communities around the world face many social, economic, political and legal inequalities arising out of ongoing colonial legacies. In the case of Canada, the presence of paternalistic legislation designed to subvert complex systems of Indigenous governance has created enduring conditions of dependency as First Nation, Métis and

Inuit communities have been subordinated under the oversight and administration of the federal government. While Indigenous resistance to colonial administration has been constant throughout Canada's history, in the past 50 years there has been a shift in the relationship between Indigenous peoples and the Canadian state. Bolstered by the emergence of an international Indigenous rights movement [19], Indigenous peoples have taken steps to assume greater control over governance and policy-making within their communities, albeit with overarching institutional apparatuses of colonial administration still intact. While the assertion of the right to self-determination has become a prominent feature of Indigenous politics in Canada, variation exists in the approaches Indigenous communities take to achieve self-determination and their capacity to pursue it.

Numerous strategies and approaches have been taken to achieve self-government and enhance self-determination. One strategy is to take larger steps such as the signing of self-government agreements and land claim negotiations, while a second type of approach is more incremental, characterized by smaller steps involving the devolution and decentralization of decision-making into the hands of Indigenous communities and stakeholders. Literature on Indigenous politics has mostly focused on the former set of approaches, exploring the "high politics" of self-determination and self-government, emphasizing formal agreements and negotiations between Indigenous communities and other levels of government [17]. Far less attention has been given to the smaller, less-visible steps that communities are taking to achieve the same ends. Aided in part by legislative opportunities created by the federal government, an increasing number of Indigenous communities across Canada are enacting iterative steps toward the development of self-determination through the ratification of community-based legislation [11]. In recent years the iterative approach has become increasingly possible through the adoption of online voting as a tool to enhance voter engagement and pass key pieces of legislation. We explore this process and its impacts in this article in the context of First Nations in Canada.

3 Indigenous Governance, Digital Technology and Online Voting

3.1 Indigenous Governance

First Nations in Canada face an array of governance and participation challenges stemming from Canada's history of colonization and continued colonialism. While beyond the scope of this article to summarize in full, this history has left previously autonomous Indigenous nations with truncated forms of territorial sovereignty and decision-making authority over their communities [4, 18]. The legislative framework under which most First Nations are governed is the federally written *Indian Act*. Originally devised by representatives of the Crown in 1867, the *Indian Act* allowed for the forcible removal of First Nation peoples from their traditional territories while replacing previous forms of Indigenous governance with colonially-imposed band councils. Under the terms of the *Indian Act*, First Nations are given the ability to democratically-elect representatives for their communities. However, the *Indian Act's* legal framework effectively limits the governing authority of these representatives by granting the federally-appointed Minister of Indian Affairs the authority to approve or disallow many decisions passed by band councils [16]. Furthermore, the original terms of the *Indian Act* provide the Minister with the ability to replace democratically-elected band council representatives and assume authority over First Nations. This has infused an inherent element of instability into First Nation governance.

While the majority of First Nations in Canada continue to operate under the *Indian Act's* legal framework, substantive efforts have been made to revitalize on-reserve governance and improve political engagement. These efforts have come in many forms including amendments to the *Indian Act* itself and intergovernmental negotiations [1, 2, 27]. While many First Nations have replaced the *Indian Act* in its entirety with self-government agreements, most have pursued a more incremental approach. This incremental approach has focused on increasing the autonomy and self-government capacity of First Nations through targeted reforms to specific provisions of the *Indian Act* and negotiated agreements with the federal government that allow for the decentralization of on-reserve services to First Nation governments [27]. These changes have provided opportunities for communities to take iterative steps toward self-government, negotiating with the federal government to gradual develop their governance capacity and assume control over service delivery in areas such as health, housing, education and social services. This incremental approach does not include systemic reform to broader legal and political frameworks. Change instead comes largely through targeted reforms to specific provisions of the *Indian Act* or the negotiation of agreements between individual or collective groups of First Nations. While these changes tend to be smaller and less visible, they represent important evolutions in governance and Indigenous sovereignty often overlooked by post-colonial or neo-Marxist scholars [3, 5].

To date more than 90 Indigenous communities in Canada and the United States have deployed online voting. Decisions to adopt online ballots have been primarily motivated by a desire to improve political participation [14]. Under the terms of the *Indian Act*, however, voting in elections and referendums is permitted only by paper ballot (either in-person at a poll location or by mail) though it is allowed for other types of votes, such as ratification votes or community polls.

3.2 Digital Technology and Online Voting

In recent years, digital technologies have emerged as important tools for First Nations pursuing incremental approaches toward self-government. Digital technologies have allowed First Nations to strengthen governance capacity while addressing social, political and economic challenges. Scholarly literature has explored the use of technology in the areas of healthcare, education, social services, economic development and cultural renewal [20, 21, 23, 26, 28]. These studies have demonstrated the resourcefulness of First Nations in overcoming digital divides through the creation of innovative funding and ownership models [19]. This body of research has also drawn connections between digital technology and self-determination, exploring the ways in which technology has been used to support broader political goals. For example, several scholars have noted how technology has been used by First Nations to improve administrative capacity to assume greater control over service design and delivery. For First Nations, digital technologies are not only an avenue to improve service delivery or public outreach, but are also understood as tools within a broader decolonizing struggle to roll back the power of settler governments and realize self-determination [22].

To date, few scholars have examined the effects of online voting on Indigenous communities. Research in this context mostly focuses on First Nations in Canada [9, 10, 13] despite the fact that Indigenous communities in the United States and New Zealand are embracing the technology. Existing work has pointed to a number of benefits in Indigenous contexts. Studies have documented improved political engagement through enhanced voter accessibility [9, 10, 13], albeit with small sample sizes, and improved community connectedness by stimulating intergenerational communication among youth and elders [9]. While studies of online voting use in municipal elections in Canada has shown that the voting method can increase turnout by 3.5% points [15], other analyses in comparative contexts that employ similar methodological approaches find no increase [12]. It is unclear whether we could expect the same effect in First Nations as in Canadian municipalities given the unique context and since online voting is used less frequently for Chief and Council elections given legislative limitations and more so for other types of votes (referenda, agreement votes etc.).

Beyond engagement, online voting has also been shown to positively benefit the governance capacity of First Nations. By allowing communities to engage a larger number of their citizens, online voting has supported communities in reaching difficult quorums required to ratify legislation [8, 9]. Further, online voting has also been shown to benefit local governance and strengthen administrative capacity by expediting tabulation of results and by generally including a wider group of community members [14]. Though self-determination has been an important theme in research on online voting in First Nations, it has been relatively underexplored compared to issues of participation and engagement.

Despite benefits covered in the literature, recent research also highlights the unique challenges First Nations face with online voting deployment. First, access to quality broadband is a concern, especially because many communities are located in rural or remote areas [8]. Second, the tendering of online voting contracts to private sector vendors has raised issues especially with respect to data governance and ownership. In addition, the fact that some communities have limited technical resources and capacity has made adequately vetting suppliers more challenging. In response to this a recent report has called for the development of online voting standards to boost technical capacity in First Nations [8]. Finally, it is important to point out that voters' unfamiliarity with online voting can pose a challenge to implementation. While issues with the novelty of online voting are not unique to First Nations, there is the potential that unfamiliarity coupled with pre-existing feelings of distrust or suspicion toward government may deter uptake.

4 Methodology

4.1 A Community-Engaged Approach

For this study we employed a Community-Engaged Research (CER) approach which seeks to overcome some of the power inequities that exist between researchers and Indigenous communities through the development of research partnerships which promote empowerment, inclusivity, and respect [6, 7]. Such projects share underlying goals of influencing social change, and equitably involving community partners throughout the research process from the inception of the project through knowledge mobilization [24]. Our study employs a qualitative research design, which is considered ethical, respectful, applicable, authentic, beneficial and relevant to the experiences of Indigenous peoples.

We began building a relationship with Wasauksing First Nation in March 2016. This included a number of phone conversations, contributions to community newsletters, attendance and presentations at community events, and presentations to Chief and Council. In addition to receiving university ethics approval, Chief and Council also approved and were supportive of the research. Community members were provided with information about the purpose of the project, data collection process, responsibilities, risks or inconveniences, benefits, assurances of confidentiality and any additional information requested. The practice of gift giving, whether for ceremony or for community events, is common in Indigenous communities [25]. We felt that gift giving was an important part of maintaining positive community relationships and building trust. As a result, we raffled off door prizes at each community meeting, including a number of gift cards and tablets.

4.2 Data Collection

The data for this article comes from semi-structured interviews undertaken with political and bureaucratic leaders in the community, participant observation on voting day, and voter exit surveys. All questionnaires were constructed in active consultation with the community and specific items were added based on their needs.

Interviews asked questions about the process of adopting online voting, challenges and benefits and the role of digital technology in self-determination and self-governance. Notes taken during the interviews and observation were analyzed using NVIVO qualitative data analysis software. Transcripts were uploaded to the software and analyzed using a multi-stage inductive approach, which involved identifying core themes in the transcripts related to community views toward the introduction of online voting. These core themes were then used as coding categories to sort and analyze our interviews with the community. This inductive method of analysis is consistent with the broad CER approach taken in our overall study and allowed for community per-spectives and voices to be expressed clearly in the research findings. Our analysis uncovered 3 core themes related to the introduction of online voting: innovation and community modernization, community connectedness, and self-determination and self-governance.

Voter exit surveys were administered to online and paper voters once they had cast a ballot. All persons who voted online or in-person at the polls were offered the option to participate, and completion was voluntary. To support participant recruitment six youth research assistants and one elder interpreter were hired and completed a training course on data collection at the polls. Online voter surveys were administered online. The survey was open for completion during the online voting period, which lasted from December 10th, 2016 until 8:00am on the primary voting day, February 25th, 2017. Paper voters casting a ballot on voting day were encouraged to complete the survey by iPad, but could also fill out a paper copy or complete the survey orally with the assistance of an interpreter. Paper surveys were also offered to voters on December 10th as part of in-person advanced voting.

Survey questions probed voter satisfaction, rationale for use, concerns, likelihood of future use, digital access and literacy, participation histories and standard socio-demographic items. A total of 15 online voter surveys were completed, representing a response rate of 20%, and 66 paper voter surveys for a response rate of 66%.[1] Respondents self-selected for both surveys and so may have been more likely to like or dislike online voting. Given the self-selected nature of the sample, and the small N's,[2] descriptive statistics are used to analyze data where appropriate. These limitations prevent us from drawing broad conclusions about online voting's affect on voter engagement in a First Nations context and should be taken as suggestive evidence that could be further explored in future studies.

As part of the knowledge mobilization strategy for this project, Wasauksing was provided with written reports of survey results. Findings were also presented to Chief and Council and the Lands Management committee. These efforts are in line with a CER approach and intended to ensure that the research process and results are meaningful, respectful and relevant, and that they reflect community concerns and interests.

5   Wasauksing First Nation and Their Land Code Ratification

Wasauksing First Nation (WFN) is an Ojibway, Odawa and Pottawatomi community located near Parry Sound, Ontario, Canada. The community has a land base of approximately 7,875 hectares and a total population of 1,090 with 369 community members residing on reserve. The community is currently engaged in two land claim negotiations with the federal and provincial governments to extend the boundary line of

---

[1] The paper voter sample includes more women (64%) than men (34%), with 2% identifying as 'other'. Paper voter respondents have a median age of 46 years, household income range of $20,000 to $29,000, median education level of "some technical community college", and are likely to reside on reserve. The sample of online voters, by comparison, also contains more women (71%) than men (29%). This sample also reports a median age of 46, household income range between $80,000 and $99,000, median education of completed "technical, community college", and are more likely to live off-reserve.

[2] While the N's are small, they are very good based on the size of the community.

the reserve to cover an additional 223 hectares of traditional land. The *Indian Act* presently governs elections and referendums in WFN.

In addition to the land claims, WFN has sought to extend its control over its reserve land by signing on to the *Framework Agreement on First Nation Land Management*. The framework agreement was initially signed in 1996 between 13 First Nations and the Minister of Indian Affairs and Northern Development. Since then, the it has been ratified as part of the *First Nations Land Management Act* (1999) and expanded to include an additional 125 First Nation signatories. As a signatory, each First Nation is provided the opportunity to develop land code legislation to replace sections of the *Indian Act* related to the governance and management of reserve lands. The agreement is a sectoral self-government agreement that provides First Nations with the legal status and powers to govern and manage their lands and resources through the passage of laws under their own land code.

Once a community has signed on to the framework agreement, they are tasked with developing and drafting their own land code legislation. This legislation covers a number of areas related to land management including general rules and procedures, occupation of reserve lands by members and non-members, financial accountability measures for revenues, and laws and regulations related to environmental protection. Land codes empower communities by setting out the rules and procedures for making and publishing their own land laws, while also diverting funding and fees collected from the administration of land back to the community instead of to the federal government. Passing a land code represents removal from 25% of the *Indian Act*.

The penultimate step once a First Nation has drafted land code legislation is to negotiate and sign an Individual Agreement with the Government of Canada. The Agreement establishes the specific terms of the transfer of management of reserve lands from the federal government to the First Nation. After this has been reached, the First Nation must proceed to ratify the proposed Land Code legislation and Individual Agreement by holding a ratification vote. The ratification vote must include all eligible or registered band members aged 18+. Although legislation passed by parliament in December 2018 has softened the requirements to pass a land code, at the time of WFN's vote at least 50% + 1 of registered voters were required to vote, with at least 25% + 1 of all eligible voters casting a yes vote. Historically, meeting this quorum has been difficult [9] and has resulted in failed votes [14].

WFN signed on to the framework agreement in December of 2013 and held a ratification vote on the Land Code in February 2017. Ratification of the Land Code required 178 yes votes from the community's 725 eligible electors. To bolster engagement, WFN decided to offer online voting as a complementary voting method for advanced voting. Paper ballots at the polls and by mail-in were also offered. The final tally resulted in 191 ballots cast in support of the Land Code and 60 against its passage, Table 1. WFN was successful in ratifying the proposed land code legislation by meeting the required quorum of registered and eligible voters.

Interestingly, 151 ballots (75 internet and 76 mail) were cast remotely, while 100 were cast in person at traditional poll locations. This suggests that remote voting methods were the preferred voting channel for community members and may be important for community engagement. This is explored more fully in the following section.

Table 1. Total counts in Wasauksing first nation land code ratification vote

Votes Received	Yes	No	Totals
Internet	69	6	75
Paper (76 received by mail)	122	54	176
Totals	191	60	251

6 Findings

Examination of interview and participant observation data using NVIVO reveals three prominent themes: innovation and community modernization, community connectedness, and self-determination and self-governance. In the section that follows we discuss the findings according to these three themes and reflect on implications for governance and participation in Wasauksing and the future well-being of the community.

6.1 Innovation and Community Modernization

One key theme identified was the connection between online voting adoption and the modernization of First Nation governance. The deployment of online voting in the Wasauksing Land Code referendum was discussed not just as a one-time novelty to help the community reach quorum, but also as part of a more generalized approach that First Nations are taking to meet citizens' needs and modernize local governance. Most commonly, interviewees discussed the challenge posed by off-reserve residency. Like many First Nations, a large portion of Wasauksing's members reside off-reserve, posing challenges for political involvement such as potentially being less informed and engaged. As one community leader explained:

> "Our demographics of our population, that's a real challenge to us. It might even be a 60/40 or 50/50 that live on-off reserve. We try to maintain all the data on our off reserve members but that's a challenge because we find historically that, our people move with the seasons. So a lot of people still move that way and so we might have multiple addresses on an annual basis. So that's one of the challenges, tracking our people that are off reserve and they, to some degree, they hold the big piece of the mandate. So we want to ensure that we can reach out to them, have a tool or a method of reaching out."

Community leaders and administrators discussed the role online voting has played to diminish these challenges by reaching citizens off-reserve or whose residency changes frequently. Specifically, officials remarked that online voting provides an effective low-cost avenue to keep community members informed and engaged.

In addition, interview data clearly reveals the connection between political modernization and online voting. For Wasauksing, online voting represents a natural evolution of the community's engagement with digital technology as a means of adapting governance to the changing realities of member's lives. As one senior administrator who has worked with land code issues in several First Nations told us, online voting has become standard procedure when undertaking community referenda:

"So currently, every First Nation that is in the development process will be doing e-voting. There are none that are opting out of it. Every one of them is going that route. The way I see it going is that it will replace mail in ballots, we won't have that cost anymore. So it will just become that. Post land code, I think all the votes on referendums may have some component of in person voting, whether that be a show of hands, because we can do that. But I think e-voting may become the one avenue where all the votes are done through e-voting. So it will just be a more streamlined, economical, efficient way of doing things and so that's where I see it's going. But every community that I've been working with, they're all embracing e-voting. It's not a question of should we do this, it's just we're doing it."

As this quote illustrates, the adoption of online voting is inextricably linked to the community's vision for future governance. Online voting represents a continuation of local innovation that First Nations have been experimenting with.

However, while the leaders and administrators we spoke with voiced mostly favourable views of online voting, concerns and issues were also raised. Many interviewees discussed concerns similar to what has been observed in non-Indigenous contexts [13] such as breaches in security or privacy posed by potential hacking or interference. Administrators also pointed to confusion and challenges associated with requiring online registration prior to casting a ballot, especially in situations where quorum involves reaching benchmarks of both registered and eligible voters. Comments also focused on the changing nature of voting verifiers in First Nations votes. As one local administrator explained:

"The registration part of it that's more of challenge because now online, you registered whereas with the paper registration, you had the name of the witness and both signed. So the mindset, not so much of the administrators, not so much of the ratification officers and not so much of the eligible voters, we have an additional person who's like a scrutineer, their verifier. And so, in their role, they go from reviewing the land code to making sure it's compliant with the framework agreement to then ensuring that the community ratification process is followed. So then in their minds it becomes "Okay, if there is a challenge based on e-voting, how do I verify that?"

The issues with registration and voter verification stem from administrative confusion that can arise when tallying both paper and online ballots and breaking from traditional processes. None of the administrators we spoke with viewed issues with registration and voter verification as insurmountable challenges, and most stressed that with education and clear communication among administrators, verifiers and electors potential issues could be avoided.

Perhaps the most serious set of issues regarding trust of online voting have nothing to do with the technology, but rather stem from the history of colonialism and Indigenous politics in Canada. Interviewees stated that many citizens who expressed mistrust toward online voting did so on the basis that any change, even one made independent of non-Indigenous governments, may work against the broader political interests of the community and consolidate colonial power dynamics. When explaining this apprehension, one administrator told us:

"I've used online voting a few times, there's not a large response to it and I think that's because it's new. I also find that our communities resist change. And that's probably because in the past in dealing with the government, whenever we agreed to change, it didn't work to our benefit, it worked to our detriment. So we're apprehensive about change and even though online voting can be a good thing, it's a change from the traditional system on how we did it by voting coming in person and voting on paper. So it will take a while for that."

This fear of introducing online voting highlights the unique political concerns facing First Nations. These are broader concerns that may not be relevant to other jurisdictions, but which First Nations must be acutely aware of and contemplate deeply. These complex and historically situated heuristics fundamentally alter the calculation for enacting any sort of reforms, even one that seemingly extends participation and legal jurisdiction in the community. As one administrator explained:

> "That's right and we don't really look at change in the way that it could benefit us, such as online voting. That may not be a detriment, it's change. And so we're apprehensive, we don't jump at the chance to change the way."

These concerns highlight the tension that exists between innovating voting processes with online voting and traditional norms and practices within a First Nation context. The political fissures created by colonialism and threats posed to Indigenous rights lead many First Nation citizens to view political reform with suspicion out of fear that it will lead the community astray from traditional ways of practicing politics. This poses a challenge to the success of online voting use in First Nations, particularly amongst those who may already be disenfranchised or distrustful of governments. As one administrator communicated, face-to-face interaction and the voter experience plays an important role in First Nations:

> "I did hear from some community members that weren't in favour of the use of online voting, that they didn't like it because one of the big things with voting in person is that it brings the community together and the people get to see each other again and talk and to have that bit of discussion."

While none of the tensions between modernization and traditional practices were expressed as fatal to the long-term prospects of online voting, it highlighted that online voting should not be viewed as a direct replacement for pre-existing practices and opportunities to participate. Rather, for online voting to be accepted it must be integrated with traditional cultural structures and norms in a supplementary fashion. This was crystallized by Wasauksing's Chief when speaking about his experiences using social media:

> "Social media is one of the tools that we use. Again, some of our approaches to a big change like this, have to go through our structure, our community structure. So again, it's not so easy when a Chief and Council have an idea and going to a community or the elders, there is a structure in our community and we try to utilize that. That's going to our elders first and trying to get an idea of what they're thinking and how they feel and then they infiltrate their families. So that was one of the approaches as well that we do traditionally. I guess it's my duty, as Chief, to touch base with our elders in regards to that."

Overall, interviewees positioned online voting as part of the broader modernization of governance practices in the community. Community leaders and administrators were optimistic about the prospects of online voting to improve community connection in local politics.

6.2 Improving Community Connectedness

The second major theme that emerged from interview and participant observation data is the potential for online voting to improve community connectedness by better engaging some members and enhancing community well-being. Improving voter turnout is a commonly cited motivation for the introduction of online voting [12, 13]. For Wasauksing's leadership, there was hope online voting would improve voter access and enhance participation, but implementation was more focused on better connecting community members by more fully bringing off-reserve members into the policy discussion. Wasauksing's Chief emphasized this point when asked to reflect on the community's experience with online voting:

> "It gives us that opportunity to be able to connect with them [off-reserve members] and make them feel like they're part of the reserve and they're still part of the voting processes and they're still part of the governance of the reserve and the community and their people. One of the big things with people living off reserve is of course employment and that's an issue and it doesn't mean that they don't want to be part of the reserve, it just mean that for their own financial gains and for their own life circumstances, they, for whatever reasons, aren't living on reserve anymore. But it doesn't mean that they don't want to be connected...the online voting, I think that really helped to increase the involvement and the participation of those off reserve members."

In addition, interviewees stressed hopes of augmenting community connectedness with on reserve citizens. In speaking about her experiences with other First Nations, one senior administrator explained that online voting can be a key tool to engage on-reserve members who may not otherwise make it out because they are less engaged. She commented that uptake was equally high among those living on reserve lands:

> "On reserve yeah. And you do door-to-door with the mail in ballots or with the VIN numbers or whatever and they attend to participate that way, because these are people who don't come out to council meetings, they don't come out to community meetings, to the annual general meeting. They just don't like to participate or they're intimidated or they're quieter people or they're shy or whatever, this allows them to participate without having to [I: Put themselves out there.] Yeah, yeah. I find, they participate greatly with the online voting but I think it's the on reserve that we've seen a lot of uptake..."

While the assessment of greater uptake by on reserve members is unexpected, it highlights the compatibility and usefulness of technology within a First Nation context.

Looking at Wasauksing's voter survey data, however, shows that paper voters are more likely to reside on reserve while those that chose to vote online are more likely to live off-reserve. In addition, as outlined above, of the 251 votes cast 151 of these were cast remotely – 75 by internet and 76 by mail-in ballot. This suggests that in Wasauksing online voting appeals to off-reserve members and that remote voting methods are important for enabling engagement [14]. This is reinforced by the fact that the primary reasons internet voters cast a ballot online, and why paper voters would consider doing so, include enhanced convenience and accessibility.

In addition, paper voters were asked if they would use online voting in a future vote. Sixty-three percent said they would. Of these, 28% said they would do so "in all circumstances" while 35% noted they would use it under "special circumstances" such as in instances where they were sick, away, or too busy to make it to a traditional poll location. This signals that online voting may be increasingly important to provide access to, and equality of, the franchise. Put a different way, paper voters were asked how they would prefer to vote if they could not attend a physical poll location. Forty-nine percent of respondents chose online voting, 22% voting by mail, 10% said they would vote by proxy, 5% by telephone and 5% reported that they would abstain in such circumstances.

Finally, reflecting on community connectedness by age among both paper and online voters we see that while paper voting is a preferred voting channel for the youngest and oldest voters, online voting had significant uptake from middle-aged voters. This implies that both voting methods are important to connect and engage community members in votes. Reported satisfaction with paper and online voting emphasizes this point. One hundred percent of online voters reported being satisfied with the online voting process, while 89% of paper voters expressed satisfaction with paper voting at the polls. Overall, available survey data from paper and online voters in Wasauksing supports the finding online voting is a tool to engage off-reserve members. It also indicates that online voting is an option paper voters want to see to improve their future voting access, and suggests it could be a means to better connect middle-aged voters with these types of policy discussions.

The importance of community voice was emphasized by the Chief when he reflected that "Chief and Council cannot do it alone". He noted it was essential citizens shared and discussed information regarding the land vote as a way to increase the collective knowledge about the proposal and extend the number of participating citizens. Overall, for Indigenous communities that face challenges with members located on and off of community lands findings from Wasauksing's land code experience suggest that the voting method can improve community connectedness and contribute to enhanced community well-being regardless of where members reside. This is consistent with earlier findings published about Wasauksing and other First Nations in Canada [14].

6.3 Self-determination and Self-government

The third and final theme that emerged in our analysis is the connection between online voting use and the community's pursuit of self-determination and self-government. For Wasauksing, understanding the potential gains in self-determination and self-governance by leveraging online voting was a key motivation in partnering with our project. Their goal was not only to understand how online voting could support the community in reaching the quorum to ratify the Land Code, but also to understand whether online voting could be harnessed to create a vibrant and connected citizenry and contribute to long-term sustainable gains in self-determination. As the Chief explained, one of the foremost challenges to enacting self-determination and decision-making is difficulties consulting with community members:

"I know within our nations, I do speak with the regional chiefs and at multiple levels of leadership within the First Nations; we all have issues with reaching out to our off reserve voters. We, as I mentioned, we might be 50/50. I know of communities that are 75/25, 75 living out of their community. So they have real challenges when they need a ratification vote, they don't have the statistics to hold the data [I: They need a threshold, yeah.]. So they go nowhere in their development, their governance, their development. I guess, to some degree, it's really, really tough for them to govern and move their communities forward."

Interviewees viewed online voting as a strategic tool to overcome these challenges, offering an effective and cost-efficient way to foster inclusiveness and enhance connectivity amongst Wasauksing's membership. Moreover, the use of technologies such as online voting is understood as a viable and necessary pathway to support First Nations in achieving self-determination and seeking recognition of Indigenous rights. For example, as the Chief commented, "The UN Declaration guarantees our inherent rights. We're taking back jurisdiction on many fronts and developing laws, and asserting our rights but we'll need digital tools to do this." In the context of the land code ratification vote, online voting played a critical role in enabling the community to reach the quorum necessary to ratify the legislation. More significantly, however, the community's ability to deploy online voting and define the terms of its referendum represented an important enactment of self-determination in its own right. This was made clear to us by a senior administrator:

"It's huge...I'll try to go back to the reasons why we've been able to utilize those platforms is because we're not guided by the Indian Act rules for elections or under the referendum regulations. So under the framework agreement under First Nation Land Management, First Nations have really taken on the role of developing their own community ratification process. So that has allowed them to take advantage of all the emerging technology, e-voting. I've been doing this since 2001. So in 2001, I actually did approach Elections Canada and asked them 'What do you know about e-voting and where's that at?' 'Nowhere.' And they're still nowhere. But First Nations have really been able to take this on and municipalities too."

Interviewees discussed the role of online voting and technology more broadly in assisting the community in moving out from under the *Indian Act*. For Wasauksing, the Land Code referendum was viewed as a preliminary step toward future gains in self-governance. The impetuses to pursue a Land Code *by* the community and *for* the community was made clear by one administrator:

"The motivation is actually very simple, it's jurisdiction. We're not asking for anything new, this is returning to how things used to be before the *Indian Act* was imposed on us before the oversight of Indian Affairs or Aboriginal Affairs or Indigenous Affairs; however you want to call them."

Broadly, interviews with political and bureaucratic officials in the community illustrate the usefulness of online voting for enhanced self-determination and progress toward self-government in two distinct respects: (1) enabling the passage of legislation that builds community autonomy and capacity, and (2) that the adoption of online voting is an empowering process in and of itself. On the one hand, passing legislation to gain autonomy and move away from governance under the *Indian Act* is a crucial step as part of an iterative approach to self-government. Yet, as outlined, passing such legislation has often been difficult to accomplish with historically imposed quorums. With growing numbers of community members living off-reserve land, connecting members to participate in these processes has become challenging and resulted in failed votes [8]. In this sense, online voting has played a crucial role in connecting community members and enabling their engagement in such votes, without which the passage of these types of community-oriented legislation would not have been possible.

Second, the process of adopting online voting as a complementary voting method and new digital initiative is itself a process of empowerment that enhances self-determination. The process of the community introducing its own chosen tools to enhance its self-determination results in improved capacity on its own.

7 Conclusion

By drawing on community experiences and narratives, this article contributes to our understanding of how online voting affects Indigenous communities, notably the relationship between governance and digital technology. Findings lead us toward optimistic conclusions about online voting positively advancing Indigenous self-determination and community capacity. In the case of Wasauksing First Nation's Land Code referendum, the community accrued significant capacity to reach out to and involve its membership by leveraging online voting. In addition, community leaders and administrators identified online voting as a strategic tool essential in pursuing an iterative approach to self-government.

Wasauksing's experiences with online voting mirror many of the findings and discussions in the scholarly literature focused on notions of digital decolonization and self-determination [22]. For the community, the land code vote represented an opportunity to decentralize authority and decision-making over lands from the federal government. The use of online voting helped the community ensure that the land code process was inclusive by promoting consultation with members living both on and off-reserve. While there are tensions and challenges with online voting use in a First Nation context, our engagement with Wasauksing finds no evidence of online voting conflicting with traditional norms and decision-making practices and its adoption in no way superseded important cultural protocols of community consultation. Rather, the technology was introduced in a manner consistent with the pre-existing decision-making structures that centered on community deliberation and openness. The success of online voting in this case is largely due to the fact that the community dictated the terms of its introduction. This ensured the voting method would be deployed in a manner consistent with the community's broader political goals and that members could be educated and socialized toward the technology.

While these findings are not meant to argue that online voting can be successful in all First Nations, they suggest that by employing an appropriate approach online voting can be a useful tool in the pursuit of Indigenous self-determination. They also emphasize what previous research has underscored about the potential to engage off-reserve membership [14] and the extent to which this enhances community capacity. While some research has explored good practices regarding Indigenous deployment of online voting [8, 13] additional studies are needed to determine the conditions and steps which best ensure online voting serves the interests of First Nations, particularly in other jurisdictions such as the United States or New Zealand. Future research could also more systematically examine how online voting affects voter turnout in Indigenous communities and whether these differ from findings of local government elections [12, 15]. Finally, comparative assessments of how online voting impacts Indigenous governance and self-determination in other contexts could support the results of this article.

Acknowledgement. All authors contributed equally to this research. Authorship is listed alphabetically. We extend our deep thanks to Wasauksing First Nation for taking part in this research. Research undertaken for this article was financially supported by the Social Sciences and Humanities Research Council of Canada and Chelsea Gabel's Canada Research Chair in Indigenous Well-Being, Community-Engagement and Innovation.

References

1. Abele, F., Prince, M.J.: Four pathways to Aboriginal self-government in Canada. Am. Rev. Can. Stud. **36**(4), 568–595 (2006)
2. Alcantara, C., Davidson, A.: Negotiating aboriginal self-government agreements in canada: an analysis of the inuvialuit experience. Can. J. Polit. Sci. **48**(03), 553–575 (2015)
3. Alfred, T., Corntassel, J.: Being Indigenous: resurgences against contemporary colonialism. Gov. Opposition **40**(4), 597–614 (2005)
4. Asch, M.: On being here to stay: treaties and Aboriginal rights in Canada. University of Toronto Press, Toronto (2014)
5. Coulthard, G.S.: Red skin, white masks: rejecting the colonial politics of recognition (2014)
6. Dickson, G., Green, K.L.: Participatory action research: lessons learned with Aboriginal grandmothers. Health Care Women Int. **22**, 471–482 (2001)
7. Ermine, W., Sinclair, R., Jeffery, B.: The Ethics of Research Involving Indigenous Peoples. Indigenous Peoples' Health Research Centre, Saskatoon, Saskatchewan (2004)
8. Gabel, C., Goodman, N.: Indigenous Experiences with Online Voting. Report (2019)
9. Gabel, C., Goodman, N., Bird, K., Budd, B.: Indigenous adoption of internet voting: a case study of Whitefish River First Nation. Int. Indigenous Policy J. **7**(3), 3 (2016)
10. Gabel, C., Goodman, N., Bird, K., Budd, B.: The impact of digital technology on First Nations participation and governance. Can. J. Native Stud. **36**, 107–127 (2016)
11. Gabel, C.: Towards Healthier Aboriginal Health Policies? Navigating the Labyrinth for Answers. Ph.D. Dissertation, McMaster University (2012)
12. Germann, M., Serdült, U.: Internet voting and turnout: evidence from Switzerland. Electoral. Stud. **47**, 1–12 (2017)
13. Goodman, N., Pyman, H.: Understanding the effects of internet voting on elections: Results from the 2014 Ontario municipal elections. Technical Paper, Centre for e-Democracy (2016)
14. Goodman, N., Gabel, C., Budd, B.: Online voting in Indigenous Communities: lessons from Canada. In: Krimmer, R., et al. (eds.) E-Vote-ID 2018. LNCS, vol. 11143, pp. 67–83. Springer, Cham (2018). https://doi.org/10.1007/978-3-030-00419-4_5
15. Goodman, N., Stokes, L. C. Reducing the cost of voting: an evaluation of internet voting's effect on turnout. Br. J. Pol. Sci. 1–13 (2018)
16. Imai, S.: The Structure of the Indian Act: Accountability in Government. Research Paper for the National Centre for First Nations Governance, Ottawa, ON (2007)
17. Ladner, K.L.: Understanding the impact of self-determination on communities in crisis. Int. J. Indigenous Health **5**(2), 88–101 (2009)
18. Ladner, K.L.: Political genocide: Killing nations through legislation and slow-moving poison. In: Colonial Genocide in Indigenous North America eds. Alexander Laban Hilton, Andrew Woolford and Jeff Benvenuto. Duke University Press, Durham NC (2014)
19. Lightfoot, S.: Global Indigenous Politics: A Subtle Revolution. Routledge, New York (2016)

20. Lockhart, E., Tenasco, A., Whiteduck, T., O'Donnell, S.: Information and communication technology for education in an Algonquin First Nation in Quebec. J. Community Inf. **10**(2) (2013)
21. McMahon, R., LaHache, T., Whiteduck, T. Digital data management as Indigenous resurgence in Kahnawà:ke. Int. Indigenous Policy J. **6**(3) (2015)
22. McMahon, R.: From digital divides to the first mile: indigenous peoples and the network society in Canada. Int. J. Commun. **8**, 25 (2014)
23. McMahon, R., Gurstein, M., Beaton, B., O'Donnell, S., Whiteduck, T.: Making information technologies work at the end of the road. J. Inf. Policy **4**, 250–269 (2014)
24. Minkler, M., Wallerstein, N.: Community Based Participatory Research for Health. Jossey-Bass, San Francisco (2003)
25. Moore, C., Castleden, H.E., Tirone, S., Martin, D.: Implementing the tri-council policy on ethical research involving indigenous peoples in Canada: so, how's that going in Mi'kma'ki? Int. Indigenous Policy J. **8**(2), 4 (2017)
26. O'Donnell, S., Beaton, B., McMahon, R., Hudson, H.E., Williams, D., Whiteduck, T.: Digital technology adoption in remote and Northern Indigenous Communities In Canada. Canadian Sociological Association Annual Conference. University Of Calgary, Calgary, Alberta, June (2016)
27. Papillon, M., Bakvis, H., Skogstad, G.: Canadian Federalism: Performance, Effectiveness, and Legitimacy, pp. 284–301. Oxford University Press, Oxford (2012)
28. Sweet, M., Pearson, L., Dudgeon, P.: IndigenousX: a case study of community-led innovation in digital media. Media International Australia **149**(1), 104–111 (2013)

Online Voting in Ontario Municipal Elections: A Conflict of Legal Principles and Technology?

Anthony Cardillo[1], Nicholas Akinyokun[2], and Aleksander Essex[1(✉)]

[1] Department of Electrical and Computer Engineering, Western University,
London, ON, Canada
{acardill,aessex}@uwo.ca

[2] School of Computing and Information Systems, The University of Melbourne,
Melbourne, Australia
oakinyokun@student.unimelb.edu.au

Abstract. This paper presents the first comprehensive study of the use of online voting technology in the province of Ontario, Canada. Despite having one of the largest concentrations of online voters globally, its use is not governed by any federal or provincial standards. This has left many municipalities to make decisions largely in isolation, relying on for-profit vendors to set their own bar for cybersecurity and public accountability. This study presents important observations about online voting use in the 2018 Ontario municipal election and questions whether the legal principles are being met by the technology deployed in practice.

1 Introduction

In an era characterized by foreign interference in national elections, it can be easy to lose sight of the cybersecurity of elections held at the municipal level. With much of our attention squarely focused on state-level threat actors, we must occasionally remind ourselves of a more fundamental threat to our democracies: loss of confidence in the process itself. This idea is summarized expertly by the Supreme Court of Canada:

> Maintaining confidence in the electoral process is essential to preserve the integrity of the electoral system, which is the cornerstone of (our) democracy. ... if (electors) lack confidence in the electoral system, they will be discouraged from participating in a meaningful way in the electoral process. More importantly, they will lack faith in their elected representatives. Confidence in the electoral process is, therefore, a pressing and substantial objective.[1]

This paper is an extended abstract. The full version is available online: https://whisperlab.org/ontario-online.pdf.

[1] Harper v. Canada (Attorney General), [2004] 1 SCR 827, 2004 SCC 33 (CanLII). Available online: http://canlii.ca/t/1h2c9.

© Springer Nature Switzerland AG 2019
R. Krimmer et al. (Eds.): E-Vote-ID 2019, LNCS 11759, pp. 67–82, 2019.
https://doi.org/10.1007/978-3-030-30625-0_5

In this paper, we study online voting in the context of Ontario's 2018 municipal elections in which as many as one million voters cast a ballot online. In the absence of almost any federal or provincial government standards or oversight, municipalities and their private for-profit vendors are primarily left to set their own bar for cybersecurity and public accountability in their elections.

We present several observations about the election and question whether the associated practices align with the legal principles established in case law. We believe these observations will prove significant to municipalities, since, as the Chief Electoral Officer of Ontario recently pointed out:

> As the public becomes more informed about software, malware, and manipulation of technology data systems, they are increasingly interested in knowing exactly how election technology preserves the integrity of our electoral process and the confidentiality of their personal information [5].

This leads to the central thesis of this work: purposeful, malicious interference, or fraud is not necessary to undermine an election. Nor is the honest discharge of an election sufficient to prevent it. Given enough time, a seed of doubt in an otherwise faithfully executed election may eventually grow to accomplish what even the best threat actor cannot. With the goal of preventing this outcome, we hope this work will serve as an encouragement to Ontario municipalities and others contemplating online voting to develop standards to address these issues.

Contribution. We present the first comprehensive study of the cybersecurity of online voting in Ontario's 2018 municipal elections, including a complete accounting of municipalities, ballot options, vendor partnerships, and the extent of municipalities affected by emergency extensions to the voting period on election night. We present findings showing issues with weak voter authentication; poor transparency of election results; and, a general lack of disaster-preparedness which resulted in nearly one million voters receiving an emergency extension to the voting period due to a misconfiguration in the online infrastructure on election night. We study date of birth as a login credential and show that it could by used to uniquely re-identify up to 50% of online voters in the 2018 election.

2   Background

Canada does not offer online voting at the federal level, and cybersecurity is a significant factor in that position. The parliamentary Special Commission on Electoral Reform (ERRE) reviewed the possibility of online voting in 2016 and recommended against its introduction on cybersecurity grounds [3,18].

2.1   Online Voting in Ontario Municipalities

Municipalities in the provinces of Ontario and Nova Scotia have held online elections since 2003 [10]. Since then, adoption in Ontario has followed an exponential trend, nearly doubling with each election cycle. As of the 2018 municipal election, we observed 45% of municipalities (accounting for 29% of the province's 9.4 million voters) offered online voting. Furthermore, 33% of municipalities (accounting for 16% of all voters in Ontario) eliminated paper ballots completely. While hard numbers of turnout by voting method have not been made publicly available, we estimate the number of Ontario voters casting a ballot online between 2–4 times higher than Estonia (see Sect. 3.3).

Despite concerns about the use of online voting, the Communications Security Establishment (CSE) assesses threats to municipal elections as "very likely to remain at its current low level," [3], which is often cited by municipal councils and clerks favoring the adoption of online voting. While the report considers conventional threat actors (nation-states, hacktivists, cybercriminals, terrorist groups, political actors), it overlooks others, such as election officials, system manufacturers, and system operators (cf. [17]). Nor does it consider the inherent threat to confidence posed by the use of non-transparent election technology.

Furthermore, no technical standards currently exist within Canada for designing, testing, or certifying online voting systems, nor auditing or otherwise independently verifying the result they produce. Nor do the federal or provincial governments provide guidance on the procurement and operation of such systems. As we discuss in Sect. 3.1, Ontario offers almost no oversight to the degree that they do not even track which municipalities offer online voting.

Finally, the population difference between the largest and smallest municipalities in Ontario is *four* orders of magnitude. While some municipalities have the resources to perform security reviews of vendor proposals,[2] others rely almost entirely on their vendors for cyber-expertise.

2.2 Legal Context

A commonly used expression in Ontario municipal politics is that "cities are creatures of the province," which references the fact that the province legislates their existence.[3] Municipalities are categorized by three tiers: single, lower, and upper. Upper-tier municipalities correspond to counties or regional municipalities, which consist of multiple lower-tier municipalities. Municipal councils exist at all three tiers; however, elections are only conducted by single- or lower-tier municipalities. The composition of upper-tier councils is either determined automatically, e.g., as a council of all the mayors of the constituent lower-tiers (as in Bruce County) or by a direct ballot question in the constituent lower tier-elections (as in the election of the Regional Chair of Durham).

Ontario has 444 municipalities: 30 upper-tier, and 414 lower- and single-tier. In the 2018 Ontario Municipal Election held on October 22nd, each single- and

---

[2] Security Assessment of Vendor Proposals, Toronto, 2014. Available online: https://www.verifiedvoting.org/wp-content/uploads/2014/09/Canada-2014-01543-security-report.pdf.

[3] Municipal Act, 2001, S.O. 2001, c. 25. Available online: https://www.ontario.ca/laws/statute/01m25.

lower-tier municipality was responsible for organizing and delivering its own independent election. This means up to 414 municipal councils made up to 414 individual decisions about the use of online voting in their election.

Municipal Elections Act (MEA). The main piece of legislation governing municipal elections in Ontario is the Ontario Municipal Elections Act (MEA).[4] Although online voting is not explicitly mentioned in the MEA, it allows a municipal council to pass by-laws authorizing the use of "an alternative voting method, such as voting by mail or by telephone, that does not require electors to attend at a voting place in order to vote," (MEA sec. 42). Additionally, it grants municipal clerks the power to establish procedures for alternative voting methods.

Whereas the MEA provides extensive language surrounding the delivery of paper-ballot elections and other electoral matters such as the use of rank-choice ballots, it provides no guidance regarding how to deliver an online election. The Act does not even contain the words "online," or "internet."

This contrast between specificity for paper-ballot in-person elections on the one hand and ambiguity toward online voting on the other leads to an apparent contradiction in places between the letter of the law, and the technology being used in practice. For example, the Act requires that "no person shall communicate any information obtained at a voting place about how an elector intends to vote or has voted," (MEA, Sec. 49 (2)c). However, the act of casting a ballot in an online voting system communicates—in the literal network communication sense—information to the online system about how an elector has voted.

Legal Principles. Democratic and legal principles provide an important lens through which to interpret the use of technology in elections (cf. [1]), especially in the absence of technical standards. The principles of the MEA are not included in the MEA itself, but have been inferred from its provisions and set out in case law as follows:[5]

- **Ballot secrecy**. The secrecy and confidentiality of the voting process is paramount,
- **Fairness**. The election shall be fair and non-biased. Voters and candidates shall be treated fairly and consistently,
- **Accessibility**. The election shall be accessible to the voters,
- **Integrity**. The integrity of the voting process shall be maintained throughout the election,
- **Certainty**. There is to be certainty that the results of the election reflect the votes cast,
- **Eligibility**. Valid votes are counted and invalid votes are rejected so far as reasonably possible.

---

[4] Municipal Elections Act, 1996, S.O. 1996, c. 32, Sched. Available online: https://www.ontario.ca/laws/statute/96m32.

[5] Cusimano v. Toronto (City), 2011 ONSC 2527 (CanLII) at para. 67. Available online: http://canlii.ca/t/fl5pg.

3 Election Statistics

3.1 Initial Survey of Available Data

Several months before the election, we set out to obtain a list of which cities were intending to use online voting. We wrote to the Ontario Ministry of Municipal Affairs and Housing (MAH) in March 2018 and were surprised to discover this list did not exist. Although the MEA requires local municipal councils to formally pass a by-law authorizing the use of an alternative voting method in the year prior to the election, we were informed in an email response that "municipalities are not required to declare their intentions to the province ... the Ministry does not have a list of municipalities that will be using internet voting in the 2018 municipal election." Several of the vendors had commented publicly on the total number of their municipal clients, but none offered a breakdown. One of our colleagues requested such a breakdown from one of the vendors, but they refused to provide it. It was evident that we would need to collect the data ourselves.

3.2 Data Collection Methodology

Correcting the Municipal List. Our first step was to obtain a complete list of Ontario's 444 municipalities, their tier-status, and associated URL. We consulted MAH's online list[6] and quickly discovered many URLs were incorrect or outdated. For example, many municipalities had switched from the older `city.on.ca` form to the newer `city.ca` form. Some cities no longer owned the URL listed. For example, the URLs listed for Mattawan and Larder Lake directed to Japanese-language websites. We had to inspect each of the 444 URLs for correctness manually. We wrote to MAH around the time of the election and received an acknowledgment that they would undertake to update their list. Six months later, many of the errors we identified remained uncorrected.

Tracking Down Voting Website URLs. Our next step was to determine which municipalities were planning to use online voting, which vendor they contracted, and the URL of the voting website. We were concerned that finding the URLs would be challenging, since many municipalities we observed made it a practice never to list it anywhere online, revealing them only in the voter information package mailed to voters before the election. Sample voter information packages found online used a placeholder URL (e.g., `anytown.election.ca`), and candidate social media fairly consistently respected this approach. We believe the practice of concealing URLs was meant as a cybersecurity protection to make the voting site harder to find by non-residents.

We made inquiries with colleagues in the province about the URL of the voting site in their respective cities and observed a trend in which vendors were encoding a municipality's voting website either into sub-domain (e.g., Intelivote

---

[6] List of Ontario Municipalities. Ontario Ministry of Municipal Affairs and Housing. http://www.mah.gov.on.ca/page1591.aspx.

used the form `city.evote2018.ca`), or sub-directory (e.g., Dominion used the form `intvoting.com/city`). We then wrote a collection of automated scripts that used the municipal list to search for the existence of voting sites based on the particular URL form a vendor was using. For municipalities encoded into sub-domains, we performed passive DNS lookups. For names encoded as sub-directories, we attempted to fetch the HTTP header from the server and inferred whether the page existed from the response code.

For any municipalities not captured by the bulk search, we conducted a labor-intensive manual web search of online municipal documents, including meeting minutes of councils and voter accessibility documentation. This allowed us to identify municipalities using custom domain names (e.g., `kenoravotes.ca`), and abbreviations (e.g., Elizabethtown-Kitley used `ektwp.evote2018.ca`). The only URL we were not able to find with this approach was Markham's, who were partnered with Scytl, so there was no obvious way to infer the URL from others. Furthermore, staff and candidates made a seemingly flawless effort of not mentioning the URL in online documents, social media, etc. Ultimately, however, we found it (`evote.markham.ca`) by searching certificate transparency logs.

Cross-validation and Corrections. After the election, the Association of Municipalities of Ontario (AMO) published a list of municipalities broken down by election results, number of eligible voters, and voting methods offered.[7] Rather than being made available as a single downloadable data file, the figures were spread across 444 individual web-pages, which we scraped in order to cross-validate against our list.

We found a few mistakes in the AMO list. For example, the municipalities of Belleville, Bracebridge, and Timmins were reported as not using online voting when, in fact, they did. The township of Machin was reported as using online voting when it did not. We shared this information with the AMO. We also discovered three municipalities with active websites on Intelivote's domain for which no election was held as the races were acclaimed. We also initially falsely concluded that Newmarket had contracted Intelivote since there was an active website on the `evote2018.ca` domain. The Newmarket deputy clerk later confirmed they contracted Scytl instead.

In terms of the correctness of self-declared vendor figures, we observed three of the four vendors reporting more municipal clients than actual elections run. See the full report for further discussion.

3.3   Results: Who Used Online Voting?

Of the 444 municipalities, 30 upper-tier municipalities do not hold elections, and 23 single-/lower-tier municipal councils were acclaimed and therefore did not run an election. In total there were 391 elections involving 9,444,628 eligible voters.

---

[7] https://elections.amo.on.ca.

Table 1. Voting methods offered in the 2018 Ontario municipal election.

Voting method	Municipalities		Eligible voters	
Electronic ballot only	131	(33.5%)	1,512,076	(16.0%)
Electronic and paper	46	(11.8%)	1,230,019	(13.0%)
Paper ballot only	214	(54.7%)	6,702,533	(71.0%)
Total	391		9,444,628	

Of those, 177 offered an online voting option, of which 131 were completely paperless. Our full dataset is available for download online.[8]

Table 1 shows the number of municipalities and eligible voters by voting method. These consisted of electronic ballot options (online and telephone ballot casting), paper ballot options (incl. optical-scan and postal mail-in), or a combination of options. Combining the AMO's population data with our observations, our results show that online voting was available to approximately 2.74 million voters, or 29% of the voting population. Of these, approximately 1.51 million voters, or 16% of the voting population experienced a completely paperless ballot, cast either online or by telephone.

Most municipalities did not report turnout categorized by voting method. However, if we combine our numbers with the AMO's province-wide turnout rate of 38.2%, we estimate the total number of voters who cast ballots online to be between 0.5–1 million, which is approximately 2–4 times the online ballots cast in the 2019 Estonian parliamentary elections.[9]

We observed 4 vendors active in the 2018 Ontario election: Dominion Voting Systems, Intelivote Systems, Simply Voting, and Scytl. Intelivote and Scytl worked together in partnership, although the extent of their business relationship remains unclear to us. Though ostensibly distinct business entities, we observed both Scytl Canada Inc. and Intelivote Systems Inc. have a registered office at the same mailing address in Dartmouth, NS. Additionally, we observed a considerable portion of Intelivote's web content (Javascript, images) and infrastructure (IPs, domains) appears to have been provided by Scytl. Of the municipalities offering online voting, Table 2 shows the relative market share.

4 Election Observations and Findings

In this section we present three significant findings. Additional findings are presented in the full version.

---

[8] https://whisperlab.org/ontario-online.csv.
[9] https://www.valimised.ee/en/archive/statistics-about-internet-voting-estonia.

Table 2. Online voting market share in the 2018 Ontario municipal election.

Vendor	Municipalities		Eligible voters	
Dominion Voting Systems	49	(27.7%)	1,323,194	(48.3%)
Intelivote Systems	98	(55.4%)	860,985	(31.4%)
Simply Voting	28	(15.8%)	304,479	(11.1%)
Scytl	2	(1.1%)	253,437	(9.2%)
Total	177		2,742,095	

4.1 Disaster Preparedness

One open question was how municipalities were preparing for the possibility of a disaster in the online voting infrastructure (accidental or otherwise), especially in the absence of standards. Our initial examination of municipal documents found no mention of a disaster recovery plan. We raised this issue in the media six months prior to the election [8]. Several clerks were also interviewed but "could not provide a disaster plan to be implemented in case the election is hacked, or irregularities tip the balance in favor of a candidate who should not have been elected." The clerk of Sarnia acknowledged, "I don't have a disaster plan in place right now, I'd have to talk to my vendor about that." The clerk for St. Thomas added, "We're hoping nothing does happen."

Election Night Emergencies. As it turned out, something significant did happen. Starting around 6 p.m. on election night, the voting websites of 43 municipalities experienced a dramatic slowdown. Just before 6 p.m., we performed a network capture of the login page for Hanover's voting site, and after 2 min the page load timed out. Although the static content appeared to load, the dynamic content loads dragged on, and some eventually timed out.

In the face of an unavailable voting website, and with many affected municipalities without any paper ballot option as a back-up, many clerks made the extraordinary decision to declare emergencies to extend the voting period. In some cases, voting was extended later into the evening by 1–2 h. The majority of affected municipalities, however, extended voting by a full 24 h [12,20].

A statement by Dominion on the night of the election attributed the slowdown to their co-location provider (an IT sub-contractor) "placing an unauthorized limit on incoming voting traffic that was roughly 1/10th of the system's designated bandwidth." Dominion did not disclose the names of the affected cities, so we assembled this list manually by examining multiple news sources and municipal websites. A complete list is available in the full version. The number of municipalities and affected voters are shown in Table 3. A complete list of municipalities who extended voting periods is provided in the full version.

Five months after the election we were invited to present preliminary results of this paper to the Association of Municipal Managers, Clerks and Treasurers of

Table 3. Emergency extensions due to Dominion's election night slowdown

Emergency extension	Municipalities	Eligible voters
24-h extension	35	575,022
Same-evening extension	8	422,085
Total	43	997,107

Ontario (AMCTO). We spoke to several clerks and a representative from Dominion. None were willing or able to provide any explanation for the events that lead to the co-location provider's bandwidth restriction, nor even the provider's identity. According to Sudbury's post-election report, however, the slowdown was determined to be a "miscommunication between Dominion and the service provider."[10]

Conflict with Principles. The outage may contradict the accessibility principle on the basis that the voting websites became inaccessible to voters. The unexpected nature of the outage may contradict the fairness principle on the basis that the emergency extensions to the voting periods allowed some voters an additional day to form a decision relative to those who had cast their ballots just prior to the slow-down.

4.2   Voter Authentication

Voter lists at the municipal level are largely derived from the Municipal Property Assessment Corporation (MPAC), whose primary business is not voter list management. This mismatch of focus has lead to inaccurate municipal voter lists over the years, and numerous news stories ran prior to the election on the subject. Because the lists are derived from property ownership, we heard anecdotal accounts of rental tenants who did not receive their online voting login credentials, whereas non-resident adult children away in college did. Other accounts described land owners of multiple properties receiving multiple login credentials. One news story reported a deceased dog in the town of Mono received a PIN [7].

Online Voting Credentials. The primary credential needed to cast a ballot online consisted of a knowledge factor (a PIN and/or ID) transmitted to the voter in a voter information package via postal mail. To our knowledge, the sole exception was the city of Cambridge, which sent PINs via email. In almost all cases a second knowledge factor (date of birth) was required. See Table 4 for a breakdown of credentials used by the vendor.

---

[10] City of Sudbury. Post Election Report. Jan 21, 2019. Available: https:// agendasonline.greatersudbury.ca/index.cfm?pg=feed&action=file&agenda=report& itemid=25&id=1312.

Table 4. Credentials needed to vote online

Vendor	Primary credential (mailed)	Secondary credential
Dominion	13-digit ID & 8-digit PIN	Date of birth
Intelivote	16-digit PIN	Date of birth
Scytl	16-digit PIN	Date of birth
Simply Voting	9-digit PIN	Date of birth

The use of single credential for voter authentication is inadvisable since access to the voter information package is sufficient to cast a ballot on another's behalf. Furthermore, some voters observed that the PINs were legible through the envelope when held up to bright light. See Fig. 1. In order to mitigate this risk, most municipalities required a date of birth as a secondary credential. Note that authentication is still considered single-factor (as opposed to multi-factor) authentication since both credentials are knowledge factors.

Dates of birth, however, make a poor login credential for several reasons. Aside from the significant privacy implications (which we discuss in Sect. 5), they are low entropy, cannot be changed, and typically are not very secret, especially when considering one's co-habitants (i.e., friends and family) are potential threats. Aside from the widespread practice of sharing dates of birth on social media websites, some US states such as Ohio include dates of birth in voter registries which are freely available for download online.

Much of the voting literature on eligibility and authentication focuses on threats like coercion and vote selling. In practice, however, it appears that a far more pervasive version of these threats is also more casual.

Voting on someone else's behalf is an offense under the MEA. Nevertheless, we heard anecdotal accounts from several independent sources of parents who voted on behalf of children living in another city, or people who voted on behalf of their spouse while they were at work. We also heard accounts of individuals gifting their unopened voter information packages to friends and family.

Ultimately, knowledge of a PIN or date of birth does not establish a voter's identity. It merely establishes to the voting server that some entity on the other end of the connection knows a secret. Secrets, of course, can be transferred or intercepted. Indeed, the fraudulent interception of online voting PINs is currently the subject of a criminal investigation in Alberta [6,15].

Conflict with Principles. This form of voter authentication and eligibility verification may contradict a number of principles. The use of dates of birth evidently contradicts the ballot secrecy principle (see Sect. 5). The multiple anecdotal accounts of individuals voting on behalf of others would seem to contradict the principles of fairness and eligibility.

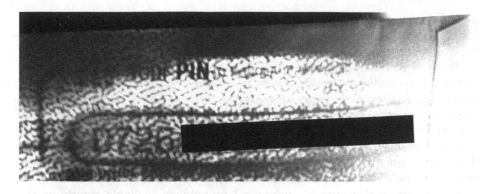

Fig. 1. Voter login credentials visible through mail envelope

4.3   Transparency and Accountability

The opportunity for an independent evaluation of security claims and implementations is vital to the public interest. There are numerous examples in the academic literature of improperly implemented software leading to critical vulnerabilities in online voting technology (see, e.g., [9,16,19,21]).

As a substantial illustration of this point, academics recently discovered several critical implementation vulnerabilities in Scytl's software as implemented for the proposed Swiss Post national online voting system [11,13]. These included, among other things, the possibility of the election provider creating a valid-looking mathematical proof of a fake election result. On March 29, 2019, Swiss Post announced that it would suspend its e-voting system as a result of critical "errors in the source code." Importantly, these findings were possible because Swiss Post made the system and source code available for independent review not only to the general public but to the international community (Swiss Post reported 3,200 participants from 137 countries).[11]

No such opportunity for independent review was provided in the election. This fact is troubling, as we found numerous municipal documents in circulation which made security claims which were: short on detail; mostly non-technical; and, largely unverifiable by members of the public.

Result by Fiat? For several months after the election, we received phone calls from council candidates from around the province asking how they could verify the correctness of the online vote totals. Many of them had experienced an unexpected loss, and although they all acknowledged there were entirely legitimate possible explanations for the outcome, they were understandably in search of answers.

Unfortunately, however, there appeared to be little objective evidence either supporting or disputing a particular online election result beyond the clerk's

---

[11] https://www.post.ch/en/about-us/company/media/press-releases/2019/swiss-post-temporarily-suspends-its-e-voting-system.

declaration of results itself. None of the deployed online systems produced an accompanying paper trail, and there is currently no online equivalent of risk-limiting audits [14].

Based on URLs found in municipal documents obtained under access to information, clerks accessed election results by logging into their vendor's web admin portal, where they could generate reports of events, activity, and results. The extent of objective evidence the clerks received (if any) remains an open question. Many of the public documents we examined either pointed to the existence of an independent auditor who performed basic logic and accuracy testing, or to third-party firms who performed routine penetration testing of the online system. Aside from neither of these constituting proof of an election outcome, our search of municipal documents uncovered no publicly available reports on the topic. What reassurance do audits provide the public if their scope, methodology and findings are entirely unavailable?

After the election, several residents and former candidates in Wasaga Beach contacted us to share their deep concern about an unexpected election loss. Among other things, we suggested they inquire as to whether there were any IPs responsible for casting an unusually large proportion of ballots in the election. Initially, residents contacted the vendor but were referred to the city clerk. We then helped them write a freedom of information request. The clerk responded that they could not provide this information because the municipality did not have any such records.

Conflict with Principles. Our observations point to what we believe is a serious concern over the degree of certainty of results achievable in the current online voting setting. If there ever was evidence of an incorrect result or fault (whether due to error or otherwise), some of the experiences we heard suggest that it would exist beyond the reach of the public.

As Elections Ontario pointed out in its study of alternative voting technologies, unless the implementation of an online voting system provides auditable evidence of the election results, then "the process is open to question" [4]. Perhaps the most pressing issue for Ontario municipal elections is whether online voting in the next election can provide candidates an objective measure of certainty in the results they will have worked so hard to achieve.

5   Analysis of Voter Confidentiality and Ballot Secrecy

A significantly overlooked question in the online voting conversation in Ontario has been to what extent an online voting vendor can associate a voter's identity with their ballot selection. Recalling the MEA principle stating secrecy of the ballot is paramount, in this section we ask how unique is a voter's date of birth (DOB) within their particular municipal election.

Data Collection. As part of our study leading up to the election we collected basic web data from each of the 180 active voting websites we found.

This included the IP addresses, TLS certificates, HTTP headers, and static HTML of the login pages. We examined the source code of each web page for elements that indicated the presence of a DOB field. Most voting sites loaded the DOB field dynamically. We did not wish to burden on the election servers by capturing full HTTP sessions of the login pages of every municipality. Loading the login page of a single Dominion municipality, for example, required over 100 separate GET requests, so we opted to capture a single municipality per vendor. As a result do not have a complete accounting of which municipalities used DOB as a login credential, though our sampling of municipal documents suggests a large majority did.

We used a web proxy on the evening of the election to capture HTTP messages sent by the voting client to the election server when the login button was clicked. We used breakpoints so that we could intercept and examine POST messages without actually forwarding them to the server. At the time of capture, we were unable to complete a load of Dominion's login page (see Sect. 4.1).

We found that within a single web session the server receives information about: the voter's city (from the URL itself), their date of birth (from the login), and how they voted. We now examine the degree to which this information could be used to associate voter and vote.

5.1   Re-identifying Voters with City and Date of Birth

As a rough estimate, there are approximately 30,000 possible dates of birth in a voting age population (365 days times 80 years). Considering that many of the municipalities who ran online voting had voting populations numbering in the low thousands, it seemed likely that many voters would have a unique DOB in their town. To model this, we used the AMO's data on eligible voters in each municipality, combined with a sizable real-world DOB dataset to create a distribution from which we could run experiments to study the uniqueness of dates of birth within each municipality.

Modeling Date of Birth Distribution. Our experiment required a DOB distribution representative of a general population of voting age individuals. In the US, many states provide public access to voter registries. Most include names and postal addresses, and some even include birth dates. We decided to use the statewide Ohio voter registry, which is a large publicly available dataset (>7 million records) containing voter DOB information.[12]

For each municipality, we ran the following experiment: we uniformly sampled dates of birth from the Ohio voter registry equal to the number of eligible voters in the given municipality. To determine the uniqueness of each record, we counted the frequency of each DOB in the sample, and then counted the number of times each frequency value was recorded. The result was a probability distribution of finite outcome, where the probability of each outcome represented the likelihood

---

[12] Ohio statewide voter files. Available: https://www6.sos.state.oh.us.

Table 5. Degree to which voters were uniquely identifiable ($k = 1$) or near-uniquely identifiable ($k = 5$) by the use of date of birth as a login credential

Vendor	Eligible voters	$k = 1$		$k = 5$	
		Max affected	% of eligible	Max affected	% of eligible
Dominion	1,323,194	531,758	(40.2%)	1,181,876	(89.3%)
Intelivote	860,985	613,999	(71.3%)	847,876	(98.5%)
Simply Voting	304,479	190,097	(62.4%)	294,912	(96.9%)
Scytl	253,437	32,880	(13.0%)	123,712	(48.8%)
Total	2,742,095	1,368,734	(49.9%)	2,448,376	(89.3%)

that a DOB record would have exactly that many matches in the election. We ran 1,000 trials for each municipality, generating a cumulative distribution where the probability of each outcome represented the likelihood that a particular DOB would have up to that many matches in the election. We estimate the number of re-identified voters within a cell size of k by multiplying the number of eligible voters in a given municipality by the probability of k or fewer matches from its cumulative distribution.

Results. The repeated trial experiment was run for each municipality, determining the maximum number of affected voters that were uniquely identifiable (i.e., $k = 1$). We also considered an *almost* uniquely identifiable case ($k = 5$), which we chose as the smallest cell size found in industry, although a cell size of $k > 20$ is typical [2]. A breakdown of our findings by vendor is shown in Table 5. Of 9,444,628 eligible voters in the province, 2,742,095 (29.0% of the total voting population) were at some risk of being re-identified by the combination of their city and DOB. Of these, up to 1,368,734 voters (49.9% of the total affected population) could be uniquely identified, and 2,448,376 (89.3% of the total affected population) could be near-uniquely identified. That these numbers are so high is reflective of the fact that much of the 1.4 million voters were spread across numerous small towns, significantly increasing the chance of a unique city/DOB combination. If we were to simulate this effect for the entire province in the scenario where municipalities used online voting, we estimate that up to 2,638,340 voters (27.9%) would be uniquely re-identified and up to 5,302,183 (56.1%) would be near-uniquely identified.

In conclusion, roughly half of the voters eligible to cast online ballots in the 2018 Ontario municipal election were uniquely re-identifiable by their date of birth and town. Given this information is transmitted to the voting server in the same web session as the voter's cast ballot, there is a strong case to be made that dates of birth as login credentials conflicts with the principle of ballot secrecy.

6   Conclusion

There is significant work to be done in Ontario if online voting is to continue in the long term. As one clerk of a large city acknowledged to us, it may take as little as one successful cyber attack for online voting to be banned permanently. The observations made in this study, however, point to a more likely failure mode without hackers, malice, or fraud. Until the technological practice inhabits the same universe as the legal principles, the absence of standards for online voting in Ontario may lead it to collapse on its own.

Acknowledgments. We are grateful to a many individuals in Ontario and beyond for important insights on technology, policy and law. Special thanks to Jane Buchanan. See the full version of the complete list of acknowledgments.

References

1. Handbook for the Observation of New Voting Technologies. Organization for Security and Cooperation in Europe (OSCE) Office for Democratic Institutions and Human Rights (2013). ISBN 978-92-9234-869-4
2. De-identification guidelines for structured data (2016). https://www.ipc.on.ca/resource/de-identification-guidelines-for-structured-data
3. Cyber threats to Canada's democratic process. Canada. Communications Security Establishment, Canada (2017). http://publications.gc.ca/site/eng/9.838566/publication.html
4. Alternative Voting Technologies report. Elections Ontario (2019). ISSN 978-1-4606-2017-5
5. Modernizing Ontario's Electoral Process: Report on Ontario's 42nd General Election. Elections Ontario (2019). https://www.elections.on.ca/en/resource-centre/reports-and-publications.html
6. Anderson, D., Dunn, C., Dempster, A., Labby, B., Neveu, A.: Fraudulent emails used to cast votes in UCP leadership race. CBC News, Published 10th April 2019. https://www.cbc.ca/news/canada/calgary/ucp-leadership-voter-fraud-membership-lists-data-1.5091952
7. Boisver, N.: Dead dog registered to cast vote in upcoming mono, ont. election. CBC News, Published 11th October 2018. https://www.cbc.ca/news/canada/toronto/decease-dog-voting-pin-1.4859489
8. Butler, C.: Ontario civic elections: the problem with online voting. CBC News, 4th April 2018. https://www.cbc.ca/news/canada/london/london-ontario-online-voting-1.4598787
9. Chang-Fong, N., Essex, A.: The cloudier side of cryptographic end-to-end verifiable voting: a security analysis of Helios. In: 32nd Annual Computer Security Applications Conference (ACSAC 2016), CA (2016)
10. Goodman, N., Pammett, J.H., DeBardeleben, J.: Internet voting: the canadian municipal experience. Can. Parliam. Rev. **33**(3), 13–21 (2010)
11. Haenni, R.: Swiss post public intrusion test: undetectable attack against vote integrity and secrecy (2019). https://e-voting.bfh.ch/publications/2019/
12. Laucius, J.: Election night glitch points to the 'wild west' of online voting, says cybersecurity expert. Ottawa Citizen, 25th October 2019. https://ottawacitizen.com/news/local-news/election-night-glitch-points-to-the-wild-west-of-online-voting-says-cybersecurity-expert

13. Lewis, S.J., Pereira, O., Teague, V.: How not to prove your election outcome (2019). https://people.eng.unimelb.edu.au/vjteague/HowNotToProveElectionOutcome.pdf

14. Lindeman, M., Stark, P.B.: A gentle introduction to risk-limiting audits. IEEE Secur. Priv. **10**(5), 42–49 (2012)

15. MacVicar, A.: Alberta NDP calls for special prosecutor to oversee RCMP investigation of UCP leadership race. Global News, Published 2nd May 2019. https://globalnews.ca/news/5233913/notley-special-prosecutor-ucp-leadership-race/. Accessed May 2019

16. Nemec, M., Sys, M., Svenda, P., Klinec, D., Matyas, V.: The return of copper-smith's attack: practical factorization of widely used RSA moduli. In: Proceedings of the 2017 ACM SIGSAC Conference on Computer and Communications Security, pp. 1631–1648. ACM (2017)

17. Regenscheid, A., Hastings, N.: A Threat Analysis on UOCAVA Voting Systems. Number NISTIR 7551. US National Institute of Standards and Technology (2008)

18. Scarpaleggia, F., et al.: Strengthening Democracy in Canada: Principles, Process and Public Engagement for Electoral Reform, Canada. Parliament. House of Commons. Special Committee on Electoral Reform (2016). http://publications.gc.ca/site/eng/9.828533/publication.html

19. Springall, D., et al.: Security analysis of the Estonian Internet voting system. In: Proceedings of the 2014 ACM SIGSAC Conference on Computer and Communications Security, pp. 703–715. ACM (2014)

20. Warren, M.: Online voting causes headaches in 51 ontario cities and town. Toronto Star. Published 23rd October 2019. https://www.thestar.com/news/gta/2018/10/23/internet-voting-causes-headaches-in-51-ontario-cities-and-towns.html

21. Wolchok, S., Wustrow, E., Isabel, D., Halderman, J.A.: Financial Cryptography, chapter Attacking the Washington, D.C. Internet Voting System, pp. 114–128 (2012)

The Swiss Post/Scytl Transparency Exercise and Its Possible Impact on Internet Voting Regulation

Ardita Driza Maurer(✉)

Centre for Democracy Studies Aarau, University of Zurich, Zürich, Switzerland
ardita.drizamaurer@uzh.ch

Abstract. In Switzerland, internet voting has been in the experimental phase for over fifteen years. With a view to putting an end to trials and normalizing its use alongside the paper-based channels (polling station and postal voting), a thoroughly updated federal regulation entered into force in January 2014. Only systems that are formally certified and offer complete verifiability can be authorized to propose internet voting in an unrestricted manner, i.e. to all the electorate. Furthermore, since July 2018, the publication of the source code of fully verifiable systems is mandatory. A major transparency exercise took place in February – March 2019. The first system to introduce complete verifiability – the Swiss Post/Scytl system – was submitted to a public intrusion test (PIT), open to anyone interested. In a parallel development, the source code of the same system was published on the internet. Researchers found critical errors in the source code of both individual and universal verifiability. The PIT revealed other, less critical issues. This experience has fuelled the already heated debate over the future development of internet voting in Switzerland. It questions the procedures for controlling verifiability solutions and, ultimately, the consensus to develop such solutions. Lessons learned will most probably be reflected in the future update of the regulation.

Keywords: Switzerland · Internet voting · Regulation · Security · Transparency · Public intrusion test (PIT) · Source code publication

1 Introduction

Debate on internet voting in Switzerland focuses on security and transparency. After initial experiences with "black-box"[1] internet voting systems in political elections in several countries, including Switzerland, at the beginning of 2000, consensus emerged within the research community that end-to-end verifiable voting systems are a necessary condition for internet voting [1].[2] Systems started to be developed that may allow the voter and anyone else to verify important aspects of the election, namely his/her

---

[1] We use this term to characterise first generation internet voting systems introduced in the beginning of 2000 which did not provide for independent, transparent verifications.

[2] See also the 2007 Dagstuhl Accord, http://drops.dagstuhl.de/portals/index.php?semnr=07311. **All links were last checked on 28 June 2019**.

© Springer Nature Switzerland AG 2019
R. Krimmer et al. (Eds.): E-Vote-ID 2019, LNCS 11759, pp. 83–99, 2019.
https://doi.org/10.1007/978-3-030-30625-0_6

own vote and the final tally, while protecting the secrecy of the vote, without introducing any additional danger of improper influence of the voter as compared to postal voting and without relying on trust in persons, processes, devices or software. According to this consensus, the challenge for government and civil society should be to find ways to foster development and testing of new election paradigms in general and to allow them to be assessed and expeditiously rise to meet their potential to improve elections, the goal being to develop systems that increase transparency regarding the correctness of the election results and yet maintain secrecy of individual votes. Improved voter confidence may follow.[3] Proper implementation of such systems as well as voter education are considered important to avoid misuse. Recent developments in Switzerland show that control of end-to-end verifiability solutions and requirements thereof are crucial.

Complete verifiability is required by federal regulation if a system is to be authorized to cover more than 50% of the cantonal electorate [2].[4] It is the sum of extended individual verifiability and universal verifiability. Extended individual verifiability allows the voter to ascertain whether their vote has been manipulated or intercepted on the user platform or during transmission. Voters must receive proof that the server system has registered the vote as it was entered by the voter on the user platform as being in conformity with the system. The proof must also confirm to the voters that the data relevant to universal verification has reached the trustworthy part of the system. Voters (rather "electors" in this case, i.e. persons with voting rights but who did not vote) must be able to request proof after the electronic voting system is closed that the trustworthy part of the system has not already registered a vote cast using their client-sided authentication. For universal verification, the auditors receive proof that the result has been ascertained correctly. The proof must confirm that the result ascertained: a. takes account of all votes cast in conformity with the system that were registered by the trustworthy part of the system; b. takes account only of votes cast in conformity with the system; c. takes account of all partial votes in accordance with the proof generated in the course of the individual verification.[5] Verifiability relies on several trust assumptions.[6]

The development of end-to-end verifiable systems provides valuable real-world experience. One of the two Swiss internet voting systems, the Swiss Post/Scytl system, became the first to allegedly introduce complete verifiability[7] after it had been certified to offer individual verifiability.[8]

---

[3] *Ibid.*

[4] The definition of complete verifiability is to be found in article 5 read in combination with article 4 of the federal Chancellery Ordinance on Electronic Voting (VEleS), RS 161.116.

[5] *Ibid.*

[6] See e.g., art. 4 para. 4 and 5 as well as art. 5 para. 3 let. c and para. 5 and 6 VEleS.

[7] https://www.post.ch/-/media/post/evoting/dokumente/complete-verifiability-security-proof-report.pdf?la=fr&vs=1.

[8] Individual verifiability is required for authorization for more than 30% of the cantonal electorate, whereas complete verifiability is required for more than 50% (art. 27*f* PRO and articles 4 and 5 VEleS). The Swiss Post system was the first and eventually only system (as Geneva decided to stop developing its system) to be certified for more than 30% of the cantonal electorate. See fn. 14.

The Swiss Post set the objective to present a system offering complete verifiability by the end of 2018.[9] In this context, it underwent the most complete transparency exercise organized so far on a Swiss internet voting system and, to our knowledge, the most complete on an internet voting system for political elections. The system was submitted to a public intrusion test (PIT) decided by the federal Chancellery and the cantons[10] which took place from 25 February to 24 March 2019.[11] In a parallel development, the Swiss Post and its partner, the Spanish firm Scytl, published the source code of their software on 7 February 2019,[12] in accordance with the federal requirement to do so which came into force in July 2018.[13] The publication of the source code should take place when the system has the property of complete verifiability in terms of article 5 VEleS and after successfully passing the examinations foreseen in article 7 VEleS.[14]

A group of researchers discovered significant flaws in the source code [3].[15] As for the PIT, a total of 16 responses were classified as breaches of best practice. According to the federal Chancellery, they do not constitute major risks.[16]

---

[9] https://www.post.ch/en/business/a-z-of-subjects/industry-solutions/swiss-post-e-voting?shortcut=evoting.

[10] https://www.bk.admin.ch/bk/en/home/dokumentation/medienmitteilungen.msg-id-73898.html. See also   https://www.evoting-blog.ch/en/pages/2019/public-hacker-test-on-swiss-post-s-e-voting-system.

[11] See https://onlinevote-pit.ch and https://pit.post.ch/en.

[12] https://www.post.ch/en/business/a-z-of-subjects/industry-solutions/swiss-post-e-voting/e-voting-source-code?shortcut=evoting-sourcecode.

[13] Article 7a and 7b of the federal Chancellery Ordinance on Electronic Voting (VEleS).

[14] Two types of examinations are foreseen: for less than 30% of the electorate (paragraph 3) and for more than 30% (paragraph 2). The Swiss Post system had successfully passed a number of examinations required by paragraph 2 of art. 7 VEleS for more than 30% of the electorate, in May and June 2017. The certificates issued end June 2017 are valid till end June 2020. The information is published   on   https://www.post.ch/en/business/a-z-of-subjects/industry-solutions/swiss-post-e-voting. The examinations/certificates published are the following:
- Verification of the cryptographic protocol https://www.post.ch/-/media/post/evoting/dokumente/zertifikat-pruefung-des-kryptographischen-protokolls.pdf?la=en&vs=1
- Verification of functionality https://www.post.ch/-/media/post/evoting/dokumente/zertifikat-pruefung-der-funktionalitaet.pdf?la=en&vs=1
- Verification of infrastructure and operation https://www.post.ch/-/media/post/evoting/dokumente/zertifikat-pruefung-infrastruktur-und-betrieb.pdf?la=en&vs=1
- Verification of protection against attempts to infiltrate the infrastructure https://www.post.ch/-/media/post/evoting/dokumente/zertifikat-pruefung-des-schutzes-gegen-versuche-in-die-infrastruktur-einzudringen.pdf?la=en&vs=1
We could not find information on the internet about the examination required by art. 7 paragraph 2 let. e (printing offices) and f (control components) VEleS on the internet. We take for granted that "the disclosed source code relates to the implementation of the cryptographic protocol for complete verifiability at application level" (see https://www.post.ch/en/business/a-z-of-subjects/industry-solutions/swiss-post-e-voting/e-voting-source-code) and that all preconditions for doing so (art. 7a VEleS) were respected.

[15] https://www.bk.admin.ch/bk/en/home/dokumentation/medienmitteilungen.msg-id-74307.html.

[16] https://www.bk.admin.ch/bk/en/home/dokumentation/medienmitteilungen.msg-id-74508.html.

The federal Chancellery declared itself satisfied that these measures (PIT and publication of source code) led to the discovery of weaknesses and allowed important findings to be made. It also declared that it would conduct a review namely of the licensing and certification procedures for e-voting systems. The Swiss Post decided to suspend internet voting until the source code and other identified errors are addressed and not to offer e-voting at 19 May 2019 federal vote. The federal Chancellery considered the decision on the part of Swiss Post not to make its system available for the vote on 19 May to be logical under the circumstances.[17]

The next federal vote is the federal (National Council) election of 20 October 2019. Requirements for authorizing use of e-voting at federal elections are stringent [4]. The correction of the source code most probably classifies as "substantive change" which should be followed by tests and a new certification [5].[18] The certification requirements are currently under review by the federal Chancellery.[19] Given this, it is questionable whether the Swiss Post system can be ready in time for the 2019 federal election. The federal Government will decide on authorizing the Swiss Post system to use electronic voting in the federal election of 20 October foreseeably on 14 August 2019, provided cantons working with the Post will apply for such an authorization.[20]

The second system belongs to the canton of Geneva and is operated by its administration. It offers individual verifiability but not the universal one. Geneva system was used for the 19 May 2019 vote. It has not been formally certified so far and is authorized for less than 30% of the cantonal electorate. End November 2018, the Geneva Government announced it would cease operating its e-voting system in 2020 for lack of financial support to upgrade it to a fully compliant system, namely, to set up a new system that offers complete verifiability and have it certified.[21] On 19 June 2019 the Geneva Government decided to stop e-voting with immediate effect because of uncertainties around the possible authorization by the federal Government to use e-voting at the October 2019 federal election. The canton of Geneva and the other cantons working with it on internet voting estimated that the expected moment for the federal Government decision (14 August 2019) did not leave enough time to adapt the procedures in case the decision would be negative.[22]

Another potentially disruptive development started in March 2019: the collection of signatures in support of a popular initiative – the so-called e-voting moratorium initiative – to stop any form of e-voting for at least five years.[23] The initiative aims at changing the federal Constitution to prohibit e-voting. It foresees a possible ban lift by the federal Parliament, through a law, which can be introduced at the earliest five years

---

[17] *Ibid.*

[18] See article 27 *l* 2 PRO and article 7 paragraph 1 VEleS.

[19] https://www.bk.admin.ch/bk/en/home/dokumentation/medienmitteilungen.msg-id-74508.html.

[20] This was still pending on 28.06.2019 when this paper was last reviewed. See https://www.swissinfo.ch/ger/schweiz-demokratie-volksabstimmungen-evoting/45061040.

[21] https://www.ge.ch/document/point-presse-du-conseil-etat-du-28-novembre-2018.

[22] https://www.ge.ch/document/point-presse-du-conseil-etat-du-19-juin-2019.

[23] Initiative populaire fédérale « Pour une démocratie sûre et fiable (moratoire sur le vote électronique) », FF 2019 2081 (*"FF" is an abbreviation of the Swiss Federal Gazette*).

after the introduction of the ban. Several cumulative conditions should be fulfilled to lift the ban, namely: e-voting should offer at least the same level of security against manipulations than paper voting; it should allow voters without specialized knowledge to verify the main steps of the e-voting procedure and enable count-as-cast of cast-as-intended votes while also respecting vote secrecy; the system should exclude external influences and should make sure that results are unequivocal and unfalsified; results can be verified in a sure manner and without special knowledge through new counting; it should be possible to exclude results that do not respect the beforementioned requirements. One of the conditions, namely the possibility for the layman to understand and control every important step without specialized knowledge, seems, at first reading, impossible to achieve.[24] The 18 months signature collection period ends on 12 September 2020. If the initiative committee gathers the required one-hundred-thousand valid signatures, the fate of internet voting will be decided in a popular vote by the majority of the people and cantons.

These developments unfold in the context of the implementation of a federal Government's decision of April 2017 to introduce internet voting into regular operation alongside the postal and polling-station voting.[25] The federal Council submitted in December 2018[26] a proposal to modify the federal Act on political rights (PRA) [6] in this sense. The proposed modification upheld the current requirements for internet voting and proposed to improve the structure of the regulation by bringing core principles of complete verifiability, transparency, certification, risk assessment framework and accessibility to the level of the law instead of having them at the ordinances' level, as is currently the case. The normalized use of e-voting would have put an end to the experimental phase that lasts since 2004. The proposed revision of the PRA was submitted to a consultation procedure from 19 December 2018 to 30 April 2019. Cantons and interested organizations were invited to comment on the proposal. The results of the consultation were published end June 2019.[27] They show that developments around the Swiss Post transparency exercise influenced the debate. The consultation revealed that most respondents, including a clear majority of the cantons and political parties, support the introduction of e-voting in principle. However, most respondents, including political parties which support e-voting in principle, also considered its introduction into regular operation to be premature. On 26 June 2019, the federal Council took the decision "to provisionally forgo introducing electronic voting into regular operation" and "not to proceed with the partial revision of the Political Rights Act at the present time".[28] Internet voting's introduction as a regular voting channel is thus technically delayed. The federal Council also commissioned the federal Chancellery "to amend the general conditions for future trials" namely "to redesign the

---

[24] A few months earlier the federal Parliament had refused such a "layman control" on e-voting https://www.swissinfo.ch/eng/boost-for-expat-swiss-group_opponents-of-e-voting-suffer-setback-in-parliament/44395904.

[25] https://www.bk.admin.ch/bk/fr/home/documentation/communiques.msg-id-66273.html.

[26] https://www.bk.admin.ch/bk/fr/home/documentation/communiques.msg-id-73491.html.

[27] https://www.newsd.admin.ch/newsd/message/attachments/57568.pdf.

[28] https://www.bk.admin.ch/bk/en/home/dokumentation/medienmitteilungen.msg-id-75615.html.

way in which the trials are operated, and to present the results in a report by the end of 2020. The aim is to establish stable trial operations using the latest generation of systems. Other measures include extending independent audits, increasing transparency and trust, and greater involvement of scientific specialists".[29]

The following sections focus on lessons learned from the PIT and the publication of source code, from a regulatory point of view. After an overview of the federal legal requirements on security and transparency (Sect. 2), we present the PIT and the publication of the source code and related events (Sect. 3). The results call into question the current regulation, particularly the control requirements for end-to-end verifiable systems and, ultimately, the consensus on the role and adequacy of such solutions. The experience has already had an impact on regulation as it prevented the amendment of PRA and the introduction of e-voting into regular operation. It will continue to have an impact as the federal Chancellery is expected to amend the conditions for future trials and decide later on its transformation into a regular voting channel (Sect. 4).

2   Internet Voting Development in Switzerland

2.1   Federal Regulation of Internet Voting

Switzerland has adopted a cautious approach to internet voting which is reflected in the long experimental phase. E-voting has been tested with binding effect in political votes and elections for more than 15 years. The motto is "security before speed". At the same time, Switzerland has a unique situation: its direct democracy system imposes frequent votes at all levels of government. Electors, i.e. the persons with voting rights, are invited to vote on issues or elect representatives at local, cantonal (state) and federal levels an average four times a year. It is thus important to find ways and means to offer effective voting channels to a maximum of electors, including those living abroad and those with special needs.

At the beginning of the years 2000 Swiss authorities concluded that any use of internet voting in the political field required a legal basis [7]. Federal regulation of internet voting, including a dedicated article (art. 8*a*) and other modifications in the political rights Act (PRA) [6] and a dedicated chapter (art. 27*a* ff.) in the political rights ordinance (PRO) [5] was introduced in 2002 and has been in force since 1st January 2003. Swiss cantons started internet voting trials in 2003 (cantonal votes) and 2004 (federal votes). The federal Council (federal Government) evaluated the trials in 2006 [8] and 2013 [9].[30] In 2006 it decided to continue to experiment internet voting and extend the trials to include the Swiss abroad and new cantons. New forms of cooperation developed between cantons with an internet voting system (Geneva, Zurich and Neuchâtel) and those without system. Fifteen out of the 26 cantons have tried internet voting so far; the majority outsources the internet voting service to another canton with a system (Geneva until June 2019) or to a privately held system (currently, the Swiss

---

[29] *Ibid.*

[30] All evaluations can be found at https://www.bk.admin.ch/bk/fr/home/droits-politiques/groupe-experts-vote-electronique/rapports-et-etudes-concernant-le-vote-electronique.html.

Post). In its third evaluation report of 2013, the federal Council decided to continue to use internet voting but to gradually replace the "black box" first generation systems with "end-to-end verifiable" systems. As a result, the federal regulation was thoroughly modified in December 2013: the federal Ordinance on Political Rights (PRO) was updated and a new instrument, the Ordinance of the federal Chancellery on e-voting (VEleS) was introduced,[31] both in force since 15 January 2014. An additional requirement became mandatory as of 1st July 2018: the publication of the source code of the software of complete verifiability as well as the procedure for its publication (see articles 7a and 7b VEleS).[32]

Regulation is based on the idea that e-voting must respect all principles applicable to democratic votes and elections and the ensuing legal requirements.[33] The federal regulatory framework for e-voting has a cascade structure that includes the Constitution and the higher-level formal law (PRA), the federal Council ordinance (PRO) that implements the PRA and, further down, the federal Chancellery ordinance on electronic voting (VEleS) and its Appendix which contain detailed provisions that implement the higher level requirements to e-voting. This structure allows for a relatively quick adaptation of the detailed provisions (VEleS) to reflect technical developments and good practices which are considered important in the security area.[34] Generally speaking, the federal regulation requires that e-voting systems and their security are state of the art, as stated in art. 27 l para. 1 let. b PRO.

According to federal regulation, use of internet voting at federal votes is furthermore subject to authorization by the federal Council and agreement by the federal Chancellery.[35] Different levels of compliance and respective limitations are foreseen.[36] The Swiss Post system became the first to be formally certified compliant with regulation for systems providing individual verifiability, potentially allowed to cover up to 50% of the electorate. End 2018 it was expected to become fully compliant with the federal regulation for systems providing complete (individual and universal) verifiability which opens the door to authorization to cover up to 100% of the electorate.[37] At this point, it was required to pass two important tests: a public intrusion test (PIT)[38] and

---

[31] RO 2013 5365 and RO 2013 5371.

[32] RO 2018 2279.

[33] At the federal level e-voting must comply namely with the principle of free elections of art. 34.2 of the federal Constitution (Cst., RS 100), the principles mentioned in article 8a PRA, which is the legal basis for introducing e-voting, and the detailed provisions of articles 27a ff PRO, of VEleS and its appendix.

[34] The VEleS Appendix contains several references to good/best practice.

[35] Art. 8a para. 1 and 1bis PRA, art. 27a and 27e PRO.

[36] Art. 27f PRO. See also the discussion in Puiggali/Rodriguez-Pérez (2018).

[37] On its web page, the Swiss Post says that the advantage of its e-voting solution is that it "offers state-of-the-art technology and, in its most advanced phase of development, meets all statutory provisions". To the attention of cantons and municipalities it says that its solution is "Certified for all eligible voters resident in Switzerland and abroad", https://www.post.ch/en/business-solutions/e-voting/the-e-voting-solution-for-cantons.

[38] See fn. 10.

the publication of the source code of the software for complete verifiability in compliance with the VEleS requirements for doing so.[39]

We do not refer to cantonal legislation as it is less detailed and mainly a repetition of federal provisions. In principle, cantons have important autonomy in the electoral field [10]. However, with respect to internet voting, the main requirements, namely those related to security, are defined at the federal level and are the same across the country and the systems.

2.2 Federal Requirements on Security and Transparency

The federal regulation of internet voting introduced in 2002 was quite a detailed piece of legislation which also inspired the development of the Council of Europe 2004 Recommendation on e-voting [11, 12]. Electoral authorities controlled the implementation of security related requirements. External audits were conducted but the findings were not published.[40] Privileged players, i.e. federal authorities in the context of the authorization procedure and the electoral commission in cantons where it existed, had access to the documentation. Political parties represented at the electoral commissions, namely in Geneva and Neuchâtel, could access the documents, which is a good practice.[41] A form of peer-control was provided by federal groups accompanying each cantonal e-voting project whose members are e-voting specialists from other cantons. However, security and transparency of first generation systems, and indirectly the regulation on which they were based, was criticized by research which referred to them as "security by obscurity" approach [13].[42] To sum up, first generation systems introduced in the beginning of 2000 did not provide for independent, transparent verifications. They were not submitted to federal requirements to divulgate the source code or security relevant documents.[43]

---

[39] Art. 7b VEleS.

[40] In its second report on e-voting the federal Government said that "the technical documentation including evaluations of an e-voting system and its security are cantonal confidential documents that are annexed to the request for authorization addressed by a canton to the federal Council. These documents are not public. Cantons that apply the transparency principle can attach conditions to the consultation by the public of these documents and source codes or even refuse access to the extent that they contain sensitive security information or trade secrets. This practice has been upheld by the federal Court" (our translation), FF 2006 5205, 5215. In its third report, the federal Council reminds that only one canton (Geneva) had introduced legislation on limited access to the source code, FF 2013 4519, 4596 f. The federal Council notes that the mid and long-term objective is to achieve maximum transparency without violating legal or contractual obligations.

[41] Third report of the federal Government on e-voting, point 5.4.4, FF 2013 4519, 4600.

[42] For an overview of major weaknesses that technical research identified in first generation systems and proposals to correct them in second generation systems, see in particular Dubuis, Haenni, Koenig (2012), pp. 10 ff, in particular points 1, 2, 5 and 11.

[43] Security was mainly based on measures taken by the voter to protect her own computer, on the discouraging effect of penal law provisions and on the security provided by the system itself at the structural, functional and technical levels. The fact for e-voting to be only a complementary voting method, not an exclusive one, was considered relevant to its security: See the first report of the federal Government on e-voting, FF 2002 612, 632 ss, 640.

The thoroughly revised regulation introduced in December 2013 resulted from close cooperation with research.[44] It has the following general approach to security and transparency issues. The higher-level principles that e-voting should satisfy[45] are as many objectives that an e-voting system and program should fulfil to receive federal authorization. The objectives take into account the weaknesses inherent to the underlying technology, as well as main threats, both internal and external ones. Threats include malware on the client or server side, DNS spoofing, MITM attacks, administrator attacks both on the content of votes and on the secrecy of the information, criminal organisations' attacks, DOS etc. Switzerland having already a generalised system of distant postal voting, threats related to "family voting" are not considered as they are not specific to e-voting [9].[46] Risks must be constantly evaluated and kept at an acceptable level by the cantons. A risk arises if a weakness in the system can be exploited by a threat and therefore the fulfilment of a security objective is potentially jeopardised. Threats and vulnerabilities inherent to e-voting should be monitored permanently and appropriate countermeasures are introduced whenever necessary by federal and cantonal authorities.[47]

The regulation admits that absolute security is impossible to achieve in e-voting, or in any other voting channel for that matter.[48] Optimum security is the objective.[49] It rests on three pillars: strong requirements (federal regulation of e-voting refers to state of the art solutions), controls by independent and competent bodies of the conformity of the system with requirements (incl. formal certification)[50] and the possibility to detect possible problems that may still arise during the voting or counting process (plausibility and verifiability checks).[51] If more than 30% of the cantonal electorate are to be authorised to participate in e-voting, the system and its operation must be

---

[44] The main novelties of the new regulation introduced in 2013, namely verifiability and formal certification, as well as the source code publication introduced in 2018, reflect proposals by technical research. The federal Chancellery accompanied the publication of the Berner Fachhochschule study on the concept and implications of verifiable e-voting systems of 21 February 2012 with a note saying that, although the full implementation of the proposals of BFH is to be considered in the long term, nothing prevents (the authorities) from integrating them already in the daily work of improving the systems (our translation), https://www.bk.admin.ch/bk/fr/home/droits-politiques/groupe-experts-vote-electronique/rapports-et-etudes-concernant-le-vote-electronique.html.

[45] Mainly found in art. 27b PRO. Some of them, such as the publication of source code are currently to be found in the lower level VEleS. The proposed modification of PRA aimed at bringing the main principles from PRO and VEleS up to the PRA level. As discussed above, the Government decided on 26 June 2019 to postpone the PRA amendment.

[46] This being so, critique on end-to-end verifiable systems related to secrecy does not affect the Swiss verifiability solution. With respect to such critique, see e.g. Jones D.W.: Some problems with end-to-end voting (2009).

[47] VEleS Appendix, point 3 "Security requirements".

[48] Already the first report of the federal Government on e-voting in 2002 noted that «permanent and absolute security is illusory», FF 2002 612, 639.

[49] VEleS Appendix, point 3 "Security requirements".

[50] Art. 27l PRO.

[51] art. 27i PRO.

examined in particular detail with regard to several criteria:[52] control of the crypto-graphic protocol which can be done by a highly specialised institution upon approval by the federal Chancellery; control of other aspects (functionalities, security of infrastructure and operation, protection against attempts to infiltrate the infrastructure, requirements for printing offices and control components) which is to be carried out by an institution accredited by the Swiss Accreditation Service (SAS).[53]

A third provision, important for security, came into force in July 2018: the pub-lication of the source code of systems that offer complete verifiability. The source code should be published only after the system has been certified. In the words of the federal Chancellery, a trustworthy control prior to publication guarantees that the advantages of the publication of the source code outweigh the potential risks associated with it [14].[54] Further, the publication should be done in line with good practice to make sure that interested persons have effective access to the source code and the time needed to analyse it and to submit remarks. In particular, the source code should be prepared and documented in line with good practice.[55] Access should be simple and free.[56] The documentation on the system and its operation must explain the relevance of the individual components of the source code for the security of electronic voting. The documentation must be published along with the source code.[57] Finally, anyone is entitled to examine, modify, compile and execute the source code for ideational pur-poses, and to write and publish studies thereon.[58] This provision integrates and goes beyond good cantonal and international practice.[59] The legal requirement to publish the source code marks a new approach in e-voting security, in line with good practice and suggestions from research: security is no longer linked to secrecy but to openness and independent verification [15].

To summarize, the regulation requires state-of-the-art security measures. Control of compliance with the regulation and detection of problems rely mainly on certification, verifiability and publication of the source code. These controls are expected to prove a system's conformity with requirements and the absence/presence of potential problems during implementation and should themselves be conducted in a state-of-the-art fashion. The Swiss regulation on security and transparency of internet voting is quite detailed and integrates research recommendations and good practice. It is the first standardisation and certification framework for online voting systems [16]. However, the PIT and source code publication revealed lacunae and raise questions.

---

[52] Art. 7 para. 2 VEleS.

[53] Appendix VEleS, chapter 5.

[54] See in particular comments on art. 7a, al. 2, VEleS in reference [14].

[55] Art. 7b para. 1 VEleS.

[56] Art. 7b para. 2 VEleS.

[57] Art. 7b para. 3 VEleS.

[58] Art. 7b para. 4 VEleS.

[59] Canton Geneva introduced legislation on source code publication already in 2016. An important previous milestone was the publication of the source code of the Norwegian system.

3 Public Intrusion Test and Publication of the Source Code of the Swiss Post/Scytl System

Intrusion tests are required by federal regulation to check a system's security. They should be organized at least every three years and be conducted by an accredited organism as part of the certification process.[60] The federal Chancellery and cantons decided to organize a public intrusion test (PIT), open to anyone, to check the security of the Swiss Post system offering complete verifiability.[61] The PIT took the form of a "bug bounty" with the Swiss Post committing financial compensation to participants who would be the first to reveal a relevant vulnerability. The Confederation contributed a substantive amount (250'000 Swiss francs) to the "bug bounty" fund. The PIT lasted one month, from 25 February to 24 March 2019. Around 3,200 people from 137 countries participated.[62] The PIT was accompanied and monitored by a management committee composed of members of the Confederation and the Cantons. The management committee should prepare a final report to the attention of the Steering Committee of the federal internet voting project.[63] The PIT participants discovered least severe vulnerabilities which include findings that show uncritical optimization opportunities.[64]

The most critical vulnerabilities were discovered by examining the source code of the Swiss Post system, whose publication was done in line with the newest requirements of VEleS. According to researchers of the Berner Fachhochschule, these vulnerabilities were already apparent in the system specification documentation; the PIT and publication of source code only played a secondary role in their detection.[65]

The code was published[66] on the platform GitLab and made available upon registration and acceptance of the terms of use, among which the requirement to publish the findings only 45 days afterwards.[67] The published code "leaked" in the sense that researchers who did not accept the terms of use, received it from others and were able to examine it. A group of them detected major vulnerabilities affecting the universal

---

[60] Point 5.5 of Appendix to VEleS.

[61] Fn. 10.

[62] Swiss Post press release of 29 March 2019 "Facts and figures on the public intrusion test on the e-voting system", https://www.post.ch/en/about-us/company/media/press-releases/2019/swiss-post-temporarily-suspends-its-e-voting-system.

[63] Federal Chancellery's information on the PIT https://www.bk.admin.ch/bk/en/home/politische-rechte/e-voting/oeffentlicher_intrusionstest.html.

[64] The 16 accepted vulnerabilities published on the PIT page https://www.onlinevote-pit.ch/stats/ are classified as breaches of best practice which do not constitute major risks. See "Qualifying vulnerabilities" on https://www.onlinevote-pit.ch/conduct/.

[65] Dubuis, E.: Schwachstellen im E-Voting-System der Post entdeckt, https://www.societybyte.swiss/2019/03/25/schwachstellen-im-e-voting-system-der-post-entdeckt/.

[66] https://www.post.ch/en/business/a-z-of-subjects/industry-solutions/swiss-post-e-voting/e-voting-source-code?shortcut=evoting-sourcecode.

[67] La Poste Suisse, Accord d'accès au code source de la solution de vote électronique, Janvier 2019.

and individual verifiability [3].[68] They communicated their findings ongoing on Twitter, after a short advance notice to the Post, thus in breach of the 45 days deadline. Although the distribution of the source code to third parties who have not accepted the terms of use is prohibited according to the terms of use, the Swiss Post and the federal Chancellery didn't mention this detail in their communications and took notice and reacted after each published finding.[69]

The first critical error discovered related to universal verifiability.[70] A trapdoor was found that would allow the system operator or any person with access to the system to modify any number of votes in a way that cannot be detected by the verifiability mechanisms. According to the Post, this vulnerability had already been pointed out two years earlier by Swiss researchers of BFH but still persisted. They said regretting that the technology partner, Scytl, which is responsible for the source code, had not made the correction in full earlier.[71] The trapdoor was found in the new version of the system (for +50% of the electorate) which has never been used so the vulnerability couldn't have been already exploited to falsify a vote. This time, according to the Swiss Post, Scytl rectified the error, in full and immediately.[72]

A second vulnerability was found that affects individual verifiability. Someone could theoretically invalidate votes without being detected. Individual verifiability is part of the system that has already been used. However, the Swiss Post relativized saying that exploiting this vulnerability would have produced invalid votes which cannot be accepted by the system and would have been noticed.[73] The question remains: why was it not detected by certification and other tests?

The group of researchers noted that their control was limited as they could only examine a very small percentage of the source code documents, enough though to find two critical vulnerabilities. They would not be surprised to find others. They question other controls which proved successful such as cryptographic and symbolic proofs of verifiability properties,[74] the role of trust assumptions,[75] and suggest solutions to rectify the trapdoor [17].[76]

Lewis, Pereira and Teague also highlighted the extremely complex structure of the source code (6000 documents). Other researchers also mentioned that in addition to the security issues, namely the fact that the code allowed manipulations that could have gone unnoticed, a quick examination of the source code revealed other problems,

---

[68] https://www.bk.admin.ch/bk/fr/home/documentation/communiques.msg-id-74508.html.

[69] See the two Press releases of the federal Council of 12 March and 29 March 2019, resp. https://www.admin.ch/gov/en/start/documentation/media-releases.msg-id-74307.html and https://www.bk.admin.ch/bk/en/home/dokumentation/medienmitteilungen.msg-id-74508.html.

[70] *Ibid.* Press release of 12 March 2019.

[71] https://www.post.ch/en/about-us/media/press-releases/2019/error-in-the-source-code-discovered-and-rectified.

[72] *Ibid.*

[73] https://www.evoting-blog.ch/en/pages/2019/new-finding-in-the-source-code.

[74] https://decryptage.be/2019/03/svote/.

[75] *Ibid.* See also the Berner Fachhochschule experts' conclusions in https://www.societybyte.swiss/2019/03/25/schwachstellen-im-e-voting-system-der-post-entdeckt/.

[76] See also fn. 74.

namely: the code is not clear; the documentation does not comply with the standards; all building blocks (code) must be individually configured (by the Post or cantons) which makes it prone to errors; the documentation must not be cited which makes it impossible for researchers to inform and discuss about errors. This last condition clearly does not comply with the VEleS requirements on publication of the source code.[77]

Eventually, the Swiss Post decided to temporarily suspend e-voting and not provide the service to the cantons for the vote of 19 May. It informed it will correct the source code and have it reviewed again by independent experts.[78] The federal Chancellery invited the Swiss Post to review its security related procedures. It decided to re-examine the certification and agreement procedures.[79] On 26 June 2019 the federal Council mandated the federal Chancellery to amend the general conditions for future trials.[80]

4 Lessons Learned and Questions

The publication the of source code and the PIT were meant to confirm an already certified system and help discover potential errors that certification and other tests could not detect. Instead, examination of the code has shown that certification and other controls had failed to notice some critical vulnerabilities in both individual and universal verifiability. No complete evaluation of the experience has been published so far. There will certainly be important lessons and conclusions that will be drawn on the technical side. E-voting supporters hope that this will make the system/s more secure. The experience also raises more fundamental legal and policy questions.

4.1 Controls

The Swiss regulation on internet voting is an advanced example of designing internet voting requirements to achieve end-to-end verifiable systems in conformity with good practice on security and transparency. The practical implementation shows that, despite good will and the important means dedicated to this, we have not yet obtained an end-to-end verifiable system free of errors. Of course, experts note that these errors would not be there had state-of-the-art solutions been used [e.g. 3, 13, 17].[81] Yet, experts are

---

[77] Kolly, M.-J. based on a discussion with Stiller, B. and Killer, Ch. of the Zurich University: Der Quellcode des E-Voting-Systems ist problematisch, und das hat nicht nur mit Sicherheit zu tun. NZZ, 12 March 2019, https://www.nzz.ch/schweiz/e-voting-der-quellcode-ist-undurchsichtig-sagen-experten-ld.1461406.

[78] Swiss Post press release of 29 March 2019: https://www.post.ch/en/about-us/company/media/press-releases/2019/swiss-post-temporarily-suspends-its-e-voting-system. See also Scytl press release of 1st April: https://www.scytl.com/en/statement-related-to-the-recent-decision-to-place-evoting-temporarily-on-hold-in-switzerland/.

[79] Fn. 69.

[80] Fn. 28.

[81] See also fn. 77.

puzzled by the fact that other cryptographic proofs and controls (other than certification) failed to notice the vulnerabilities.[82] And they also question one of the basic building blocks of verifiability as practiced here – the trust assumptions.[83] This raises a first question of principle. The lay person considers end-to-end verifiability as the way to verify the result of the election given the impossibility to certify that a system, as implemented during e-voting, can be considered 100% secure. If the control of the end-to-end verifiability solution and its implementation presents difficulties similar to those related to controlling the system itself, is end-to-end verifiability a good solution?

Second, the regulation requires state-of-the-art solutions on all aspects related to security, including its control. A constructive dialogue has taken place between cantons, the Confederation and technical research, who have been actively involved in designing and evaluating the two systems. Yet, introducing state-of-the-art solutions in a timely manner is very challenging, as shown by this experience. Certification procedures for end-to-end verifiable solutions were designed end 2013 and allegedly respected good practice at that time. According to researchers, at least by the end of 2018, it became clear that procedures should be redesigned. However, this has not yet been done and the certification of the Swiss Post system was conducted according to the 2013 regulation. According to researchers of the Berner Fachhochschule, this, among others, explains why the system got the certification, despite the flaws.[84] This shows that, although the Swiss federal internet voting regulation is built in a cascade structure which allows the federal Chancellery to rapidly adapt VEleS to take into account technical developments, it still takes some time to adapt the regulation and the processes. This is unavoidable. Regulation cannot follow technique without delay and there will always be a time lag. In our case this was very detrimental as it allowed certification of a flawed system. State-of-the-art that requires adaptations of regulation cannot be implemented without a time lag. Legality seems to weaken the state-of-the-art requirement. Quid?

A third issue is the definition of good practice and state-of-the-art. Researchers for instance pointed out the complexity and quality of the source code of the solution [3]. Certification bodies are expected, according to regulation, to control that the system and security measures are state-of-the-art and respect good practice.[85] Is this possible at all? Is certification the right instrument for doing this? If yes, is such a certification possible within reasonable time and financial costs? If not, who should define what is state-of-the-art at a given moment and who should check this? Additional questions relate to partial implementation of state-of-the-art and consequences for doing so.

A fourth, crucial issue, relates to the cost of state-of-the-art security. In Switzerland they are covered by the cantons mainly, who organize and conduct elections, including federal ones. As security requirements are determined at the federal level and can vary

---

[82] Fn. 74.

[83] Dubuis, E.: Schwachstellen im E-Voting-System der Post entdeckt, https://www.societybyte.swiss/2019/03/25/schwachstellen-im-e-voting-system-der-post-entdeckt/.

[84] *Ibid.*

[85] Art. 27*l* para. 1 let. b PRO and references to good practice in VEleS.

according to risk evaluation, there is increasingly a friction which may result, as in the case of Geneva, in a decision to abandon internet voting.[86] The relation between security requirements, which should be uniform and determined at the federal level, and financial means, which come from cantons (states), needs further clarification.

4.2   Transparency

The publication of the source code was the starting point for discovering the most critical vulnerabilities. This highlights the importance of this transparency exercise. The "leaked code" experience shows that restrictions to publication of source code, such as the 45 days silence period, may be unenforceable.

Despite its importance, the publication of the source code and its examination is not a full and systematic control of a system's security. Researchers indicated that they could only examine a very small fraction of the code. Time and resources fail to do more. Unlike the PIT, the source code examination was not designed as a "bug bounty", so incentives to detect and report vulnerabilities may be lower. As publication of the source code of systems offering complete verifiability is permanent, conditions may be reconsidered to integrate lessons learned from this first exercise.

4.3   Future Directions?

Putting an end to the experimental phase and transforming e-voting into an ordinary voting channel similar to the postal and polling station voting proves to be very challenging. On 26 June 2019, the federal Government decided to delay its introduction as a regular voting channel and reframe the trial phase. Depending on the outcome of the recent popular initiative to introduce a moratorium on e-voting and the interpretation of its requirements, e-voting may even become impossible until its control by the layman is ensured.[87]

Cooperation with research has been crucial in developing second generation systems that offer verifiability and transparency. However, cooperation is important not only in order to develop and evaluate solutions that respect the federal regulation. More should be done already when defining an e-voting policy and regulation. The last decision of the federal Government announced "greater involvement of scientific specialists". This seems to point into the right direction and should be welcomed.

---

[86] Following the cantonal government's decision of fall 2018 to stop using their own system and outsource the internet voting service to an external provider from the beginning of 2020, on 14 May 2019 the cantonal parliament voted a draft law, which requires that the design, management and exploitation of an internet voting system remains in public administration's hands. The Government of Geneva expressed this position – of an internet voting system in public hands – at the consultation on the proposed amendment of PRA (see fn. 27). On 19 June 2019 the cantonal Government decided to advance the deadline and stop using the Geneva system with immediate effect.

[87] For the time being however the task of verifying the security of internet voting can be conducted by specialists.

The contribution of end-to-end verifiability to the security of the internet voting needs a new reflection. Does researchers' consensus on developing end-to-end verifiable systems need an update? Are elections appropriate playground to try and test end-to-end verifiability? Are there undisputed techniques to achieve "optimum" security?

References

1. Benaloh, J., Rivest, R., Ryan, P., et al.: End-to-end verifiability (2014). http://arxiv.org/abs/1504.03778
2. Federal Chancellery Ordinance on Electronic Voting (VEleS), RS 161.116. https://www.admin.ch/opc/en/classified-compilation/20132343/index.html
3. James Lewis, S., Pereira, O., Teague, V.: Trapdoor commitments in the SwissPost e-voting shuffle proof. https://people.eng.unimelb.edu.au/vjteague/SwissVote
4. Federal Chancellery, Catalogue des exigences à remplir pour recourir au vote électronique lors de l'élection du Conseil national en 2019, Version 5 April 2018. https://www.bk.admin.ch/dam/bk/fr/dokumente/pore/Anforderungskatalog%20NRW%202019.pdf.download.pdf/Catalogue_des_exigences_ECN_2019_FR.pdf
5. Federal Ordinance on Political Rights (PRO), RS 161.11. https://www.admin.ch/opc/fr/classified-compilation/19780105/index.html
6. Federal Act on Political Rights (PRA), RS 161.1. https://www.admin.ch/opc/en/classified-compilation/19760323/index.html
7. Federal Council: «Rapport sur le vote électronique. Chances, risques et faisabilité», FF 2002 612, 9 January 2002 (2002). We refer to it as "first report"
8. Federal Council: «Rapport sur les projets pilotes en matière de vote électronique», FF 2006 5205, 31 May 2006 (2006). We refer to it as "second report"
9. Federal Council: «Rapport du Conseil fédéral sur le vote électronique. Evaluation de la mise en place du vote électronique (2006–2012) et bases de développement», FF 2013 4519, 14 June 2013 (2013). We refer to it as "third report"
10. Driza Maurer, A.: Internet voting and federalism: the Swiss case. In: Barrat i Esteve, J. (Coord.) El voto electronic y sus dimensiones jurídicas: entre la ingenua complacencia y el rechazo precipitado, Iustel, Madrid, pp. 261–288 (2016)
11. Braun, N.: E-voting: Switzerland's projects and their legal framework in a European context. In: Prosser, A., Krimmer, R. (eds.) Electronic Voting in Europe. Technology, Law, Politics and Society, Lecture Notes in Informatics (LNI) - Proceedings Series of the Gesellschaft für Informatik (GI), vol. P-47, pp. 43–52 (2004)
12. Driza Maurer, A.: Ten Years Council of Europe Rec (2004)11. Lessons learned and outlook. In: Krimmer, R., Volkamer, M. (eds.) Proceedings of Electronic Voting 2014 (EVOTE 2014), pp. 111–120. TUT Press, Tallinn (2014)
13. Dubuis, E., Haenni, R., Koenig, R.: Konzept und Implikationen eines Verifizierbaren Vote Électronique Systems (im Auftrag der Schweizerischen Bundeskanzlei) (2012). https://www.bk.admin.ch/bk/de/home/politische-rechte/e-voting/berichte-und-studien.html (see "Von der Bundeskanzlei in Auftrag gegebene Studien", "Konzept Berner Fachhochschule")
14. Federal Chancellery: Vote électronique: publication du code source. Rapport explicatif sur la modification de l'ordonnance de la ChF sur le vote électronique (VEleS), du 30 mai 2018, https://www.bk.admin.ch/bk/fr/home/droits-politiques/groupe-experts-vote-electronique/criteres-pour-les-essais.html (see "Adaptation des dispositions légales 2018", "Rapport explicatif OVotE")

15. Driza Maurer, A.: E-voting source code publication: a good practice becomes a legal requirement. In: Jusletter IT 26. September 2018
16. Puiggali, J., Rodriguez-Peréz, A.: Designing a national framework for online voting and meeting its requirements: the Swiss experience. In: Krimmer, R., et al. (eds.) E-Vote-ID 2018 Proceedings, pp. 82–97. TUT Press, Tallinn (2018)
17. Haenni, R.: Swiss Post Public Intrusion Test Undetectable Attack Against Vote Integrity and Secrecy (2019). https://e-voting.bfh.ch/publications/2019/
18. Haenni, R.: Swiss Post Public Intrusion Test: Generating Random Group Elements (Best Practice) (2019). https://e-voting.bfh.ch/publications/2019/

How do the Swiss Perceive Electronic Voting? Social Insights from an Exploratory Qualitative Research

Emmanuel Fragnière[1,2]([⊠]), Sandra Grèzes[1], and Randolf Ramseyer[1]

[1] University of Applied Sciences and Arts Western Switzerland (HES-SO),
Sierre, Switzerland
{emmanuel.fragniere,sandra.grezes,
randolf.ramseyer}@hevs.ch
[2] School of Management, University of Bath, Bath, UK

Abstract. Electronic voting is enjoying growing interest within the scientific community. However, the focus is on systems (algorithms, mathematical cryptographic models, user experience, reliability, traceability, security, etc.). Consequently, the purpose of this exploratory research on e-voting is not to address aspects that have already been well-studied by scientists, but rather to understand, through a qualitative research, bottlenecks and sociological obstacles. This understanding will help to explain the reasons that might prevent its adoption by Swiss citizens and also the dissemination of e-voting in the digital age. Based on 25 semi-directed interviews (in German, French and Italian) that we have analyzed, we are able to provide new insights that are more sociological than technological. These insights are essentially related to the social acceptance of e-voting. We observe in particular that the vote in Switzerland has an almost sacred dimension and that the trust that surrounds the voting "ritual" is of supreme importance.

Keywords: Democratic values · Field studies · Self-Determination ·
Social acceptance · Perception · E-Voting operations

1 Introduction

1.1 Context

Electronic voting is enjoying growing interest within the scientific community. However, the focus is on systems (algorithms, mathematical cryptographic models, user experience, reliability, traceability, security, etc.). Estonia has become a well studied and known case since it has been systematically using it for many years. Switzerland could also become a reference in this field since it already represents a life-size laboratory because of its internationally recognized status as a semi-direct democracy. However, even if a law allows it, the Federal Chancellery remains extremely cautious about these developments. Last June 2019, the e-voting project has been postponed until the end of 2020. As a matter of fact arguments are often used to undermine the credibility of electronic voting, such as its unreliability (amplified hacking in the case

© Springer Nature Switzerland AG 2019
R. Krimmer et al. (Eds.): E-Vote-ID 2019, LNCS 11759, pp. 100–115, 2019.
https://doi.org/10.1007/978-3-030-30625-0_7

of the last presidential elections in the United States), or people's tradition and attachment to the voting physical process that are known and understood for a long time. The intergenerational digital divide is also an argument frequently used by some political parties. Thus, our intention regarding this exploratory research on e-voting is not to address aspects that have already been well-studied by scientists, but rather to understand, through a qualitative field research, bottlenecks and sociological obstacles. This understanding will help to explain the reasons that prevent this type of development, as well as its adoption by citizens, in Switzerland. While postal voting has not caused any such resistance, and its use is well accepted and widespread, this is not the case with electronic voting.

1.2 Research Purpose and Contribution

The research project's purpose consists in providing the Swiss parliament and government with sociological rather than technical elements to develop a relevant public policy on electronic voting in Switzerland. Indeed, for the time being, within the framework of the Swiss e-voting project, the Confederation has only surrounded itself with experts (academics, the Confederation and the Cantons), with the aim to implement a fully functioning e-voting system. However, it is indispensable to integrate the opinions, perceptions and the rationale of the Swiss population, as the final users of e-voting is the population who is entitled to vote. Hence, this is also a matter of social acceptance of the new voting system by the population. Our project therefore has the advantage of questioning the population in depth (practically this has been done through 25 semi-structured interviews administered in the three national languages, respectively, German, French and Italian, during the period from January to June 2019). Moreover, it is important to take into account the cultural and socio-demographic characteristics of the different profiles interviewed, to consider all the stages of the different operational processes leading to the vote (ballot box, postal voting, electronic voting), to also integrate the major changes in all sectors of society caused by the global phenomenon of digitalization. Through the analysis of the interview transcripts, we have produced a synthesis of the main findings of this field study. This will allow us to develop, in a next step of this research, a theoretical model explaining the population's perceptions about the development of electronic voting in Switzerland. In a third step, everything will be ready to set up a national quantitative survey to validate the assumptions of our theoretical model in order to make statistical inferences at the national level.

From a scientific point of view, our study would be, to our knowledge, the first of its kind corresponding to a qualitative research taking into consideration the different Swiss cultures (French-speaking, German-speaking and Italian-speaking) that would allow the generation of "meanings" explaining the public's perceptions about the development of electronic voting. Indeed, the scientific literature on this subject is rather sparse compared to that with a more technical orientation. Even if we focus on a small country, Switzerland nevertheless represents a highly relevant and credible "democratic laboratory" on a global scale. It is indeed the country where the most votes are cast in the world and since 2000 more than 200 electronic voting trials have already been carried out (https://www.admin.ch/gov/fr/accueil/documentation/dossiers/E-Voting.html).

1.3   An Approach Anchored on the Notion of Voting Operations

The usual way to form a political opinion in Switzerland is to read official documentation and follow traditional media such as television or the press and recently the Internet. We are also largely influenced by poster campaigns and all-household distributions. However, new media as well as digitized democratic processes are completely changing the situation. Switzerland is the country with the highest number of popular votes in the world. The traditional process consists of a preparation period that can be quite long (about 6 months) in which parties and the media contribute to the formation of voters' opinions. They send their ballot papers by post in advance or go to a voting room, where booths will be made available during the weekend of the vote, as well as voting materials and the ballot box to cast their ballot. Over the years, there has been a decline in participation in these elections, especially among the younger generation. At the same time, our economy is currently undergoing very intense digitization. We are increasingly talking about the "ubiquitous" nature of the economy, which changes the roles assigned to each person and redefines what an expert, a provider or an agent is. In terms of information and opinion forming, roles are also changing with a transformation of the role of the journalist, editorialist and expert. The scandals in the last US presidential elections and the Brexit vote highlighted the fragility of our democratic processes. We intend to address the topic of electronic voting from the perspective of a business process (i.e. voting operations), while focusing on the human aspects. In Switzerland, at the present time, two voting options are available: either the voter goes to the polling station or the voter votes by mail. A third possibility, electronic voting, has recently been accepted in Switzerland, after years of testing. Due to recent developments, the e-voting process is on hold [1]. In the coming years, it could (or not) become a fully-fledged voting option on a par with the two options already in place. Electronic voting is based, like ballot box voting and postal voting, on an operational process, except that most of the steps are dematerialized, since they are digitized. This is called a digital process.

1.4   Organization of the Text

This paper is organized as follows, In Sect. 2, we present a brief literature review about e-voting. In Sect. 3, we describe the methodology that has been employed in this research. In Sect. 4, we present an overview of the main elements of electronic voting perception. In Sect. 5, we present an overview of the main elements of electronic voting security. In Sect. 6, we present an overview of the main elements of electronic voting operations. In Sect. 7, we provide a discussion about the notion of trust and confidence in the voting process. Finally, we conclude and provide directions for further research.

2   Literature Review

2.1   The Digitalization of Service Operations

Electronic voting refers to any process that benefits from the use of electronic technology by electoral authorities for the conduct of elections [2]. As part of our research, it is important to place electronic voting in a broader field of investigation that generally concerns the digitalization of society. Digitization can be defined as the integration of multiple digital technologies into all aspects of daily life that can be digitized by the conversion of analogue information into digital form so that information can be processed, stored and transmitted through circuits, equipment and networks digital [3]. Thus, referring to the concept of digitization (or digitalization), rather than talking about digital processes, implies that it is an emerging transformation process, in progress, still in the development phase rather than a completed and clearly defined process [4]. These authors believe that digitization corresponds to the characteristic of the information society, as defined by [5], i.e. it is not simply something that is imposed on individuals and organizations, but something that individuals and organizations "do" and produce themselves through daily practice and social interaction. Therefore, if we consider e-voting as a phenomenon of digitalization of our democratic society, we must also analyze it in its integration into the life of voters and in the context of the social interactions in which it is integrated. We live in a digital age, because digital technologies are used today in almost every aspect of life [6] and they play a key role in shaping and regulating societies, communities, organizations and individuals [7].

2.2   Research on the Topic of E-Voting

Let us now return to scientific research that focuses more specifically on the field of electronic voting. We note that the production of scientific articles on this subject over the past decade is very abundant [8], with pioneering scientific works already published at the beginning of the new millennium [9]. One country, Estonia, is a precursor in this field, having made it possible to use electronic voting in its elections since 2005 [10, 11]. However, it should be noted that Estonia has developed strongly from the point of view of digitalization in all sectors of society. This Estonian practice attracts the attention of all regions of the world. This is particularly the case in Europe. The Council of Europe has also issued a specific recommendation on this subject. The Recommendation "Rec (2004)11" on legal, operational and technical standards for electronic voting is a unique reference source in this field. Europe, through the Organization for Security and Cooperation in Europe (OSCE), has sent experts to Switzerland to observe the various test phases that have been planned since 2005. Switzerland can thus be considered as a kind of laboratory for the process of digitizing votes, which has made it possible to develop original scientific research [12, 13].

Most of the scientific contributions in the field of electronic voting deal mainly with technical aspects. There are many articles on the following themes: design and evaluation of electronic voting systems, identification and authentication of voters, reliability, security and safety issues, end-to-end traceability, etc. A recent article [14] provides a comprehensive literature review on all these technical and usability aspects. Research on e-voting also incorporates the "Blockchain" to address supposed vulnerabilities inherent in most existing systems [15]. Some researchers even argue that traditional paper-based voting is subject to the same security problems. However, since we have been using paper for a long time, people are no longer even aware of security problems related to paper-based voting [16].

2.3 Taking into Account the Human Factor in E-Voting

What is not much studied in academic research, however, is everything that touches on the human aspects of electronic voting, and in particular the public's perception of this new possibility of voting. However, some rare studies of this type exist. This is the case with a survey conducted in Australia that shows that there is a correlation between perceived ease of use and perceived utility of e-voting technologies to determine their acceptance and use [17]. A Malaysian study on a campus shows that when students use e-voting to express themselves on university activities, there is a need to have confidence in the electronic system to ensure a real commitment to voting [18]. As part of this research project, we employ qualitative research to identify and explain the perceptions of e-voting by Swiss citizens about the widespread adoption of electronic voting. To our knowledge, no scientific study has yet been carried out on this subject specifically.

3 Methodology

3.1 Methods

The aim of this study is first of all, through documentary analysis, to better understand the innovations linked to the mode of democratic process that does not lead to digitalization within our societies. It is therefore a question of taking stock of the e-voting initiatives carried out at the global level. Through this documentary research, it was also necessary to understand the situation in Switzerland (legal bases, parliamentary debates, motions, party politics, test phases carried out in the various cantons, etc.). Secondly, we have conducted field research based on an ethnographic approach. Ethnography represents the descriptive study of the activities of a specific human group. More specifically, we use ethnomethodology, which is not based on an a priori theoretical framework. Ethnomethodology makes it possible to identify the latent needs of the target population, to detect social trends for the design and improvement of given public service processes and finally to write scenarios to highlight intangible elements that bring added value to users. In practice, we have launched a field research based on 25 semi-structured interviews administered in German, French and Italian to directly question citizens about their perceptions regarding electronic voting. This research approach is therefore essentially based on the notion of constructivism (or interpretivism). Its main objective is to understand how and why electronic voting, as a new method of voting (on a par with voting by depositing it in the ballot box and voting by post), is at the root of skepticism and opportunities. We therefore believe that this inductive approach is the most appropriate for our research. It is indeed well adapted to the understanding of the perception we have of the environment under study. The data collected through semi-structured interviews have been analyzed on a content analysis basis (with the help of RQDA and NVivo) according to the codes or code categories used for the analysis of the transcripts. On the basis of the synthesis of the results, we will develop in a subsequent research a new theoretical model to explain the public's major concerns about the adoption of electronic voting. In a third phase of research the generated model will be validated through a quantitative survey.

3.2 Purposeful Sampling Strategy and Interview Guide

For this qualitative research, we used the purposeful sampling technique [19]. The aim is not to be representative of the population studied in order to draw statistical inferences, but rather to "go around the issue". Indeed, a qualitative field research has an exploratory purpose and not the validation of research hypotheses. For inductive and exploratory research, qualitative methods are most suitable, as they can lead to hypothesis building and explanations. Qualitative research also delivers better understanding of motivations, values and attitudes on a given context. Data collected from a small number of carefully selected samples on relevant issues can be sufficient in this case, as it demands a limited number of observations to explain different aspects of the problem area. Low numbers are justified to do an in-depth study [20].

Nevertheless, in our case, we have tried to take into account Swiss cultural diversity (14 interviews in German, 8 in French and 3 in Italian). To have broad social insights, we chose people from different cantons. Moreover, to understand the perceptions of different generations, we chose people covering an age spectrum from 29 to 75 years. Apart from that, the other socioeconomic parameters are not representative of the Swiss population since the sampling strategy was purposeful. All of the interviewees are highly educated [21], most of them have a University diploma and they appear to vote on a regular basis. In our sample, there are solely a few people who are Swiss living abroad and who have already experience with e-voting, to enlarge our insights concerning e-voting. The main topics, guided by authors' discussions (translated into 14 questions) addressed during our semi-structured interviews were: e-voting "customer journey/mode of operation", personal views about electronic voting, trust and security aspects, meaning of e-voting in relation to democracy, habits related to digitization, e-voting for Swiss abroad/disabled people, obstacles and barriers to e-voting. Choices of the different dimensions retained in our interview guide have been based on discussions taking place before the fieldwork and on the literature review of Sect. 2.

4 Findings Regarding E-Voting Perception

4.1 Different Attitudes Towards E-Voting

The qualitative analysis of the interviews revealed different attitudes towards electronic voting. In the following, we tried to identify some patterns of attitudes towards e-voting.

Type 1 is a strong supporter of the e-voting system. He or she is accustomed to the use of digital devices for many daily activities and e-administration, such as e-banking. He or she rather or strongly trusts the political system and/or e-voting. One respondent e.g. has been eager for years to vote electronically: "I would love it. It makes everything more flexible and easier for me" (German-speaker from Valais, female). Respondents of this type of attitude relativize the risks associated to e-voting, as an interviewee underlines "If someone wants to manipulate, he or she will succeed in doing it, no matter the voting type" (German-speaker from Bern, male).

On the other side of the spectrum, type 4 is totally against e-voting and would never vote like that. However, there was only one person who has this attitude among those questioned. This person argues that "a voice cannot be reduced to an action on Internet" (German-speaker from Valais, male). Another argument of this person is that via e-voting "not only Swiss can manipulate the vote, but theoretically the whole world" (German-speaker from Valais, male).

In between this spectrum of supporter and opponent of e-voting, there are different nuances of attitudes towards e-voting. Such a profile (type 3) is rather skeptical towards e-voting. However, this type acknowledges the convenience aspects of e-voting and trusts the system for better or for worse by being aware of the various risks associated with this system. One respondent says: "I have always been very skeptical, because I asked myself: is it really enough secure?" (German-speaker from Solothurn, male). Then, we could identify another type of attitude (type 2) that is characterized by a limited interest in e-voting and do not have a strong feeling of support of or opposition of e-voting systems. The reasons for this attitude can be different. Some of them say that "the introduction of e-voting corresponds to modern times" (German-speaker from Schaffhausen, female/German-speaking from Valais, female). People with this attitude think that e-voting is a logical consequence of current technological developments, which also influence the way people vote. Another reason can be that "they have not yet had the time to deal with that topic" (German-speaker from Basel, female/German-speaker from Fribourg, male). One respondent mentioned that he has not yet become accustomed to this "e-government logic" (German-speaking from Fribourg, male). Yet, these latter persons are also aware of the risks associated with e-voting.

Several interviewees mentioned that they are more or less obligated to trust the system, as they have not the time, nor the interest or competence to understand in detail the technological process of e-voting. Therefore, interviewees trust the system in general, but one of the respondents says that a lack of security would indeed be a no-go. Another interviewee says "if there is somewhere a chance, to forge the vote, then it is a no-go for me." (German-speaker from Schaffhausen, female).

4.2   Pros and Cons of E-Voting in General

When asked about the advantages of e-voting (see Table 1), respondents stressed in particular the flexibility (independence in terms of time and place) and the efficiency and simplification of the process (German-speaker from Aargau, male). One respondent says "you do no longer have an excuse for not going to vote" (Italian-speaker from Ticino, male). Some respondents also mentioned the environmental aspect, which means that less paperwork is needed. However, some interviewees wondered whether it really would be a simplification of the process. They are therefore a little skeptical on this point. An atypical answer was that one advantage would be that "the envelope does not have to be licked like during the postal vote" (German-speaker from Valais, male). Even if many respondents mention the convenience aspect as one of the main advantages of electronic voting, the two interviewees having already used e-voting systems (one abroad, one in Switzerland), underline that they perceived the process itself as being more complicated than the postal voting process because of additional security barriers. However, most interviewees not having used e-voting so far, think that e-voting has the potential to be easier than the other types of voting. They underline that login and password issues, loading problems or a missing confirmation, that the vote has been validated, could complicate things. Many respondents also think that the current system works very well and they wonder why it should be changed. This general lack of interest is reflected in the responses of the interviewees concerning the question, if they have already informed themselves about e-voting; a question that almost all of the interviewees denied.

Table 1. Pros and Cons of E-Voting

Pros	Cons
Better for young people	Could be a problem for elderly people
Flexibility, efficiency (process and concerning resources), simplicity Less people and resources needed	Is it really easier? Logins, passwords could be more complicated than by postal vote The current system functions very well, very easy Lack of social contact Less work for postman, at the beginning a lot of technical and financial effort
Security	Manipulation (also a problem for other vote systems), hacking, data abuse
Additional technological elements possible (like interactive tools, mistake detection, e.g. concerning elections)	You need internet (but it is a matter of course today)
More ecological	

Cons (see Table 1) are particularly related to the possibility of manipulation and hacking. The respondents mentioned that people might be afraid of not having guaranteed the anonymity of the data. However, they mentioned this point when talking about possible reasons why some Swiss citizens are not satisfied with the introduction of e-voting, not concerning themselves. Except for one person, most respondents express some concerns about the security aspects. Many of them also mention that today's systems already work very well and that there is no immediate need to change a well-functioning system to which the Swiss are accustomed. Another reason one respondent mentioned about possible concerns of the Swiss population is that they are worried that other people will not vote as seriously as they need to when voting online. Another argument is the loss of social contact, which already affects postal voting.

Respondents also mention that some time must pass before changes are implemented. Respondents also note that older people may have some difficulty voting online.

Therefore, it would be important to retain the other voting options such as postal voting and go to the ballot box. Some respondents argue that it would certainly be more interesting for younger people. One respondent stressed that e-voting is simply not trustworthy in terms of technical aspects and data abuse. Another respondent mentions the Internet's associations with electoral influence in the US and Europe. Another disadvantage of e-voting could be that paper seems to be more "binding" than voting on the Internet.

4.3   Opportunity or Risk for Democracy?

Several respondents think that e-voting is rather an opportunity for democracy than a risk, although one of them underlines the importance of security being guaranteed. Two interviewees think that e-voting will quickly become the norm. Another respondent thinks that it makes voting easier for everyone and more comfortable for Swiss people living abroad.

We also asked the respondents, if they perceive e-voting being a thread for a potential "sacred" meaning ritual dimension of current Swiss voting practices. Most of them do not think that e-voting would mean a "desacralization" of the voting process. Some of them could imagine that this could be the case for other people, who celebrate the social and ritual element of going to the ballot box. One interviewee indicated that this kind of "desacralization" has already happened by introducing the postal vote.

5   Findings Regarding E-Voting Security

5.1   Trust in Relation to Security Aspects

Except for one respondent, the majority trusts the Swiss political system and the e-voting technology. In general, interviewees tend also to trust the government and the professionals dealing with the technology. Two of the interviewees say that it is important to have confidence, as technology is far too complicated for normal citizens to be able to understand everything.

People also generally are accustomed to e-banking, which includes the management of incidents and insurance protection. Most of the interviewees are accustomed to e-banking and thus trust the system. The respondent who is totally against e-voting also uses e-banking. This respondent adds that e-voting differs from e-banking insofar as the banking system has not been hacked so far, which is however the case for the e-voting system managed by the Swiss post enterprise. This same respondent underlines that "a problem with e-voting leads to a collective damage, whereas a problem with the e-banking system only concerns the money of an individual" (German-speaker from Valais, male). Another interviewee however says that for her the personal damage would be much more important than the collective one. Even another respondent says that, normally it should be possible to realize when a vote is manipulated, as there exist surveys in the run-up to the votes that give an approximate picture of the voting results. Even if the security aspect is very important for all the respondents, some of them relativize the problem by highlighting that the risks of manipulation and loss of anonymity also exist with regard to postal vote and when going to the ballot boxes. However, some of them underline that the damage extent could be much higher with an e-voting system, especially at a national scale, whereas with the conventional types of voting (postal vote and ballot box) the risk seems to be higher at the local level. One respondent even says that e-voting seems more secure to her than the other types of voting. Moreover, some of the interviewees mention that e-voting is especially secure regarding the counting procedure.

5.2 Information Needed for Transparency

Respondents said that it would be quite important for them to be informed about the concrete procedure of the e-voting process in terms of an instruction, as well as in terms of security measures that have been taken. One interviewee however adds that the government's main aim was to reassure the citizens concerning security measures, which relativized the value of the information. Another interviewee says that an info-button dealing with security aspects could be helpful (German-speaker from Valais, female). As to the concrete procedure to vote online, some of the respondents would like to have an easy operating manual, or explanation in a video.

5.3 Influence on Voting Participation, Voting Results and Voting Decision

While most of the interviewees think that the introduction of e-voting would only slightly influence the voting participation or even not at all, one interviewee guesses that the participation from Swiss people living abroad could increase. This respondent also believes that the possibility to vote directly with the smartphone could be a reason for people to vote more often.

In general, however, the interviewees think that voting participation is a matter of interest and education rather than of the means of voting. Nevertheless, two interviewees say that they personally would vote more often, if they could do it online. In this context, it is important to bear in mind that all the interviewees have a very high participation rate in voting.

As to a potential influence on voting results, most interviewees do not think that the possibility to vote online changes the voting results in a significant way. Some of them think that it could maybe lead to a slightly higher participation of young people, but not a significant one.

We also asked interviewees what they think about e-voting influencing the voting decision of people. A majority of the interviewees guess that this could be possible in some rare cases or not at all. An example of such a rare case would be that the voter changes his or her mind regarding the voting decision later in time. Hence, when having voted electronically, he or she will not be able any more to correct his or her opinion. When doing a postal vote however, this would still be possible. However, this aspect does not seem to have a big importance for the interviewees. Moreover, one interviewee even said that the e-voting process strengthens the seriousness of voting, as one is conscious of the "seriousness of the moment and the consequences of your choice" (Italian-speaker from Ticino, male). It implies a shift of responsibility, in a digital platform all decisions are made autonomously and at one's own risk.

6 Findings Regarding E-Voting Operations

6.1 Important Aspects of the Voting Process and Suggestions for Improvement

As to the e-voting process, many respondents say that it is especially important to have an easy process. The user should receive a voting confirmation, and even if there are some loading problems, he or she should know if his or her vote was sent. Some of the interviewees also mention that e-voting via smartphone should be possible. The respondent having experience with e-voting abroad mentions that he "really appreciated to be able to choose between postal vote and e-voting" (German-speaker from Aargau, male), meaning that he did not have to choose once and for all for between the two possibilities. Another respondent suggests to use a password that can be scanned with a smartphone and that leads you directly to the right website.

However, when talking about the current voting process, most interviewees say that the process already works very well. One interviewee says that "it is important to ensure in the future that the e-voting will not be the only way but one way to vote" (Italian-speaker from Ticino, male). The most important aspects needing improvement rather concern the steps in the voting process than the voting means.

Two interviewees mention that the voting questions are sometimes asked in a confusing way. Some of the interviewees criticize the content of the brochure the federal government adds to the voting documents. This brochure summarizes the arguments of the advocates and opponents and informs the reader of the recommendations of the federal government. One interviewee thinks that there is not enough space for the people having started an initiative to express their arguments. The opinion of another interviewee goes in the same direction. He thinks that the brochure is too propagandistic and that the neutral aspect is somehow missing. One respondent thinks that there should be more options to vote about, not only yes or no.

When talking about other possibilities how technology could improve the voting process, some of the respondents said that it would be interesting to create an application that informs about the opinions of the parties, and provide access to neutral information sources. Another interviewee mentions the creation of a reward system for participation in votes to increase voting participation. Another idea is to show the party and voting financing in real time. This could make the population more aware of the differences in budget of the different parties. Another respondent says that it is not so much about how and where to vote, but about the collection of largely neutral, correct and professional information that is independent from political power struggles or economic interests. Another person says that it would be interesting if newspapers would provide online information files dealing with the voting topic. One respondent suggests an online "one-stop-shop" like an application, where you can inform yourself about different points of view, vote and see the results.

To sum up, among the respondents there was only one person who is totally against e-voting mainly out of trivialization of the process and security reasons. In general, the interviewees have not or not much informed themselves about e-voting and they are rather happy with and accustomed to the current system, being a matter of habit. Therefore, people need some time to become accustomed to e-voting. Some of them think that it could be more convenient and comfortable to vote online, but estimate the risk of manipulation of voting results as higher than with traditional voting means. In general, e-voting must provide a personal additional benefit for voters, otherwise, they are not so much interested in changing their habits. This confirms the findings of the Australian study [17].

E-voting seems to be an advantage especially for Swiss people living abroad. However, in general, most interviewees think that participation issues do not depend on the voting means, but rather on general political interest and education or on the complexity of the voting topic. Most of them guess that e-voting would not significantly change the participation or even voting results. They are also skeptical of the voting means having an influence on the decision. Some of them think that technology could be useful to improve the information collection stage, as they think that it is not an easy task to inform oneself in a neutral way about quite complex voting topics.

Moreover, the majority of the interviewees trust in the government and technology. They however agree that voting results can always be manipulated, and that the extent of manipulation increases with e-voting. Table 2 summarizes the findings of Sect. 6.

7 Discussion: Trust and Confidence in the Voting Process

The results of the interviews generally confirm that the perception of electronic voting is strongly associated and correlated with the professional demographics of voters. It is understood that the professional background of electors influences their attitude towards electronic voting. Those working in a highly digitalized world and directly witnessing the digital transformation of their businesses are likely to adopt the electronic voting system as another information and communication technology tool for democracy.

On the other hand, the perception of citizens, who work in security activities that consist in ensuring the security of people and property, with regard to electronic voting is cautious and sometimes very negative. For the latter, there is no tangible evidence of the correct recording of votes because a computer screen can display one thing and record another.

In this field research, trust is highlighted as a particularly important condition for the use of the electronic voting system. Beyond the technical malfunctions that can affect the accuracy and validity of votes, there seems to be a major concern regarding the vulnerability of electronic voting systems to manipulation by external hackers. Although manipulations can occur by internal local agents, these intrusions can only affect local and isolated structures. There are also risks with traditional voting systems with recent examples in some democracies where it was necessary to recount votes. Electronic voting opens up new possibilities for a single hacker, who may be anywhere in the world, to affect the central system disrupting the entire nation. The perception of

Table 2. Current difficulties linked to the voting process and potential of improvement along the different voting stages

1. Information collection and voting documents	
Difficulties	*Proposed solutions*
Too much, scattered and biased information, not enough time available for information	(1) Application regrouping neutral information (2) Linking e-voting platform to neutral information (3) Newspaper provide online information files (4) Interactive platforms with customized information based on one's political profile (5) State-organized sensitization with regard to the potential of being influenced by social media e.g. (to promote critical opinion forming skills) (6) Inform citizens about budget of the parties for financing their campaign (7) One stop shop for information on different points of view, reminder for votes information, results (8) A personalized digital communication, e.g. save the personal decisions of past votes
Voting questions are not clear enough	Easier formulation of questions
Complex voting topics are reduced to yes or no questions	More choice
Content of the official voting brochure not neutral enough, too easy/propagandistic	Two parts: one easy part and one more intellectual part
Forgetting about vote	Reminder via e-mail or application e.g.
2.Voting process depending on voting type	
Difficulties	*Proposed solutions*
e-voting: - Too complicated - Lack of security	It has to be as easy as possible (time-saving, comprehensible, intuitive), accessible for everyone (1) Password scanning and direct arrival on the website (2) Voting confirmation (3) Possibility to do everything orally
Postal vote: - The process is ok as it is - You have to lick the envelope, which is not comfortable - You have to put a stamp	
3. Information about results	
Difficulties	*Proposed solutions*
No particular difficulties	Inclusion in application that integrates the whole process, from information collection, to voting, to results

risk from an electronic perspective is more global, where a group of people of an individual can intervene and hack from anywhere on the planet.

The need to combine secrecy and individual verifiability is one of the most important attributes identified in this research. Indeed, unlike the e-banking system, where citizens can check their account statements at any time to ensure that all transactions are recorded correctly, one can check the accuracy of a bank transaction afterwards, by checking account statements online or by printing on official banking documents. Electronic voting operations concerning secrecy and verifiability (universal and individual) are still not clear to voters. In addition, in the event of embezzlement, the bank has insurance, through its after-sales service, to compensate its customers. All information necessary for data integrity can be stored and tracked, eliminating any secrecy between the customer and the bank. In the event of technical malfunction or external interference, these failures or manipulations may go unnoticed.

Swiss citizens will probably trust the electronic voting system and their officials. In the case of electronic voting, their trust does not need to be earned at this time, but it can only be easily lost. The technical challenges of electronic voting open doors for private companies and investors to sell their technologies. There is concern that personal data and individual voting preferences may be in their possession. It is imperative to maintain the confidence that only the government should control all systems. The government must be the sole guarantor of the entire system. With the trust established with the government, the voter is not very interested in learning more about verifiability or verification.

The results also show that the electronic voting system is accepted as a complementary means, but should not replace the postal voting system and the ballot box. This new possibility of voting will not significantly increase the number of people who participate in the vote or change their voting habits, as people vote because they want to, and not because of the different possibilities offered.

In a traditional voting system, voters have learned to trust their fellow assessors not to open the ballot box before the counting, which is a public operation understood by all voters. In the case of wrongdoing, citizens are able to accept human fault because they too can make mistakes in their own work. However, it is still difficult to accept and understand the mistakes made by software. The government official could then keep some form of electronic voting ceremony such as broadcasting live the count happening in the back-stage process.

8   Conclusion

The objective of this exploratory research was to focus on the social aspects of electronic voting. Indeed, an abundant scientific literature already covers the technical aspects of e-voting (algorithms, security, etc.). The justification for this research objective, which focuses on rather social aspects, stems first of all from the fact that electronic voting, for various reasons, is barely fully established in Switzerland, whereas many test phases have already demonstrated the feasibility of this operational process and it has recently been accepted as an official way of voting. In this research, we intended to study the perceptions of Swiss citizens regarding electronic voting, and to understand their meanings through a qualitative field research (based on semi-structured interviews). The most important findings are presented in the three following categories: electronic voting perception, electronic voting security and electronic voting operations. These insights are essentially related to the social acceptance of electronic voting. We observe in particular that the vote in Switzerland has an almost sacred dimension, as opposed to other cultural contexts, such as [5, 13, 17, 18] and that the trust that surrounds the voting "ritual" (i.e. voting operations and processes) is of supreme importance.

Through this research project on electronic voting, which focuses on the human factor dimension, we believe that this study will help to develop relevant and practical managerial precepts to better implement these digitized operations processes in the future.

Nevertheless, this study is not without limitations. As the data collection was just completed when writing the paper, more in-depth analysis iteration of database must still be completed to improve the relevancy of our conclusion. The size of the sample (25) is still too limited to draw more generic conclusions. It was however our aim to investigate the "how" and "why" of perceptions of Swiss citizens rather than percentages as it is the case in a quantitative survey. In a further research, we intend to conduct a quantitative survey based on the qualitative findings presented in this paper.

References

1. Fenazzi, S., Jaberg, S.: Le vote électronique ne devient pas un canal de vote ordinaire en Suisse. via Swissinfo.ch (2019). https://www.swissinfo.ch/fre/marche-arri%C3%A8re-gouvernementale_le-vote-%C3%A9lectronique-ne-devient-pas-un-canal-de-vote-ordinaire-en-suisse/45060752. Accessed 02 July 2019
2. Budurushi, J., Neumann, S., Renaud, K., Volkamer, K.: Introduction to special issue on e-voting. J. Inf. Secur. Appl. **38**, 122–123 (2018)
3. Gray, J., Rump, B.: Models for digitalization. Softw. Syst. Model. **14**, 1319–1320 (2015)
4. Hagberg, J., Sundstrom, M., Egels-Zandén, N.: The digitalization of retailing: an exploratory framework. Int. J. Retail Distrib. Manag. **44**, 694–712 (2016)
5. Moisander, J., Eriksson, P.: Corporate narratives of information society: making up the mobile consumer subject. Consumption, Markets Cult. **9**, 257–275 (2006)
6. Eshet-Alkalai, Y.: Real-time thinking in the digital era. In: Encyclopedia of Information Science and Technology, Second Edition, pp. 3219–3223. IGI Global (2009)
7. Liyanage, J.P.: Hybrid Intelligence Through Business Socialization and Networking: Managing Complexities in the Digital Era. IGI Global, Hershey (2012)
8. Gibson, J.P., Krimmer, R., Teague, V., Pomares, J.: A review of e-voting: the past, present and future. Ann. Telecommun. **7**, 279–286 (2016)
9. Mahrer, H., Krimmer, R.: Towards the enhancement of e-democracy: identifying the notion of the 'middleman paradox'. Inf. Syst. J. **15**, 27–42 (2005)
10. Alvarez, R., Hall, T., Trechsel, A.: Internet voting in comparative perspective: the case of estonia. Polit. Sci. Polit. **42**, 497–505 (2009)
11. Vassil, K., Solvak, M., Vinkel, P., Trechsel, A.H., Alvarez, R.M.: The diffusion of internet voting, usage patterns of internet voting in Estonia between 2005 and 2015. Gov. Inf. Q. **33**, 453–459 (2016)

12. Germann, M., Serdült, U.: Internet voting and turnout: evidence from Switzerland. Electoral. Stud. **47**, 1–12 (2017)
13. Germann, M., Serdült, U.: Internet voting for expatriates: the swiss case. JeDEM-eJournal of eDemocracy and Open Gov. **6**, 197–215 (2014)
14. Wang, K.-H., Mondal, S.K., Chan, K., Xie, X.: A review of contemporary e-voting: requirements, technology, systems and usability. Data Sci. Pattern Recogn. **1**, 31–47 (2017)
15. Tarasov, P., Tewari, H.: The future of e-voting. IADIS Int. J. Comput. Sci. Inf. Syst. **12**, 148–165 (2018)
16. Willemsen, J.: Bits or paper: which should get to carry your vote? J. Inf. Secur. Appl. **38**, 124–131 (2018)
17. Zada, P., Falzon, G., Kwan, P.: Perceptions of the Australian public towards mobile internet e-voting: risks, choice and trust. Electron. J. e-Gov. **14**, 117–134 (2016)
18. Suki, N.M., Suki, N.M.: Decision-making and satisfaction in campus e-voting: moderating effect of trust in the system. J. Enterp. Inf. Manag. **30**, 944–963 (2017)
19. Ghauri, P., Gronhaug, K.: Research Methods In Business Studies, 3rd edn. Pearson Education, England (2005)
20. Palinkas, L.A., Horwitz, S.M., Green, C.A., Wisdom, J.P., Duan, N., Hoagwood, K.: Purposeful sampling for qualitative data collection and analysis in mixed method implementation research. Adm. Policy Ment. Health Ment. Health Serv. Res. **42**, 533–544 (2015)
21. OECD Education at a glance 2014. Available via Country note (2014). http://www.rsc.org/dose/title of subordinate document. Accessed 02 July 2019

Improvements in Everlasting Privacy: Efficient and Secure Zero Knowledge Proofs

Thomas Haines[✉] and Clementine Gritti[✉]

NTNU, Trondheim, Norway
{thomas.haines,clementine.gritti}@ntnu.no

Abstract. Verifiable electronic voting promises to ensure the correctness of elections even in the presence of a corrupt authority, while providing strong privacy guarantees. However, few practical systems with end-to-end verifiability are expected to offer long term privacy, let alone guarantee it. Since good guarantees of privacy are essential to the democratic process, good guarantees of everlasting privacy must be a major goal of secure online voting systems. Various currently proposed solutions rely on unusual constructions whose security has not been established. Further, the cost of verifying the zero knowledge proofs of other solutions has only been partially analysed. Our work builds upon Moran and Naor's solution—and its extensions, applications and generalisations— to present a scheme which is additively homomorphic, efficient to verify, and rests upon well studied assumptions.

Keywords: Voting · Everlasting privacy · Zero Knowledge Proofs

1 Introduction

Electronic voting schemes have been studied extensively and ongoing research has developed schemes with increasingly strong privacy and integrity guarantees. However, at present the literature has few solutions which are simultaneously efficient, practical, and ensure the ongoing—also called everlasting—privacy of elections. By practical we mean solutions which are easy to deploy securely. Much of the existing literature relies on trusted setup or complicated recovery procedures which reduce the trustworthiness of the election.

Many schemes have sketched how to do elections with everlasting privacy. The constructions tend to use perfectly hiding commitment schemes and public key encryption; this is made verifiable by use of Zero Knowledge Proofs (ZKPs) for correct encryption and correct shuffling of ballots. At present, one of the most common commitment schemes used is not proven secure [17]. A possible method

The authors acknowledge support from the Luxembourg National Research Fund (FNR) and the Research Council of Norway for the joint project SURCVS.

R. Krimmer et al. (Eds.): E-Vote-ID 2019, LNCS 11759, pp. 116–133, 2019.
https://doi.org/10.1007/978-3-030-30625-0_8

of mixing has been suggested but the security proof is missing [9]. Further, the suggested method of mixing is not sufficiently practical. The importance of everlasting privacy has been widely recognised and prior works present constructions with competing efficiency.

We want an electronic voting system with everlasting privacy, which is also efficient to run. We introduce the following mechanisms that will enable us to design such a solution, namely Pedersen commitments [19], Sigma Protocols [8,10] and mix-nets [7]. A Pedersen commitment [19] is an informational-theoretic hiding and computational binding commitment scheme. It provides privacy regardless of the computational power of the adversary but its binding property reduces to the Discrete Logarithm (DLOG) problem. Pedersen commitments are popular in electronic voting schemes because the binding property is only relevant during the course of the election, but privacy should be assured even after the election.

Multiparty computation [25] allows the secure evaluation of a function without leaking anything more about the inputs than can be derived from the result and the inputs previously known to the adversary. ZKPs [14] are a powerful technique which allows proving the correctness of a statement without leaking any other information. The application of both multiparty computation and ZKPs to voting is obvious and commonly mentioned [9,10]. However, the general strategies for both techniques are too computationally intensive in most real elections. Hence there are tailored solutions (such as those we present here) which take advantage of the particularities of elections to construct more efficient solutions.

Sigma Protocols [8,10] are a class of protocols known to be secure under composition. They tend to be more efficient than zero knowledge protocols. A protocol of the correct form is proved to be a Sigma Protocol by showing it satisfies the following properties: *completeness*, capturing that the protocol will succeed when both parties are honest; *special soundness*, referring to the inability of the adversary to generate proofs without knowing a witness; and *honest verifier zero knowledge*, emphasising that the proof leaks negligible information.

Mix-nets were first proposed by Chaum [7], as a way to provide privacy. In the context of verifiable electronic voting mix-nets are also required to be verifiable. This is achieved by proving the correctness of the shuffle using a ZKP, of which two techniques are dominant; namely those of Bayer and Groth [4] and that of Terelius and Wikström [23]. Both techniques are general in nature and tend to be optimised for the particularities of the system in which they are used.

1.1 Related Work

Much of the everlasting privacy literature relies on and builds upon Moran and Naor's work [17], which was modified as an extension to the web-based voting Helios scheme [13]. This kind of extension reduces privacy attacks on the system (from an external adversary) to information theoretic security rather than computational. Hence, no future breakthrough in computation power, mathematics, or large-scale quantum computers will put the voters' privacy at risk.

Unfortunately, the bulk of this work relies on primitives which are somewhat unusual. Since Moran and Naor, a Pedersen commitment variant is often used but its security appears never to have been rigorously established. Indeed, there is much literature which states that Pedersen commitments and Sigma Protocols are generally required to be defined in a prime order group, which this variant is not, meaning its security should be rigorously established [3,6,20]. We denote, in the paper, the combination of Paillier encryption [18] and Pedersen commitments [19], pioneered by Moran and Naor, as the MN encryption scheme.

Arapinis *et al.* [2] recently showed in ProVerif, an automatic cryptographic protocol verifier, that various constructions achieve everlasting privacy, some of these solutions lose verifiability properties in exchange for everlasting privacy but are highly practical in those situations where these verifiability properties are not important. Cuvelier *et al.* [9] systematised much of the research by showing how certain types of primitives can be securely combined. They also present an elegant scheme called PPATC based on Abe *et al.*'s [1] commitment scheme on bilinear pairings, which they show has efficient encryption on the order of 40 times faster then existing methods. The efficiency is due to the elliptic curves which are more secure relative to their size than problems based on factorisation.

However, Cuvelier *et al.* [9] do not account for the verification complexity. We show that Moran-Naor suggestion of Paillier encryption and Pedersen commitments—refereed as PPATP in [9]—is at least as fast to verify as PPATC when using the Sigma Protocol and mix-net we will detail later. Further, the MN system supports homomorphic tallying where PPATC does not which is a significant advantage in some situations. We note that Cuvelier *et al.* [9] do sketch the same Sigma Protocol for correct encryption in their paper that we later present, but provide no proof. We also note that recent work of Hazay *et al.* [16], has made threshold key generation in Paillier practical as with PPATC.

Many of the existing solutions—except Cuvelier *et al.* [9]—are unsatisfactory in one of two ways. They complicate practical issues, by detecting issues after they have occurred rather than using ZKPs initially. Alternatively, they rely on cut-and-choose based ZKPs rather than Sigma proofs, resulting in an increase in computation and communication of about six orders of magnitude.

There are efficient mix-nets for both Paillier ciphertexts and Pedersen commitments (e.g., Moran and Naor highlight Groth's mix-net working for Paillier encryption scheme [15]). However, mixing the commitments and ciphertexts separately significantly complicates the election process and weakens security. Cuvelier *et al.* note that the general construction of Wikström [24] can be applied but do not prove the required Sigma Protocol. Further, this construction is significantly slower than the optimised constructions popular in electronic voting.

1.2   Contributions

- We present the Sigma Protocol for re-encryption of the MN cryptosystem; we also provide the proof for this Sigma Protocol and for the protocol for correct encryption [9] of the MN cryptosystem;
- We provide the first proof of security for the existing modified Pedersen commitment of semi-prime order;
- We present an efficient variant of ballot mixing;
- We give an analysis of verification efficiency of MN cryptosystem and compare with PPATC, showing MN is as fast to verify when using the mix-net and Sigma Protocols from above.

When Moran and Naor first introduced the MN cryptosystem they said "although more efficient (zero knowledge) protocols exist for these applications, for the purpose of this paper we concentrate on simplicity and ease of understanding" [17]. Unfortunately in the decade since the follow up work has continued to rely on cut-and-choose [5,13]; and, has found updating the existing zero knowledge work to the requirements of the MN cryptosystem more difficult than Moran and Naor expected. Our contribution finally closes this gap by providing efficient proofs for encryption, re-encryption and shuffling.

1.3   Road Map

In the next section, we provide the notations and definitions useful for the comprehension of the paper. In Sect. 3, we present our security proof for the modified Perdersen commitment scheme [17]. In Sect. 4, we describe our new Sigma Protocol for re-encryption, and give the security proofs for the latter as well for the Sigma Protocol for encryption [9]. In Sect. 5, we depict our verifiable mix-net, improving the efficiency of the general construction proposed in [24]. In Sect. 6, we analyse and compare the efficiency of our solution with the similar work of Cuvelier *et al.* [9]. We conclude our paper in the last section.

2   Preliminaries and Building Blocks

Due to lack of space, we let the readers refer to [14] for zero knowledge notions, and specifically to [10] for Sigma Protocols, and to [7] for mix-nets.

Notations. Natural numbers are denoted by $\mathbb{N}$ and integers by $\mathbb{Z}$. The ring of integers modulo n is denoted $\mathbb{Z}_n$, and its multiplicative group $\mathbb{Z}_n^*$. Let M denote a square matrix of order N from $\mathbb{Z}_n^{N*N}$. Let $\mathbf{v}$ be a vector of length N from $\mathbb{Z}_n^N$. Let $\langle \mathbf{v}, \mathbf{v}' \rangle = \sum_{i=1}^{N} v_i v_i'$ denote the inner product. Given a finite set S, $s \leftarrow_r S$ means a uniformly random assignment of an element in S to the variable s. A Polynomial-Time Algorithm (PPT) is a probabilistic algorithm running in time polynomial in its input size. A relationship $\mathcal{R}_*(\circ)(\diamond)$ is a subset of the

Cartesian product of the sets $\circ$ and $\diamond$. We denote by $\mathcal{R}_1 \vee \mathcal{R}_2$ the relationship consisting of the pairs $((x_1, x_2), w)$ s.t. $(x_1, w) \in \mathcal{R}_1$ or $(x_2, w) \in \mathcal{R}_2$. Let $\mathcal{R}_1 \wedge \mathcal{R}_2$ be the relationship consisting of the pairs $((x_1, x_2), w)$ s.t. $(x_1, w) \in \mathcal{R}_1$ and $(x_2, w) \in \mathcal{R}_2$.

Discrete Logarithm Assumption. Given primes p, q and $n = pq$, where $kn + 1$ is also prime, for $k \in \mathbb{N}$. Let $\mathbb{G}_n$ denote the group of order n mod $\mathbb{Z}^*_{kn+1}$ and let $\mathbb{G}_p$, $\mathbb{G}_q$ denote the groups of order p and q respectively mod $\mathbb{Z}^*_{kn+1}$. $\mathbb{G}_p$ and $\mathbb{G}_q$ are called *Schnorr groups*. The Discrete Logarithm (DLOG) assumption is believed to hold for the set of Schnorr groups.

Commitment Scheme.

Definition 1. *A homomorphic commitment scheme Π is a triple of PPT algorithms $(\Pi.\mathsf{Setup}, \Pi.\mathsf{Com}, \Pi.\mathsf{Open})$, s.t.:*

- *The Setup algorithm for a given group $\mathbb{G}$ defines a set of valid Commit Keys $\mathcal{CK}$ from which one is uniformly selected: $CK \in \mathcal{CK} \leftarrow_r \Pi.\mathsf{Setup}(\mathbb{G})$.*
- *A given Commit Key CK defines a message space $\mathcal{M}_{CK}$, randomness space $\mathcal{R}_{CK}$, commitment space $\mathcal{C}_{CK}$, and opening space $\mathcal{D}_{CK}$. The Com algorithm takes these as domain and co-domain: $\forall m \in \mathcal{M}_{CK}, \forall r \in \mathcal{R}_{CK}, (c \in \mathcal{C}_{CK}, d \in \mathcal{D}_{CK}) \leftarrow \Pi.\mathsf{Com}_{CK}(m, r)$.*
- *The Open algorithm takes a commitment $c \in \mathcal{C}_{CK}$ and opening $d \in \mathcal{D}_{CK}$ and returns either a message $m \in \mathcal{M}_{CK}$ or null $\perp$: $\Pi.\mathsf{Open}_{CK}(c \in \mathcal{C}_{CK}, d \in \mathcal{D}_{CK}) \to m \in \mathcal{M}_{CK}$ or $\perp$.*

Correctness: $\forall CK \in \mathcal{CK}, \forall m \in \mathcal{M}_{CK}, \forall r \in \mathcal{R}_{CK}$, we have $\Pi.\mathsf{Open}_{CK}(\Pi.\mathsf{Com}_{CK}(m, r)) = m$.

Homomorphism: $\forall CK \in \mathcal{CK}, \forall m_1, m_2 \in \mathcal{M}_{CK}, \forall r_1, r_2 \in \mathcal{R}_{CK}$, we have $\Pi.\mathsf{Com}_{CK}(m_1, r_1) * \Pi.\mathsf{Com}_{CK}(m_2, r_2) = \Pi.\mathsf{Com}_{CK}(m_1 + m_2, r_1 + r_2)$. The homomorphic property implies the ability to re-randomise commitments: let the ReRand algorithm be defined as $\Pi.\mathsf{ReRand}_{CK}(c \in \mathcal{CK}_{CK}, r \in \mathcal{R}_{CK}) = c * \Pi.\mathsf{Com}_{CK}(1, r)$.

Definition 2. *Perfectly hiding property of a commitment scheme: Given a group $\mathbb{G}$, a commitment scheme Π is perfectly hiding if for any adversary $\mathcal{A}$, it holds that $Adv^{hiding}(\mathcal{A}, \Pi, \mathbb{G}) = Pr[Exp_{\mathcal{A}}^{hiding-1}(\Pi, \mathbb{G})] - Pr[Exp_{\mathcal{A}}^{hiding-0}(\Pi, \mathbb{G})] = 0$ (Fig. 1).*

$Exp_{\mathcal{A}}^{hiding-b}(\Pi, \mathbb{G})$
$CK \leftarrow_r \Pi.\mathsf{Setup}(\mathbb{G})$
$(m_0, m_1, \alpha) \leftarrow_r \mathcal{A}(CK)$
$r \leftarrow_r \mathcal{R}_{CK}$
$(c, d) \leftarrow \Pi.\mathsf{Com}_{CK}(m_b, r)$
$b' \leftarrow_r \mathcal{A}(CK, c, \alpha)$

Fig. 1. Hiding experiments

Definition 3. *Binding property of a commitment scheme: Given a group $\mathbb{G}$, a commitment scheme Π is (t, ϵ) binding if no t-time algorithm $\mathcal{A}$ has $Succ^{binding}(\mathcal{A}, \Pi, \mathbb{G}) > \epsilon$ in $Exp_{\mathcal{A}}^{binding}(\Pi, \mathbb{G})$ (Fig. 2). For simplicity we will often drop t and ϵ and refer to Π as binding.*

$$
\begin{array}{l}
\hline
Exp_{\mathcal{A}}^{binding}(\Pi, \mathbb{G}) \\
\hline
CK \leftarrow_r \Pi.\mathsf{Setup}(\mathbb{G}) \\
(c, d, d') \leftarrow_r \mathcal{A}(CK) \\
m \leftarrow \Pi.\mathsf{Open}_{CK}(c, d) \\
m' \leftarrow \Pi.\mathsf{Open}_{CK}(c, d') \\
\text{if } m \neq m' \text{return } 1 \\
\text{else return } 0 \\
\hline
\end{array}
$$

Fig. 2. Binding experiment

Public Key Encryption Scheme

Definition 4. *A homomorphic public key encryption scheme Σ is a triple of PPT algorithms (Σ.KeyGen, Σ.Enc, Σ.Dec), s.t.:*

- *The KeyGen algorithm defines a set of valid key pairs ($\mathcal{PK}, \mathcal{SK}$) from which one is uniformly selected: $(PK \in \mathcal{PK}, SK \in \mathcal{SK}) \leftarrow_r \Sigma.\mathsf{KeyGen}(1^k)$.*
- *A given public key PK defines a message space $\mathcal{M}_{PK}$, randomness space $\mathcal{R}_{PK}$, and ciphertext space $\mathcal{C}_{PK}$. The Enc algorithm takes these as domain and co-domain: $\forall PK \in \mathcal{PK}, \forall m \in \mathcal{M}_{PK}, \forall r \in \mathcal{R}_{PK}, CT \in \mathcal{C}_{PK} \leftarrow \Sigma.\mathsf{Enc}_{PK}(m, r)$.*
- *The Dec algorithm takes a ciphertext $CT \in \mathcal{C}_{PK}$ and $SK \in \mathcal{SK}$ and returns either a message $m \in \mathcal{M}_{PK}$ or null $\perp$: $\forall CT \in \mathcal{C}_{PK}, \Sigma.\mathsf{Dec}_{SK}(c) \rightarrow m \in \mathcal{M}_{PK}$ or $\perp$.*

Correctness: $\forall (PK \in \mathcal{PK}, SK \in \mathcal{SK}) \leftarrow_r \Sigma.\mathsf{KeyGen}(1^k), \forall m \in \mathcal{M}_{PK}, \forall r \in \mathcal{R}_{PK}$, we have $\Sigma.\mathsf{Dec}_{SK}(\Sigma.\mathsf{Enc}_{PK}(m, r)) = m$.

Homomorphism: $\forall PK \in \mathcal{PK}, \forall m_1, m_2 \in \mathcal{M}_{PK}, \forall r_1, r_2 \in \mathcal{R}_{PK}$, we have $\Sigma.\mathsf{Enc}_{PK}(m_1 + m_2, r_1 + r_2) = \Sigma.\mathsf{Enc}_{PK}(m_1, r_1) * \Sigma.\mathsf{Enc}_{PK}(m_2, r_2)$.

We succinctly recall the IND-CPA security concept for a public key encryption scheme as intuitively meaning that the adversary cannot distinguish between the encryption of two known plaintexts.

2.1   Modified Pedersen Commitment Scheme

As we have already noted starting with Moran and Naor [17], Pedersen commitments of semi-prime order have become a significant building block for voting schemes with everlasting privacy. The construction proposed in [17] was to take two safe primes p, q (i.e. to be of the form $2p + 1$ for p prime), let $n = pq$ and work in the subgroup of order n of $\mathbb{Z}_{4n+1}^*$ where $4n + 1$ is also prime.

The modified Pedersen commitment scheme Π is the triple of PPT algorithms $(\Pi.\text{Setup}, \Pi.\text{Com}, \Pi.\text{Open})$, s.t.:

- $CK \leftarrow \Pi.\text{Setup}(\mathbb{G})$ s.t. $CK = \{\mathbb{G}, g, h\}$. Given a group $\mathbb{G}$ of semi-prime order n, let g be any generator of $\mathbb{G}$ and choose $h \leftarrow_r \mathbb{G}$ (with overwhelming probability h will be a generator).
- A given Commit Key $CK = \{\mathbb{G}, g, h\}$ defines the message space $\mathcal{M}_{CK} = \mathbb{Z}_n$, randomness space $\mathcal{R}_{CK} = \mathbb{Z}_n$, commitment space $\mathcal{C}_{CK} = \mathbb{G}_n$, and opening space $\mathcal{D}_{CK} = (\mathbb{Z}_n, \mathbb{Z}_n)$. The $\Pi.\text{Com}_{CK}$ algorithm takes $m \in \mathbb{Z}_n, r \in \mathbb{Z}_n$ and sets $c = g^r h^m$ and $d = (m, r)$.
- The $\Pi.\text{Open}_{CK}$ algorithm takes a commitment $c \in \mathbb{G}_n$ and opening $d \in (m \in \mathbb{Z}_n, r \in \mathbb{Z}_n)$. If $c = g^r h^m$ return m else return $\bot$.

2.2   A Commitment Consistent Encryption System

The encryption scheme suggested by Moran and Naor [17] is a particular kind of encryption system specialised for everlasting privacy, and commonly used in verifiable electronic voting [12,13]. The standard suggestion, which we describe below, is to use Pedersen commitments of semi-prime order and the generalised Paillier cryptosystem. This notation–while slightly unusual–is useful because it enables the direct application of various existing results, particularly those in the area of mix-nets, as we shall see later. For convenience, we shall refer to this system as the MN cryptosystem.

We now describe MN encryption scheme. Let $\Sigma = (\Sigma.\text{KegGen}, \Sigma.\text{Enc}, \Sigma.\text{Dec})$ denote a public key encryption scheme. Specifically let $\Sigma.\text{KeyGen}$ be the key generation function of the (generalised) Paillier cryptosystem [11,18] producing $PK = (n)$ and $SK = (d)$, where $n = pq$ is a RSA modulus and d is the lowest common multiple of $p - 1$ and $q - 1$. Choose k s.t. $kn + 1$ is prime, and let g, h be random generators of subgroup of order n in $\mathbb{Z}^*_{kn+1}$, denoted $\mathbb{G}_n$. We denote the ciphertext space $\mathcal{C}_{PK} = \mathbb{G}_n \times \mathbb{Z}^*_{n^2} \times \mathbb{Z}^*_{n^2}$, the message space $\mathcal{M}_{PK} = \mathbb{Z}_n$, and the randomness space $\mathcal{R}_{PK} = \mathbb{Z}_n \times \mathbb{Z}^*_n \times \mathbb{Z}^*_n$.

We quickly explain the encryption process. Let $\Sigma.\text{Enc}_{PK}(m \in \mathbb{Z}_n, (r \in \mathbb{Z}_n, r' \in \mathbb{Z}^*_n, r'' \in \mathbb{Z}^*_n))$ produce $CT = (c, ct_1, ct_2) = (g^r h^m \bmod kn + 1, (1 + n)^m r'^n \bmod n^2, (1 + n)^r r''^n \bmod n^2)$. That is we encode the message m in a Pedersen commitment hidden by the randomness r, and we encrypt the opening to this commitment in two Paillier ciphertexts. Let $\Sigma.\text{Dec}_{SK}(CT = (c, ct_1, ct_2))$ be the decryption function. First use the Paillier decryption function to retrieve m, r from ct_1, ct_2 respectively, then if $c = g^r h^m$ the result is m else $\bot$.

We first make the observation that the Σ scheme is additively homomorphic, that is $\Sigma.\mathsf{Enc}_{PK}(m_0, (r_0, r'_0, r''_0)) * \Sigma.\mathsf{Enc}_{PK}(m_1, (r_1, r'_1, r''_1)) = \Sigma.\mathsf{Enc}_{pk}(m_0 + m_1, (r_0 + r_1, r'_0 * r'_1, r''_0 * r''_1))$. Secondly, that there is a shuffle friendly map [24]: given $CT = (c, ct_1, ct_2)$ and $r = (r_0, r_1, r_2)$, $c' = c * g^{r_0}, ct'_1 = ct_1 * r_1^n, ct'_2 = ct_2 * (1 + n)^{r_0} r_2^n$. We denote this map by $(\phi_{PK}(CT, r) = \mathcal{C}_{PK} \times \mathcal{R}_{PK} \to \mathcal{C}_{PK})$. The existence of this map is necessary to apply Wikström's general mix-net construction to the cryptosystem [24].

In addition, we preserve the property of Paillier encryption and Pedersen commitments that given a ciphertext $CT = \Sigma.\mathsf{Enc}_{PK}(m_0 \in \mathcal{M}_{pk}, (r, r', r'') \in \mathcal{R}_{pk})$ and a message m_1 it is easy to compute $CT^{m_1} = \Sigma.\mathsf{Enc}_{pk}(m_0 * m_1; (r * m_1, r'^{m_1}, r''^{m_1}))$. In this case the exact effect on the randomness is a combination of multiplication and exponentiation. Lastly, since the Pailler variant we use is the variant of Damgård et al. [11], threshold decryption is also available.

3   Security Proof for the Modified Pedersen Commitment Scheme

The sketch of the security proof for the commitment scheme in [17] lacks sufficient detail to be of use in establishing the security of the commitment. Since the group n is not of prime order, given a tuple (m, r, m', r') if $GCD(|m - m'|, n) \neq 1$ and $GCD(|r - r'|, n) \neq 1$ then the sketched reduction to the DLOG problem fails. While it is not particularly surprising that the DLOG problem holds in a group whose order contains a large prime factor, it is important to show that this is indeed true and furthermore does not break any other part of the system. A correct reduction is hence needed. Moreover, we do not require the primes to be safe and thus consider a subgroup of order n of $\mathbb{Z}^*_{kn+1}$ for an integer k. Therefore, the above commitment scheme can be extended to the general case with integers k, n such that $kn + 1$ is prime. We now present the security proof of the generalization of the modified Pedersen commitment scheme.

Proposition 1. *The modified Pedersen commitment scheme Π is a homomorphic perfectly hiding commitment scheme.*

Proof. The correctness of the scheme follows immediately from the definitions of $\Pi.\mathsf{Com}$ and $\Pi.\mathsf{Open}$. The perfect hiding property of the scheme follows in the same way as normal Pedersen commitment schemes: for any two messages m_0, m_1 and commitment c there exist two unique random coins r_0, r_1 s.t. $c = g^{r_0} h^{m_0}$ and $c = g^{r_1} h^{m_1}$, and since the random coins are taken uniformly, the commitment provides no information about which message was committed to.

The key to understanding the next part on the binding property is to recall that for a cyclic group of semi-prime order $n = pq$, there are exactly two non-trivial subgroups: one is of order p and the other q. If we let $\mathbb{G}$ be the subgroup of $\mathbb{Z}^*_{kn+1}$ of order n, where $kn+1$ is prime, then the two non-trivial subgroups are two Schnorr groups. The reduction we present in the next paragraph reduces the binding property of the modified Pedersen commitment to the DLOG problem in the two Schnorr groups, which we label $\mathbb{G}_p$ and $\mathbb{G}_q$.

To show that the scheme is binding, we present a reduction in two parts. First, we show that for any t-time adversary $\mathcal{A}$ against the modified Pedersen commitment scheme Π with $Succ^{binding}(\mathcal{A}, \Pi, \mathbb{G}) = \epsilon$, we can construct an algorithm which–given a DLOG problem in $\mathbb{G}_p$, and another in $\mathbb{G}_q$–outputs the answer to at least one with probability ϵ. Then having observed against which of the two groups the better success rate is achieved, we construct an adversary against the DLOG problem in that group which succeeds with probability at least $\frac{\epsilon}{2}$. This suffices to show that the binding property of the commitment scheme cannot be broken with probability more than twice that of the DLOG problem in the weakest of the two underlying Schnorr groups $\mathbb{G}_p$ and $\mathbb{G}_q$.

There exists an efficiently computable isomorphism between the direct product of $\mathbb{G}_p \times \mathbb{G}_q$ and $\mathbb{G}_n$. The challenger takes the two subgroups of $\mathbb{G}_n$ and a DLOG problem in each. It combines these to construct the commitment key which it gives to the adversary. Since g_p and g_q are generators of their respective groups $\mathbb{G}_p$ and $\mathbb{G}_q$, if h_p and h_q are random elements (as they are in the DLOG experiment) than this is indistinguishable from the honest run. The successful adversary $\mathcal{A}(\mathbb{G}, g, h)$ outputs $(c, (m, r), (m', r'))$ s.t. $m \neq m'$. If $GCD(|m - m'|, n) = 1$ or $GCD(|r - r'|, n) = 1$ then we extract $\alpha = dlog_g h$ as normal with Pedersen commitments and calculate $dlog_{g_p} h_p = \alpha \bmod p$ and $dlog_{g_q} h_q = \alpha \bmod q$. If this is not the case, then w.l.o.g. $GCD(|r - r'|, n) = GCD(|m - m'|, n) = p$ and hence there exists unique $\delta, \gamma \in Z_q$ s.t. $\delta p = \alpha \gamma p \bmod n$ and hence $\alpha = \frac{\delta}{\gamma} \bmod q$. By the Chinese remainder theorem $\alpha \bmod q = dlog_{g_q} h_q$ and we successfully answer that. $\qquad\square$

Our solution is not only provably secure (under reasonable assumptions) but also more general with the setting $kn + 1$, with $k \in \mathbb{N}$, rather than $4n + 1$. The homomorphism of the scheme follows immediately from the group properties and the isomorphism of $\mathbb{Z}_n$ and $\mathbb{G}_n$.

4   Security Proofs for Sigma Protocols

We present two Sigma Protocols, one for correct encryption from [9] and a new protocol for correct re-encryption; we believe that proofs of both Sigma Protocols have never been published before. These proofs allow the realisation of an electronic voting scheme that is secure (compared to without ZKPs) and highly efficient (compared to the cut-and-choose solutions currently in the literature).

4.1 Sigma Protocol for Correct Encryption

The following Sigma Protocol for correct encryption was proposed by Cuvelier et al. [9], though they omit the proof. Such protocol is used to prove that given a ciphertext, one knows the inputs and uses them to generate that ciphertext.

Given $CT = (c = g^r h^m \bmod kn + 1, ct_1 = (1 + n)^m r'^n \bmod n^2, ct_2 = (1 + n)^r r''^n \bmod n^2)$, we show that we know $m \in \mathbb{Z}_n$ and $(r \in \mathbb{Z}_n, r' \in Z_n^*, r'' \in \mathbb{Z}_n^*)$:

(1) Let t_1, t_2 be random elements in $\mathbb{Z}_n$ and t_3, t_4 be random elements in $\mathbb{Z}_n^*$. The prover computes $\alpha = g^{t_1} h^{t_2} \bmod kn + 1, \beta = (1 + n)^{t_2} t_3^n \bmod n^2, \gamma = (1 + n)^{t_1} t_4^n \bmod n^2$ and sends them to the verifier.
(2) The verifier sends a challenge ξ chosen at random in $\mathbb{Z}_n$.
(3) The prover computes $s_1 = t_1 + \xi r \bmod n, s_2 = t_2 + \xi m \bmod n, s_3 = t_3 * r'^{\xi} \bmod n, s_4 = t_4 * r''^{\xi} \bmod n$, and sends these to the verifier.
(4) The verifier accepts if $\alpha c^{\xi} = g^{s_1} h^{s_2} \bmod kn + 1, \beta ct_1^{\xi} = (1 + n)^{s_2} s_3^n \bmod n^2, \gamma ct_2^{\xi} = (1 + n)^{s_1} s_4^n \bmod n^2$.
The transcript (with the elements exchanged between the prover and the verifier) is $(\alpha \in \mathbb{G}_n, \beta \in \mathbb{Z}_{n^2}^*, \gamma \in \mathbb{Z}_{n^2}^*, \xi \in \mathbb{Z}_n, s_1 \in \mathbb{Z}_n, s_2 \in \mathbb{Z}_n, s_3 \in \mathbb{Z}_n^*, s_4 \in \mathbb{Z}_n^*)$.

Security Proof

Proposition 2. *The above protocol has perfect completeness, special soundness, and honest verifier zero knowledge and is hence a Sigma Protocol.*

Proof. Completeness follows trivially and is omitted due to lack of space.

Special Soundness. Given two accepting transcripts $(\alpha, \beta, \gamma, \xi, s_1, s_2, s_3, s_4)$ and $(\alpha, \beta, \gamma, \xi', s_1', s_2', s_3', s_4')$, we show that $r = \frac{s_1 - s_1'}{\xi - \xi'}, m = \frac{s_2 - s_2'}{\xi - \xi'}, r' = (s_3/s_3')^{\frac{1}{\xi - \xi'}}, r'' = (s_4/s_4')^{\frac{1}{\xi - \xi'}}$ must be valid given that two transcripts accept. The difference $\xi - \xi'$ has no inverse with negligible probability. To calculate $r' = (s_3/s_3')^{\frac{1}{\xi - \xi'}}, r'' = (s_4/s_4')^{\frac{1}{\xi - \xi'}}$, we use our knowledge of the message in ct_1 and ct_2, extracted from s_1 and s_2, and the homomorphic property of Paillier encryption to create $ct_1' = r'^n$ and $ct_2' = r''^n$. We can directly apply the technique from Damgård et al. [11] to extract r' and r'' from the elements s_3, s_3', s_4, s_4'.

Honest Verifier Zero Knowledge. Consider a transcript $(\alpha, \beta, \gamma, \xi, s_1, s_2, s_3, s_4)$. In the honest run, t_1, t_2 are random elements in $\mathbb{Z}_n$, t_3, t_4 in $\mathbb{Z}_n^*$ and ξ in $\mathbb{Z}_n$. To simulate, choose s_1, s_2 from $\mathbb{Z}_n$, s_3, s_4 from $\mathbb{Z}_n^*$ and ξ at random from $\mathbb{Z}_n$. Set $\alpha = c_1^{-\xi} g^{s_1} h^{s_2}$, $\beta = c_2^{-\xi}(1 + n)^{s_2} s_3^n$, $\gamma = c_3^{-\xi}(1 + n)^{s_1} s_4^n$, that is a perfect simulation. Moreover, the elements β, γ are uniformly random in the honest run, and the tuple $(\alpha, s_1, s_2, s_3, s_4)$ is uniquely determined by (ξ, β, γ). In the simulation, the elements s_1, s_2, s_3, s_4 are chosen uniformly at random and consequently β, γ are uniformly at random for fixed elements ξ, c, ct_1, ct_2. $\square$

4.2 Sigma Protocol for Correct Re-Encryption

We introduce the following Sigma Protocol for correct re-encryption. It is used to prove that given a pair of ciphertexts, the second is a re-encryption of the first.

Given $CT = (c, ct_1, ct_2), CT' = (c' = c * g^{r_0} \bmod kn + 1, ct_1' = ct_1 * r_1^n \bmod n^2, ct_2' = ct_2 * (1 + n)^{r_0} r_2^n \bmod n^2)$, we show that we know $(r_0 \in \mathbb{Z}_n, r_1 \in \mathbb{Z}_n^*, r_2 \in \mathbb{Z}_n^*)$:

(1) Let t_1 be a random element in $\mathbb{Z}_n$ and t_2, t_3 be random elements in $\mathbb{Z}_n^*$. The prover computes $\alpha = g^{t_1} \bmod kn + 1, \beta = t_2^n \bmod n^2, \gamma = (1 + n)^{t_1} t_3^n \bmod n^2$ and sends them to the verifier.
(2) The verifier sends a challenge ξ chosen at random in $\mathbb{Z}_n$.
(3) The prover computes $s_1 = t_1 + \xi r_0 \bmod n, s_2 = t_2 * r_1^\xi \bmod n, s_3 = t_3 * r_2^\xi \bmod n$, and sends these to the verifier.
(4) The verifier accepts if $\alpha(c'/c)^\xi = g^{s_1}, \beta(ct_1'/ct_1)^\xi = s_2^n, \gamma(ct_2'/ct_2)^\xi = (1 + n)^{s_1} s_3^n$.

The transcript (with the elements exchanged between the prover and the verifier) is $(\alpha \in \mathbb{G}_n, \beta \in \mathbb{Z}_{n^2}^*, \gamma \in \mathbb{Z}_{n^2}^*, \xi \in \mathbb{Z}_n, s_1 \in \mathbb{Z}_n, s_2 \in \mathbb{Z}_n, s_3 \in \mathbb{Z}_n^*)$.

Security Proof

Proposition 3. *The above protocol has perfect completeness, special soundness, and honest verifier zero knowledge and is hence a Sigma Protocol for correct re-encryption.*

Proof. Completeness follows trivially and is omitted due to lack of space.

Special Soundness. Given two accepting transcripts $(\alpha, \beta, \gamma, \xi, s_1, s_2, s_3)$ and $(\alpha, \beta, \gamma, \xi', s_1', s_2', s_3')$, we show that $r_0 = \frac{s_1 - s_1'}{\xi - \xi'}, r_1 = (s_2/s_2')^{\frac{1}{\xi - \xi'}}, r_2 = (s_3/s_3')^{\frac{1}{\xi - \xi'}}$ must be valid given that two transcripts accept. The difference $\xi - \xi'$ has no inverse with negligible probability. To calculate $r' = (s_3/s_3')^{\frac{1}{\xi - \xi'}}, r'' = (s_4/s_4')^{\frac{1}{\xi - \xi'}}$, we use our knowledge of the message in ct_1 and ct_2 extracted from s_1 and s_2, and the homomorphic property of Paillier encryption to create $c_2' = r'^n$ and $c_3' = r''^n$. We can directly apply the technique from Damgård et al. [11] to extract the randomenesses r', r'' from the elements s_3, s_3', s_4, s_4'.

Honest Verifier Zero Knowledge. In the honest run, t_1 is chosen at random from $\mathbb{Z}_n$, t_2, t_3 from $\mathbb{Z}_n^*$ and ξ from $\mathbb{Z}_n$. To simulate, we instead choose s_1, s_2, s_3, ξ at random and set $\alpha = g^{s_1}(c_1'/c_1)^{-\xi}, \beta = s_2^n(c_2'/c_2)^{-\xi}, \gamma = (1 + n)^{s_1} s_3^n (c_3'/c_3)^{-\xi}$. We get the same distribution in both cases. □

5   A New Efficient Verifiable Mix-Net

Verifiable mixing is an important building block for almost all verifiable voting systems. Given a vector of ciphertexts with known relationships to the voters, mixing allows this link to be broken without allowing ballot modification or substitution.

Wikström's general result [24] shows that verifiable mixing is possible for all cryptosystems on which a homomorphic map exists and an overwhelmingly complete Sigma Protocol is known for re-encryption. However, this generic construction gives an 8-round proof, while a more optimised instance is desirable for practicality. We can take advantage of special properties from our solution and derive a secure 4-round proof. We illustrate a verifiable ballot mixing process in Fig. 3 with three mixers.

Formally we operate two mixes, one on the public bulletin board and on the secret bulletin board. At each step, the election authorities check that the two versions of the Pedersen commitments e_j and c_j match. Our solution is similar to Demirel et al. [13], but is actually shown to be secure and far more computationally efficient. The green arrows represent verifiable mixers, the red arrows represent the equality of Pedersen commitments at each stage and the blue arrow represents verifiable decryption. We now present our more efficient mixers. While there are cru-

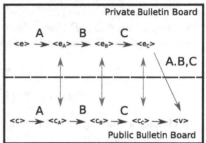

Fig. 3. Mixing with three authorities (Color figure online)

cial differences (for instance, the composite group order), our optimisations and accompanying proofs are similar to those for the optimised ElGamal version which is presented and proven by Terelius et al. [21]. We first detail the mix-net for the public board, see Algorithm 1, and then the mix-net for the private board, see Algorithm 2. We recall that π is permutation function induced by the permutation matrix M and ϕ is the re-encryption map defined in Subsect. 2.2. We use $\bar{1}$ to denote the all one vector.

We define $\mathcal{R}_{com}$ to be the relation consisting of pairs of tuples of the form commitment key CK, commitment $\mathbf{c}$, two distinct messages M, M' and two associated randomness vectors $\mathbf{r}$ and $\mathbf{r}'$ s.t. $\mathbf{c} = \Pi.\mathsf{Com}_{CK}(M, \mathbf{r}) = \Pi.\mathsf{Com}_{CK}(M', \mathbf{r}')$. We also define $\mathcal{R}_{\pi}$ to be the relation consisting of pairs of tuples of the form commitment key CK, commitment $\mathbf{c}$, message M and associated randomness vector $\mathbf{r}$ s.t. M is a permutation matrix and $\mathbf{r} = \Pi.\mathsf{Com}_{CK}(M, \mathbf{r})$. Let $\mathcal{R}_{\phi_{PK}}^{shuf}$ be the relation consisting of pairs of tuples of the form public key PK, two vectors of ciphertexts $\mathbf{CT} = (ct_1, \cdots, ct_n)$ and $\mathbf{CT}' = (ct'_1, \cdots, ct'_n)$ and a permutation π and randomness vector $\mathbf{r} = (r_1, \cdots, r_n)$ such that $ct'_i = \phi_{PK}(ct_{\pi(i)}, r_{\pi(i)})$ for all $i \in [1, N]$. Let $\mathcal{R}^{shuf}_{rerand_{CK}}$ to be the relation consisting of pairs of tuples of the form commit key CK, two commitment vectors $\mathbf{c} = (c_1, \cdots, c_n)$ and $\mathbf{c'} = (c'_1, \cdots, c'_n)$, a permutation π and randomness vector $\mathbf{r} = (r_1, \cdots, r_n)$ such that $c'_i = \Pi.\mathsf{ReRand}_{CK}(c_{\pi(i)}, r_{\pi(i)})$.

Algorithm 1. Proof of Shuffle on Public Board

Common Input: Commitment parameters $g, h, h_1, ..., h_N \in \mathbb{G}_n$, two Pedersen commitments $\mathbf{e} = (e_1, ..., e_N) \in \mathbb{G}_n^N$ and $\mathbf{e'} = (e'_1, ..., e'_N) \in \mathbb{G}_n^N$, and a permutation matrix commitment $\mathbf{c} = (c_1, ..., c_N)$.

Private Input : Permutation matrix $M = (m_{i,j}) \in \mathbb{Z}_n^{N \times N}$, randomness $\mathbf{r} = (r_1, ..., r_N) \in \mathbb{Z}_n^N$ s.t. $c_j = g^{r_j} \prod_{i=1}^N h_i^{m_{j,i}}$, and randomness $\mathbf{r'} = (r'_1, ..., r'_N) \in \mathbb{Z}_n^N$ s.t. $e'_i = e_{\pi(i)} g^{r'_{\pi(i)}}$ for $i, j \in [1, N]$.

1 $\mathcal{V}$ chooses $\mathbf{u} = (u_1, ..., u_N) \in \mathbb{Z}_n^N$ randomly and hands $\mathbf{u}$ to $\mathcal{P}$.

2 $\mathcal{P}$ defines $\mathbf{u'} = (u'_1, ..., u'_N) = M\mathbf{u}$ and then chooses $\hat{\mathbf{r}} = (\hat{r}_1, ..., \hat{r}_N), \hat{\mathbf{w}} = (\hat{w}_1, ..., \hat{w}_N), \mathbf{w'} = (w'_1, ..., w'_N) \in \mathbb{Z}_n^N$, and $w_1, w_2, w_3, w_4 \in \mathbb{Z}_n$. $\mathcal{P}$ then defines $\bar{r} = \langle \bar{1}, \mathbf{r} \rangle$, $\tilde{r} = \langle \mathbf{r}, \mathbf{u} \rangle$, $\hat{r} = \sum_{i=1}^N \hat{r}_i \prod_{j=i+1}^N u'_j$ and $r' = \langle \mathbf{r'}, \mathbf{u} \rangle$. $\mathcal{P}$ hands to $\mathcal{V}$, where we set $\hat{c}_0 = h$ and $i \in [1, N]$,

$$\hat{c}_i = g^{\hat{r}_i} \hat{c}_{i-1}^{u'_i} \quad t_1 = g^{w_1} \quad t_2 = g^{w_2} \quad t_3 = g^{w_3} \prod_{i=1}^N h_i^{w'_i}$$

$$t_4 = g^{-w_4} \prod_{i=1}^N (e'_i)^{w'_i} \quad \hat{t}_i = g^{\hat{w}_i} \hat{c}_{i-1}^{w'_i}$$

$\mathcal{V}$ chooses a challenge $\xi \in \mathbb{Z}_n$ at random and sends it to $\mathcal{P}$.

3 $\mathcal{P}$ then responds with:

$$s_1 = w_1 + \xi \cdot \bar{r} \quad s_2 = w_2 + \xi \cdot \hat{r} \quad s_3 = w_3 + \xi \cdot \tilde{r} \quad s_4 = w_4 + \xi \cdot r'$$
$$\hat{s}_i = \hat{w}_i + \xi \cdot \hat{r}_i \quad s'_i = w'_i + \xi \cdot u'_i$$

4 $\mathcal{V}$ accepts if and only if, for $i \in [1, N]$,

$$t_1 = (\prod_{i=1}^N c_i / \prod_{i=1}^N h_i)^{-\xi} g^{s_1} \quad t_2 = (\hat{c}_N / h^{\prod_{i=1}^N u_i})^{-\xi} g^{s_2}$$

$$t_3 = (\prod_{i=1}^N c_i^{u_i})^{-\xi} g^{s_3} \prod_{i=1}^N h_i^{s'_i}$$

$$t_4 = (\prod_{i=1}^N (e_i)^{u_i})^{-\xi} g^{s_4} \prod_{i=1}^N (e'_i)^{s'_i} \quad \hat{t}_i = \hat{c}_i^{-\xi} g^{\hat{s}_i} \hat{c}_{i-1}^{s'_i}$$

Algorithm 2. Proof of Shuffle on Private Board

Common Input: Commitment parameters $g, h, h_1, ..., h_N \in \mathbb{G}_n$, two ciphertexts $\mathbf{e} = (e_1, ..., e_N) \in \mathcal{C}_{PK}$ and $\mathbf{e}' = (e'_1, ..., e'_n) \in \mathcal{C}_{PK}$, and a permutation matrix commitment $\mathbf{c} = (c_1, ..., c_N)$.

Private Input : Permutation matrix $M = (m_{i,j}) \in \mathbb{Z}_n^{N \times N}$, randomness $\mathbf{r} = (r_1, ..., r_N) \in \mathbb{Z}_n^N$ s.t. $c_j = g^{r_j} \prod_{i=1}^N h_i^{m_{j,i}}$, and randomness $\mathbf{r}' = (r'_1, ..., r'_N) \in \mathcal{R}_{pk}$ s.t. $e'_i = \phi_{PK}(e_{\pi(i)}, r'_{\pi(i)})$, for $i, j \in [1, N]$.

1 $\mathcal{V}$ chooses $\mathbf{u} = (u_1, ..., u_N) \in \mathbb{Z}_n^N$ randomly and hands $\mathbf{u}$ to $\mathcal{P}$.

2 $\mathcal{P}$ defines $\mathbf{u}' = (u'_1, ..., u'_N) = M\mathbf{u}$ and then chooses $\hat{\mathbf{r}} = (\hat{r}_1, ..., \hat{r}_N), \hat{\mathbf{w}} = (\hat{w}_1, ..., \hat{w}_N), \mathbf{w}' = (w'_1, ..., w'_N) \in \mathbb{Z}_n^N$, and $w_1, w_2, w_3, \in \mathbb{Z}_n$ and $w_4 \in \mathcal{R}_{PK}$. $\mathcal{P}$ defines $\bar{r} = \langle \bar{1}, \mathbf{r} \rangle$, $\tilde{r} = \langle \mathbf{r}, \mathbf{u} \rangle$, $\hat{r} = \sum_{i=1}^N \hat{r}_i \prod_{j=i+1}^N u'_j$ and $r' = (\sum_{i=1}^N r'_{i,0} u_i, \prod_{i=1}^N r'^{u_i}_{i,1}, \prod_{i=1}^N r'^{u_i}_{i,2})$. $\mathcal{P}$ hands to $\mathcal{V}$, where we set $\hat{c}_0 = h$ and $i \in [1, N]$,

$$\hat{c}_i = g^{\hat{r}_i} \hat{c}_{i-1}^{u'_i} \qquad t_1 = g^{w_1} \qquad t_2 = g^{w_2} \qquad t_3 = g^{w_3} \prod_{i=1}^N h_i^{w'_i}$$

$$t_4 = \Sigma.\text{Enc}_{PK}(1, w_4) \prod_{i=1}^N e'^{w'_i}_i \qquad \hat{t}_i = g^{\hat{w}_i} \hat{c}_{i-1}^{w'_i}$$

3 $\mathcal{V}$ chooses a challenge $\xi \in \mathbb{Z}_n$ at random and sends it to $\mathcal{P}$.

4 $\mathcal{P}$ then responds with:

$$s_1 = w_1 + \xi \cdot \bar{r} \qquad s_2 = w_2 + \xi \cdot \hat{r} \qquad s_3 = w_3 + \xi \cdot \tilde{r} \qquad s_4 = w_4 - \xi \cdot r'$$

$$\hat{s}_i = \hat{w}_i + \xi \cdot \hat{r}_i \qquad s'_i = w'_i + \xi \cdot u'_i$$

5 $\mathcal{V}$ accepts if and only if, for $i \in [1, N]$,

$$t_1 = (\prod_{i=1}^N c_i / \prod_{i=1}^N h_i)^{-\xi} g^{s_1} \qquad t_2 = (\hat{c}_N / h^{\prod_{i=1}^N u_i})^{-\xi} g^{s_2}$$

$$t_3 = (\prod_{i=1}^N c_i^{u_i})^{-\xi} g^{s_3} \prod_{i=1}^N h_i^{s'_i}$$

$$t_4 = (\prod_{i=1}^N (e_i)^{u_i})^{-\xi} \Sigma.\text{Enc}_{PK}(1, s_4) \prod_{i=1}^N (e'_i)^{s'_i} \qquad \hat{t}_i = \hat{c}_i^{-\xi} g^{\hat{s}_i} \hat{c}_{i-1}^{s'_i}$$

Proposition 4. *Algorithm 1 is a perfectly complete, 4-round special soundness, and honest verifier zero knowledge of the relationship $\mathcal{R}_{com} \vee (\mathcal{R}_\pi \wedge \mathcal{R}_{rerand_{CK}}^{shuf})$.*

Proposition 5. *Algorithm 2 is a perfectly complete, 4-round special soundness, and honest verifier zero knowledge of the relationship $\mathcal{R}_{com} \vee (\mathcal{R}_\pi \wedge \mathcal{R}_{\phi PK}^{shuf})$.*

Proof. Due to space limitations we must omit both proofs but they will be present in the full version. Since it is infeasible under the discrete logarithm assumption to find z where $g^z = h$ or to find a pair satisfying $\mathcal{R}_{com}$, the proposition computationally implies a proof of knowledge of $\mathcal{R}_\pi \wedge \mathcal{R}_{\phi PK}^{shuf}$. $\square$

6 Comparison and Analysis of Efficiency

We study the efficiency of our solution and compare it with Cuvelier *et al.*'s results [9]. In order to accurately confront both schemes, we adopt the similar conventions to Cuvelier *et al.* The commitments used by PPATC scheme [9] require an elliptic curve with a type 3 pairing to function. Type 3 pairing is a pairing in which there exist no efficiently computable homomorphism between $\mathbb{G}_1$ and $\mathbb{G}_2$ and where the Decisional Diffie-Hellmen is hard in both groups. We assume an embedding degree of 16 such that elements of $\mathbb{G}_T$ are of size p^{16}. We, also, associate a unit cost to the multiplication of two 256 bit integers. While Cuvelier *et al.* supposed quadratic growth in the length of the operands, we assume $\mathcal{O}(n^{1.5})$, which better reflects that many BigInteger libraries support the optimised multiplication algorithms. We target a security level equivalent to 2048 bits RSA modulus N. We select $\mathbb{G}_1$ to be taken on $\mathbb{F}_p$ for a 256 bits long prime p and $\mathbb{G}_2$ to be taken on $\mathbb{F}_{p^3}$. The size of the target group is then 4096 bits, and for simplicity we take pairing to cost 10 times the effort of a multiplication in $\mathbb{G}_1$, this seems to hold for most real implementations.

We count the number of operations in Cuvelier *et al.*'s scheme and our solution. Tables 1 and 2 show these numbers for both encryption and opening verification. Let $Exp_{\mathbb{Z}_X^*}$ denote the number of exponentiations in $\mathbb{Z}_X^*$, and $Mult_{\mathbb{G}_Y}$ the number of multiplications in $\mathbb{G}_Y$. $Pairing$ is defined as the number of pairing operations.

Table 1. Total number of operations executed for encryption - Total cost is obtained according to the implementation setting.

Scheme	$Exp_{\mathbb{Z}_{kn+1}^*}$	$Exp_{\mathbb{Z}_{n^2}^*}$	$Mult_{\mathbb{G}_1}$	$Mult_{\mathbb{G}_2}$	Total cost
MN [17]	3.375	4	0	0	1024896 multiplications
PPATC [9]	0	0	9	4	114432 multiplications

Table 2. Total number of operations executed for opening verification - Total cost is obtained according to the implementation setting.

Scheme	$Exp_{\mathbb{Z}_{kn+1}^*}$	$Exp_{\mathbb{Z}_{n^2}^*}$	$Mult_{\mathbb{G}_1}$	$Mult_{\mathbb{G}_2}$	$Pairing$	Total cost
MN [17]	1.125	0	0	0	0	79488 multiplications
PPATC [9]	0	0	1	0	3	119040 multiplications

While PPATC remains faster for the encryption phase than MN scheme, the latter is 1.5 time faster for the verification phase than PPATC. In regards to mixing, which is of course a very substantial part of the verification cost, we have already shown how an optimised variant of Terelius and Wikström's approach [22] can be applied to MN cryptosystem.

Cuvelier *et al.* [9] suggested using Terelius and Wikström's approach as well. However, the efficiency of their general construction is poor compared to the optimised variants (especially when dealing with groups of composite order). The PPATC scheme of Cuvelier *et al.* is a highly elegant construction but contrary to expectations is not more efficient overall than our version of MN scheme [17]. Though, if the voting devices were unusually weak PPATC might still be preferred. In conclusion, while PPATC might still be preferred in some settings, in others where homomorphic properties are desired MN scheme with our optimised ZKPs are of comparable efficiency.

7   Conclusion

Ongoing privacy is fundamental for the proper functioning of elections but significant gaps remained. We fixed several of the outstanding issues. We showed that the modified Pedersen commitment is in fact secure and proved that the Sigma Protocols for correct encryption and correct re-encryption are safe to use. We also provided computational improvements to mixing and examined the feasibility of a secure deployment of our solution. In doing this, we help make everlasting privacy for homomorphic electronic voting a computationally feasible and rigorously secure reality. We show that this approach provides verification efficiency comparable to the most efficient non-homomorphic schemes.

References

1. Abe, M., Haralambiev, K., Ohkubo, M.: Group to group commitments do not shrink. In: Pointcheval, D., Johansson, T. (eds.) EUROCRYPT 2012. LNCS, vol. 7237, pp. 301–317. Springer, Heidelberg (2012). https://doi.org/10.1007/978-3-642-29011-4_19
2. Arapinis, M., Cortier, V., Kremer, S., Ryan, M.: Practical everlasting privacy. In: Basin, D., Mitchell, J.C. (eds.) POST 2013. LNCS, vol. 7796, pp. 21–40. Springer, Heidelberg (2013). https://doi.org/10.1007/978-3-642-36830-1_2
3. Bangerter, E., Camenisch, J., Krenn, S.: Efficiency limitations for Σ-protocols for group homomorphisms. In: Micciancio, D. (ed.) TCC 2010. LNCS, vol. 5978, pp. 553–571. Springer, Heidelberg (2010). https://doi.org/10.1007/978-3-642-11799-2_33
4. Bayer, S., Groth, J.: Efficient zero-knowledge argument for correctness of a shuffle. In: Pointcheval, D., Johansson, T. (eds.) EUROCRYPT 2012. LNCS, vol. 7237, pp. 263–280. Springer, Heidelberg (2012). https://doi.org/10.1007/978-3-642-29011-4_17

5. Buchmann, J., Demirel, D., van de Graaf, J.: Towards a publicly-verifiable mix-net providing everlasting privacy. In: Sadeghi, A.-R. (ed.) FC 2013. LNCS, vol. 7859, pp. 197–204. Springer, Heidelberg (2013). https://doi.org/10.1007/978-3-642-39884-1_16

6. Burmester, M.: A remark on the efficiency of identification schemes. In: Damgård, I.B. (ed.) EUROCRYPT 1990. LNCS, vol. 473, pp. 493–495. Springer, Heidelberg (1991). https://doi.org/10.1007/3-540-46877-3_47

7. Chaum, D.: Untraceable mail, return addresses and digital pseudonyms. Commun. ACM **24**(2), 84–88 (1981)

8. Cramer, R.: Modular design of secure yet practical cryptographic protocols. Ph.D. thesis, Aula der Universiteit (1996)

9. Cuvelier, É., Pereira, O., Peters, T.: Election verifiability or ballot privacy: do we need to choose? In: Crampton, J., Jajodia, S., Mayes, K. (eds.) ESORICS 2013. LNCS, vol. 8134, pp. 481–498. Springer, Heidelberg (2013). https://doi.org/10.1007/978-3-642-40203-6_27

10. Damgård, I.: On Σ-protocols (2010). http://www.daimi.au.dk/ivan/Sigma.pdf

11. Damgård, I., Jurik, M., Nielsen, J.B.: A generalization of paillier's public-key system with applications to electronic voting. Int. J. Inf. Sec. **9**(6), 371–385 (2010)

12. Demirel, D., Henning, M., van de Graaf, J., Ryan, P.Y.A., Buchmann, J.: Prêt à voter providing everlasting privacy. In: Heather, J., Schneider, S., Teague, V. (eds.) Vote-ID 2013. LNCS, vol. 7985, pp. 156–175. Springer, Heidelberg (2013). https://doi.org/10.1007/978-3-642-39185-9_10

13. Demirel, D., Van De Graaf, J., Araújo, R.: Improving helios with everlasting privacy towards the public. In: Electronic Voting Technology/Workshop on Trustworthy Elections, p. 8. USENIX Ass. (2012)

14. Goldwasser, S., Micali, S., Rackoff, C.: The knowledge complexity of interactive proof-systems. In: Theory of Computing, pp. 291–304. ACM (1985)

15. Groth, J.: A verifiable secret shuffe of homomorphic encryptions. In: Desmedt, Y.G. (ed.) PKC 2003. LNCS, vol. 2567, pp. 145–160. Springer, Heidelberg (2003). https://doi.org/10.1007/3-540-36288-6_11

16. Hazay, C., Mikkelsen, G.L., Rabin, T., Toft, T., Nicolosi, A.A.: Efficient RSA key generation and threshold paillier in the two-party setting. J. Cryptology **32**(2), 265–323 (2019)

17. Moran, T., Naor, M.: Split-ballot voting: everlasting privacy with distributed trust. ACM Trans. Inf. Syst. Secur. **13**(2), 16:1–16:43 (2010)

18. Paillier, P.: Public-key cryptosystems based on composite degree residuosity classes. In: Stern, J. (ed.) EUROCRYPT 1999. LNCS, vol. 1592, pp. 223–238. Springer, Heidelberg (1999). https://doi.org/10.1007/3-540-48910-X_16

19. Pedersen, T.P.: Non-interactive and information-theoretic secure verifiable secret sharing. In: Feigenbaum, J. (ed.) CRYPTO 1991. LNCS, vol. 576, pp. 129–140. Springer, Heidelberg (1992). https://doi.org/10.1007/3-540-46766-1_9

20. Shoup, V.: On the security of a practical identification scheme. J. Cryptology **12**(4), 247–260 (1999)

21. Terelius, B.: Some aspects of cryptographic protocols: with applications in electronic voting and digital watermarking. Ph.D. thesis, KTH Royal Institute of Technology (2015)

22. Terelius, B., Wikström, D.: Proofs of restricted shuffles. In: Bernstein, D.J., Lange, T. (eds.) AFRICACRYPT 2010. LNCS, vol. 6055, pp. 100–113. Springer, Heidelberg (2010). https://doi.org/10.1007/978-3-642-12678-9_7

23. Terelius, B., Wikström, D.: Efficiency limitations of Σ-protocols for group homomorphisms revisited. In: Visconti, I., De Prisco, R. (eds.) SCN 2012. LNCS, vol. 7485, pp. 461–476. Springer, Heidelberg (2012). https://doi.org/10.1007/978-3-642-32928-9_26

24. Wikström, D.: A commitment-consistent proof of a shuffle. In: Boyd, C., González Nieto, J. (eds.) ACISP 2009. LNCS, vol. 5594, pp. 407–421. Springer, Heidelberg (2009). https://doi.org/10.1007/978-3-642-02620-1_28

25. Yao, A.C.: Protocols for secure computations (extended abstract). In: FOCS, pp. 160–164. IEEE Computer Society (1982)

The Swiss Postal Voting Process and Its System and Security Analysis

Christian Killer$^{(\boxtimes)}$ and Burkhard Stiller

Communication Systems Group CSG, Department of Informatics IfI,
Universität Zürich UZH, Binzmühlestrasse 14, 8050 Zürich, Switzerland
{killer,stiller}@ifi.uzh.ch

Abstract. The Swiss postal voting system builds on trust in governmental authorities and external suppliers. The federal structure of Switzerland of cantons and municipalities leads to a distributed architecture. Detailed information on the current postal voting procedure are manifested as implicit knowledge within fragmented institutions and are not easily accessible. This work serves (*i*) as an overview of the Swiss remote postal voting system, (*ii*) a detailed insight into the process flow, and (*iii*) a respective risk assessment.

Keywords: Remote postal voting · Risk assessment

1 Introduction

Around the globe, government services are becoming increasingly digitized [1]. Naturally, these efforts include electoral processes. In Switzerland, the federal government defined strategies enabling digitization for public authorities and processes, including Electronic Voting (EV) [11,32]. Private companies collaborate with Swiss authorities to actively define standards across e-Government processes [35]. The Swiss EV typically refers to *Remote* EV (REV) carried out over the internet, which is also often referred to as Internet Voting (I-Voting) [19].

According to recent studies [32], 47% of Swiss citizens would be more likely to vote if EV were available, and almost 70% of Swiss citizens welcome an EV system [21]. Despite the positive sentiment surrounding EV, a current political position proposes a moratorium on EV in Switzerland [15]. According to their initiative [15], a REV system has to be "*at least as secure as the current remote postal voting (RPV) system*". Thus, the key question is: what exactly does such a minimal level of security involve? Which security metrics and mechanisms are mandatory? In the general public perception, EV often provokes a fear of change, presuming the current RPV system to be mostly analog and tamper-proof. However, it can be argued that the current Swiss RPV system is already partially EV, since many steps already involve distributed electronic systems. Thus, defining and comparing the security properties of a REV also requires an analysis of the current RPV system in Switzerland.

© Springer Nature Switzerland AG 2019
R. Krimmer et al. (Eds.): E-Vote-ID 2019, LNCS 11759, pp. 134–149, 2019.
https://doi.org/10.1007/978-3-030-30625-0_9

Reducing cost and increasing the voter turnout by providing a convenient way to vote are important considerations for Swiss authorities [20]. By 1994, all cantons accepted votes by postal mail. As of today, RPV is the dominant voting channel, used by approximately 90% of the voters in Switzerland [16]. Most eligible voters in Switzerland show trust in the authorities on the federal, cantonal, and municipal level to handle electoral processes and protect voter privacy [32]. The trust placed in authorities encompasses state-owned companies, which are important stakeholders in the current RPV system.

Due to the federal and decentralized structure of Switzerland, each canton and municipality autonomously manages their respective jurisdictional electoral procedures. Cantons and municipalities execute a degree of independence in decisions on how to handle certain parts of the voting process. Therefore, the current RPV system in Switzerland is neither universally documented or specified, nor homogeneous across entities.

This paper, therefore, summarizes major related work and terminology to formalize the Postal Voting Process Flow (PVPF) in Switzerland. The approach taken formalizes the PVPF in a step-based model, for which major assumptions made, such as trust, people involved, and technology applied, are made explicit, if known. The dedicated interpretation of social trust assumptions is discussed within Sect. 3, along with the risk analysis, weaknesses and strengths of a person-based RPV approach. Finally, the paper performs an overall risk assessment in Sect. 4, providing the basis for discussions of security-relevant comparisons to REV or I-Voting, while Sect. 5 draws main conclusions.

2 Legal Background and Related Work

Switzerland is organized as a decentralized system of municipal and cantonal entities, working together under the umbrella of the Federal Government. The federal structure is also mirrored in the legal framework (cf. Fig. 1). At the root rests the Federal Constitution of the Swiss Confederation, wherein Art. 39 [6] forms the basis for the Federal Act on Political Rights (BPR) [8]. In turn, Art. 91 BPR [8] is the foundation for the Federal Decree for Political Rights (VPR) [9]. On a cantonal level, the VPR builds the foundation for the Cantonal Decrees (e.g., for the canton of Aargau [7]). Every canton is an independent legal entity and defines its own constitution on the basis of the Federal Constitution.

The political system is under the authority of the cantons, i.e., cantonal laws and ordinances regarding political rights define elements for these processes. Various aspects of those elements are relevant for the RPV system in Switzerland, and each canton has its own decrees regarding political rights. The federal structure is mirrored down to the municipal level: each municipality decides on certain processes, again, aligned to cantonal laws and decrees. For instance, keeping record of the electoral register is under the authority of municipalities, leading to different approaches.

A direct comparison of the Swiss RPV system to REV was performed in [29]. Other countries discuss the usage of RPV critically because the secrecy of the

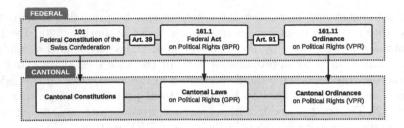

Fig. 1. Swiss legal framework

ballot cannot be fully ensured [29]. From a practical standpoint, thorough documentation is the easiest way to achieve verifiability for RPV. Supervisory bodies and authorities should check the documentation and verify it [29]. Also, trust is crucial for all voting methods. And the relationship between verifiability and trust is neither linear nor one-dimensional. Technical measures are not sufficient to create trust, sociopsychological aspects also have to be considered carefully. An extended literature review is provided in [18] with a focus on Switzerland, but also outlining the work done in Canada [22], Estonia [19], and Australia [30].

In order to analyze the RPV system with a focus on security aspects, the US National Institute for Standards Technology (NIST) serves as reference, outlining and standardizing terminology on the "Effort, Detection and Impact levels of Threat Events" [26,33,34]. Past work applied such principles to a RPV system used in the United States [25]. To consistently apply terminology, Table 1 defines the corresponding terminology used in Swiss legislation and their English translations.

Table 1. Official German terminology with corresponding English translations

German	English
Zwei-Weg Abstimmungskuvert	Two-Way Voting Envelope (VE)
Abstimmungsresultat	Voting Result (VR)
Erwahrung des Abstimmungsresultates	Legally valid determination of VR
Die Schweizerische Post	The Swiss Post (SP)
Stimmkuverts	Paper Ballot Envelope
Stimmrechtsausweis	Voting Signature Card (VSC)
Stimmregister	Electoral Register (ER)
Stimmzettel	Paper Ballot (PB)
Vertrauenswürdiger Dritter	Trusted Third Party (TTP)

3   Postal Voting Process Flow (PVPF) in Switzerland

This section details the illustrated Postal Voting Process Flow (PVPF) in-depth (*cf.* Fig. 3), containing an end-to-end process as it is currently implemented in Switzerland. The detailed sub-steps are formalized and vary between cantons and municipalities. However, the general process adheres to the federal laws and ordinances. The PVPF is divided into six main phases from A to F, each phase containing one or multiple sub-stages from 1 to N (*cf.* Fig. 2). The ensuing subsections are structured according to the PVPF within Fig. 3 and describe all the different steps in detail.

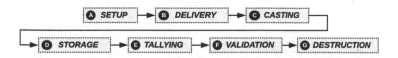

Fig. 2. Paper Voting Process Phases

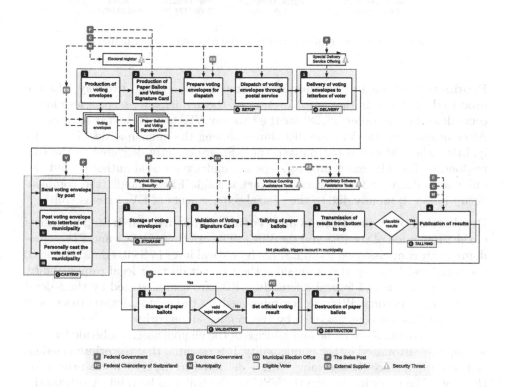

Fig. 3. Paper Voting Process Flow (PVPF)

3.1   Setup Phase

The Setup phase A contains four sub-stages 1–4 describing the production and assembly for dispatch of all necessary ballots and envelopes(*cf.* Fig. 4). The two-way Voting Envelopes (VE), the Voting Signature Cards (VSC), the Paper Ballot Envelopes (PBE), and the Paper Ballots (PB) are the physical artifacts produced in the Setup phase. The secure execution of the Setup phase is crucial, since all following phases rely on the sound production and assembly of those artifacts. The main stakeholders of this phase are the municipal and cantonal authorities supervising the process. Due to cost, time, and capability constraints, Trusted Third Parties (TTP) support the authorities during the Setup phase as External Suppliers (ES).

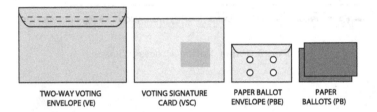

TWO-WAY VOTING   VOTING SIGNATURE   PAPER BALLOT   PAPER
ENVELOPE (VE)   CARD (VSC)   ENVELOPE (PBE)   BALLOTS (PB)

Fig. 4. Abstract representation of the necessary paper artifacts

Production of voting envelopes: In Step 1, the certified two-way VEs are produced by an ES. In the canton of Aargau, the municipality secretaries place a centralized buying order [17,28] for the two-way VEs at least a year in advance. After production, the VEs are distributed among the municipalities. In municipalities where Step 3 is outsourced, the VEs are directly delivered to the corresponding ES. The exact process steps are under municipal authority and can differ accordingly. Some cantons contract a single ES to handle the complete Setup phase A, mainly due to the special requirements of EV systems [10].

Production of Paper Ballots and Voting Signature Card: Step 2 consists of the production of the PBs and the VSCs. The printing of VSCs and PBs is predominantly commissioned to an ES. Each political layer in Switzerland (Federal, Cantonal and Municipal) commissions the PBs within their legal responsibility, *i.e.*, the production of federal referendum PBs are commissioned by the federal government, cantonal PBs are commissioned by the cantonal authorities, and municipal PBs are commissioned by the municipal authorities.

A VSC contains the name and address of the eligible voter, embedded within a template customized by the municipality. It is essential that the printed credentials are valid, since the assembled VE is delivered to the credentials printed on the VSC. The voter has to sign the VSC for the ballot to be valid. A substantial amount of ballots are not counted because many VSCs remain unsigned.

The individual VSCs are printed according to an electoral register (ER). The ER is a centralized register containing all eligible voters. The ER is under the authority of each municipality. Neither the cantonal, nor the federal authorities have copies of the ER [28].

Since most municipalities contract an ES for the printing of the VSCs, a dataset containing the eligible voters needs to be transferred to the corresponding ES. Most municipalities export a file from the ER (*e.g.*, XLS, CSV) and send the snapshot to the ES directly via email [27, 31]. The transmission of an unencrypted, unsigned dataset via standard email is critical, since the dataset could be tampered with (*e.g.*, the creation of fake identities, entries being removed), either after the export, during transmission, or when the export file reached the ES. Most ERs are administered by proprietary software systems provided by companies targeting Swiss public administrations. Some cantons also provide process checklists to municipalities. For instance, the election office (EO) of the Canton of Aargau provides such checklists [17]. These checklists state that the number of VSCs should be identical to the number of eligible voters present in the ER. If issues arise, an *in-depth* manual control should take place. Whether or not to adhere to these checklists is under the authority of the municipality. Also, since printing and assembly of the VE is mostly done by ESs, the ES should verify the integrity of the printed artifacts (*e.g.*, content and amount).

Prepare voting envelope for dispatch: Step 3 concerns the final assembly of the VEs. For each eligible voter (*i.e.*, each VSC), a VE containing the VSC, PBs, and the PBE is assembled (*cf.* Fig. 4). The assembly is a monotonous task, often outsourced to ESs or social institutions and foundations [18]. Receiving an incomplete VE increases the possibility of the voter's abstention. According to cantonal checklists [17], handing out new PBs is only allowed if the voter can *make the loss credible*. Then, the voter's credentials should be recorded to check for attempted dual voting in the Tallying phase E [17].

Dispatch of voting envelopes through postal service: The final step involves the dispatch of the assembled VEs. In some municipalities, the VEs are directly dispatched by the ES commissioned with the assembly of the VEs. The Swiss Post (SP) offers a special service [14] for the dispatch and delivery of VEs.

3.2 Delivery

In Switzerland, the postal market was partially deregulated in 2009 [13]. Still, the SP maintains a monopoly on postal letters below 50 gr. Therefore, the SP is a crucial TTP, since the secure delivery to the municipality falls under the responsibility of the SP. When using the special service provided by the SP, VEs can be dispatched on a work day in the week prior to the specified delivery week [14]. Then, the SP guarantees the delivery of the VEs will take place during the specified delivery week [14].

3.3 Casting

Phase C outlines the three different options to cast a vote. The vast majority of ballots are not cast at the urn [16]. Statistics do not indicate whether VEs arrive through postal services (I) or were delivered to the letterbox by the voter (II).

I: The most popular way to cast the vote is to *send the VE by postal mail*. Some cantons pre-stamp the VSCs, which can then be used to return VEs free of charge [3]. For the voter, it is impossible to verify whether the ballot was successfully delivered to the municipal office. The SP offers the ability to track deliveries for an additional cost.

II: Thus, a favoured alternative is to *deliver the VE into the letterbox of the municipality*, which is then emptied by municipal officials and safely stored. According to [12], this option is still a favoured option by many voters.

III: The third option is to *personally cast the ballot at the urn*, which guarantees ballot secrecy. Casting ballots at the urn remains the most secure option to cast a vote, since the PBE (containing the ballot) is directly cast into the urn and separated from the VSC (containing the voter's credentials and signature).

3.4   Storage

Phase D deals with the storage of VEs that were delivered via postal service (I), or directly cast to the municipal letterbox (II). Often, an employee is tasked to fetch the postal mail addressed to the municipal office. During votes, the VEs are collected from the SP and municipal letterbox, and then carried to the safe storage location. Past incidents describe where municipal employees misused that trust [4]. The storage safety varies heavily, depending on the municipality. The Federal Act for Political Rights (BPR) [8] does not specify any security requirements. Additional considerations include the exact definition of an access control for the VE storage, (*e.g.*, Who should have physical access to the VEs?). Also, the definition of a process for incoming VEs can increase process security (*e.g.*, How many ballots arrived at which date and time? Who got the ballots from the letterbox or postal office and transported them where?).

Thus, stricter access control and a secured ballot arrival process can maximize the physical storage security. In practice, physical storage security is not prioritized, since the municipal infrastructure is often not sufficiently equipped [27,31].

3.5   Tallying

Phase E specifies the process of tallying. The main stakeholders of phase E are the municipality and the local EO. The tallying is not regulated on a federal level and is heterogeneous among cantons and municipalities [29].

Art. 14 No. 1 BPR [8] states that every polling station should create a report containing the total number of eligible voters, the total eligible voters living abroad, the total of blank, invalid, and valid ballot papers, and the number of votes in favour and against the proposal [8]. Thus, the BPR serves as a federal guideline, without specific requirements regarding the tallying process.

Approximately 10% [23] of the ballots cast are counted with the help of Electronic Counting (e-Counting) tools, provided by ESs. The parliamentary control of the administration investigated e-Counting and concluded that the federal requirements are neither functional, nor practical, and the control mechanisms of the federal government are not sufficient [23].

Tallying of all ballots: The local EO usually hires paid and elected helpers to assist with the manual counting. In large cities, thousands of helpers are engaged to count the paper ballots [24]. The EO defines the details of the tallying process. Some municipalities use e-Counting solutions or deploy high-precision scales to weigh PBs and derive the tally from averaging the weight of (sometimes precounted) batches.

Transmission of results from bottom to top: According to Art. 14 No. 2 BPR [8], the cantonal government is responsible for compiling provisional results from the entire canton and notifying the Federal Chancellery (FC) of the results, and publishing the same result in the Cantonal Gazette (or a special issue thereof) within 13 days of the polling day. As soon as the EO concludes tallying, the result is transmitted from the municipal EO to the cantonal EO, and from there to the FC. Some cantonal EOs deploy dedicated software systems to verify results using statistical methods. Also, most cantons make use of software provided by ESs to transmit the results. Thus, this phase also includes the use of web-based assistance tools [18].

Publication of results: The tallying phase is finalized with the publication of all results on the municipal, cantonal, and federal level. Generally, the FC publishes the collected results from the Cantonal Chancelleries in the Federal Gazette. Cantons publish the results and protocols in their Cantonal Gazettes. Each municipality publishes a final tally and tallying protocol with respect to the cantonal law. Mostly, the publishing process is performed by uploading documents to a public web-server and displaying print-outs outside the municipal offices.

Validation: Art. 15 BPR [8] defines the validation and publication of the results. The official results can only be declared when no valid appeals are in process at the Swiss Federal Court. After that, the official result is published by the FC in the Federal Gazette and can not be appealed anymore.

Storage of paper ballots: Before the results are ascertained, the counted PBs and VSCs have to be safely stored in the municipalities. It is important that the ballots remain unaltered because a recount could be triggered before the official result is determined. Past cases have shown that premature destruction of the PBs and VSCs made a full re-count impossible [2].

Set official voting result: As soon as no more valid appeals are with the Federal Supreme Court, or as soon as a decision has been made on such an appeal, the legally valid voting result can be determined. According to Art. 15 No. 2 of the BPR [8], the validation decree shall be published in the Federal Gazette. The officiation by the Swiss Federal chancellery finalizes the Validation phase. Since a recount is no longer possible and the result is *untouchable*, the final phase can be started.

3.6   Destruction

The final phase, G, involves the destruction of the stored VSCs and PBs. According to Art. 14 No. 3 BPR [8], "*following validation of the result of the vote, the ballot papers shall be destroyed*". In practise, the destruction is usually done by physically shredding all PBs and VSCs [27].

4   PVPF Risk Assessment

A risk signifies the level of impact on the operation of an information system's task, given the potential impact of a threat and the likelihood of that threat occurring [5,34]. Therefore, a risk assessment (RA) serves as the identification and determination of the impact of vulnerabilities that an adversary can exploit. A threat covers any event with a potentially adverse impact on the assessed process [26]. With respect to the RPV in Switzerland, threat sources are groups or individuals who could feasibly attack the RPV system. Threat sources can stem from insiders or external adversaries. All Threat Events (TE) in the following RA are general in nature and require multiple co-conspiring hostile individuals or groups to achieve a large-scale effect. The effort for each threat defines the relative level of difficulty of performing a successful attack based on a threat [25]. Three relative levels of effort are defined:

- **Low** (−): An attack requires little/no resources or detailed knowledge of the system.
- **Moderate** (◦): An attack requires significant resources (or the ability to obtain these resources) or knowledge of the system. Inside attacks involving a small number of co-conspirators fall into this category.
- **High** (+): An attack requires excessive resources, in-depth knowledge of the system, or even access to the systems. It also requires specific tactics, techniques, and procedures [26]. Insider attacks involving a large number of co-conspirators fall into this category [25].

Detection describes the relative level of difficulty to notice whether a particular threat has been executed in an attack [25]. Thus, attacks are more severe when they remain undetected. Three estimated levels of likelihood of detection exist [25]:

- **Low** (−): An attack is unlikely to be detected without extraordinary resources.
- **Moderate** (◦): An attack may be detectable, but could require a large amount of resources and time. Such attacks are unlikely to be detected during the election.
- **High** (+): An attack would most likely be detected, given proper monitoring.

The impact on PVPF was analyzed according to [26] with the focus on confidentiality (C), integrity (I), and availability (A) as defined in [33]. Some TEs - all are shown in Table 2 - are interdependent or can be combined as depicted in Fig. 5. The following RA serves as a major discussion of potential TEs that can lead to a loss of voter confidence. The mitigation of identified TEs concerns the actions of establishing trust and confidence in a system.

Table 2. Threat events on the Swiss Postal Voting Process Flow (PVPF)

Phase	TE	Description	Effort	Detection	Impact
A	**TE1**	Delay production of physical artifacts	−	∘	$A+$
A	**TE2**	ER master records	+	∘	$I+$
A	**TE3**	ER data snapshot	∘	∘	$I+$
A	**TE4**	Forge physical artifacts	+	∘	$I\circ$
A	**TE5**	Steal assembled VEs before dispatch	∘	+	$I+$
B	**TE6**	Re-route VEs	*unknown*	*unknown*	$A+$
B	**TE7**	Steal VEs from voter letterboxes	∘	+	$A\circ$
C	**TE8**	Steal VEs from municipal letterbox	∘	∘	$I\circ$
C	**TE9**	Re-route VEs	+	∘	$C+$
C	**TE10**	Cast stolen or forged VEs	∘	∘	$I\circ$
D	**TE11**	Access stored VEs	−	−	$I+$
E	**TE12**	Manipulate tallying	+	∘	$I+$
E	**TE13**	Manipulate final tally	+	∘	$I+$
F	**TE14**	Initiate premature destruction	−	+	$I+$
G		*no major threat events identified*			

4.1 Risk Assessment Phase A

The Setup Phase A produces all the necessary artifacts for the secure execution of the whole PVPF.

TE1 describes the *malicious delay* of $A1$ and $A2$ in the PVPF. For instance, delaying the production can be achieved by targeting contracted ESs or directly attacking the municipal information systems.

TE2 describes the *tampering of the ER master records*. Often, the ER is provided and deployed by an ES. A targeted attack of an ES provider or municipal information systems with access to the ERs creates the ability to tamper with ER master records. The modification of master records can damage the integrity of ER data and the exported subset of eligible voters.

TE3 describes the *tampering of ER snapshot data*. Instead of modifying the ER master records, the snapshot used to print the VSCs can be modified. When the snapshot is neither digitally signed nor encrypted, an adversary could modify the data before, during, or after transmission to the ES.

TE4 describes the *forgery of physical artifacts* with (stolen) digital templates. If an adversary gains access to digital templates used to produce the physical artifacts, the adversary can forge VSCs and PBs. Additional information may be necessary to obtain (*e.g.*, weight and type of paper used). PBEs and VEs may also be forged, stolen, or even ordered from an ES. Since most municipalities do not perform a validation of incoming VSCs (by comparing the list of eligible voters with incoming VSCs), the attack can remain undetected. Practically executing TE4 requires a high effort and specific knowledge of the PVPF down to a municipal level.

TE5 describes the *physical theft of the assembled VEs*. By stealing assembled VEs, the adversary can either destroy or cast ballots. The detection of this threat event relies on individual voters noticing that they did not receive their VEs, *i.e.*, the detection probability increases with every voter notifying municipal authorities.

The integrity and availability of ER is crucial for the Swiss RPV. By targeting ERs, substantial damage can be inflicted on data integrity, but also on trust in local authorities and can undermine voters' confidence. Requirements for EV systems can serve as a reference for process improvements [10].

4.2   Risk Assessment Phase B

The Delivery phase *B* is a black-box. The internal processes of the Swiss Post (SP) are not publicly available. When using the dedicated SP service to dispatch and deliver VEs, the VSC design must adhere to special layout rules to facilitate automatic batch processing [14]. The special layout of VEs could simplify identification of VEs, but requires an adversary to achieve partial control of the SP routing system. To achieve such control, a hostile individual or group can create an Advanced Persistent Threat (APT) within the SP and from there, *e.g.*, identify VEs according to specific attributes and re-route identified VEs, or attempt to delay the delivery deliberately.

TE6 describes the *re-routing of VEs*. This TE requires adversarial access to internal SP systems and the capability to covertly manipulate the postal routing. A re-routing may require a co-conspiring postal employee because re-routing a large number of VEs could raise suspicion. Assuming a successful re-routing of VEs, the adversary is offered multiple options: Either to destroy the VEs, or open, modify, and re-cast them (*cf.* Fig. 5).

TE7 describes the *theft of VEs from voter letterboxes* before successful retrieval by the recipient voter. In contrast to TE5, TE7 requires the adversary to steal from individual letterboxes, not only at a single location. Similar to TE5, detection increases with every voter noticing the absence of VEs.

Phase *B* is characterized by the trust placed in one large entity, the SP. Thus, the effort and detection probability of TE6 can only be analyzed with additional information or access to internal SP systems, operations, and processes. Generally, however, an insider can achieve a low detection with moderate effort.

4.3   Risk Assessment Casting Phase C

TE8 describes the *theft of VEs from the municipal letterbox*. As shown in Fig. 5, stolen VEs can either be destroyed or opened and modified.

TE9 describes the *re-routing of VEs (before delivery to the municipality)*. Similar to TE8, re-routing offers two different options: either the adversary can decide to destroy the VEs, or open, modify, and re-cast. Similar to TE6, a co-conspiring postal employee is crucial, since delivering a large amount of VEs to a different location than the authorities may alarm an honest employee.

TE10 describes the *casting of stolen or forged VEs*. An adversary can attempt to cast stolen and modified or forged artifacts to influence the voting result. The interdependence among TEs is visualized in Fig. 5.

In official logs provided by the municipalities, there is no differentiation between channels *I* and *II*, both count as delivered by the SP. Even though 90% of votes are cast through *I* and *II*, keeping *III* remains crucial: Multiple channels strengthen confidence in results because it enables cross-channel comparison with statistical methods.

4.4   Risk Assessment Storage Phase D

TE11 describes TEs originating from *physical storage security*. Depending on the municipality, one or *N* employees have access to the cast VEs. The access to VEs offers similar options as presented in Fig. 5. Since most municipalities do not log the amount of incoming VEs, the destruction of VEs can remain undetected.

The physical access to the ballots stored allows an adversary to either destroy VEs, modify them, or open VEs and break ballot secrecy. As past incidents show [4], access control to the stored VEs is a again a question of trust.

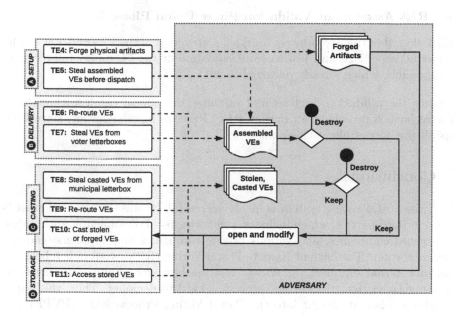

Fig. 5. Threat event interdependencies

4.5   Risk Assessment Tallying Phase E

TE12 describes the *risk of manipulation during tallying.* According to [23], over 10% of ballots cast in Switzerland are electronically counted. In 2014, sample checks identified errors in these counting mechanisms and concluded that e-Counting is neither more exact nor more secure than manual counting [23]. The manipulation of e-Counting requires an adversary to write targeted malware to influence the counting mechanism in his favor.

TE13 describes the possible *manipulation of the final tally.* Some cantons use proprietary software to handle vote transmission from municipalities to the cantonal EO [18]. An adversary with access to these tools can tamper with the final tally. Since the manual tallying process produces logs published on a municipal level, large discrepancies can be detected by attentive observers. However, a sophisticated adversary can anticipate that and tamper with all digital traces to further obfuscate detection. Hence, the risk increases when PBs were exclusively counted electronically, without any redundancy from manual counting.

The tallying phase E builds on the integrity of each and every individual member of the municipal Election Offices (EO). The distribution of trust builds the cornerstone of the Swiss RPV system.

4.6   Risk Assessment Validation Phase F and Phase G

TE14 describes the *prematurely initiated destruction* of the PBs and VSCs. The destruction of PBs and VSCs before validation by the FC makes full recounts impossible, which already occurred in 2011 [2].

Since the validation finalizes and validates the official result within Phase G, a recount is no longer an option. Also, PBs are now irrelevant, since legal appeals are impossible at this point.

5   Conclusions

The Swiss postal voting system is highly successful, because substantial trust is placed in third parties, which includes a wide range of governmental authorities, state-owned companies, and various private companies and suppliers, and the individual voter. The current Remote Postal Voting (RPV) system is inherently built on external suppliers and trusted relationships among all parties involved. For a regular citizen, the current process is hard to decipher. Thus, this paper provides a coherent insight into the Postal Voting Process Flow (PVPF) and identifies its weaknesses as well as strengths with practical examples.

The main advantage of the current RPV system is its physical decentralization, which is undercut by using centralized information systems to administer or transfer crucial data (*e.g.*, Electoral Registers (ER) or Web-based assistance tools to transmit votes). Many aspects regarding the ER, assistance tools, the

Voter Signature Card (VSC), or the physical storage of voting envelopes offer room for improvements from a security perspective.

The deployment of a Remote Electronic Voting (REV) system potentially decreases the necessary amount of trust placed in institutions and people, shifting trust to verifiable processes instead [29]. As this work showed, assessing the risks of the Swiss RPV system is reliant on the specific process across governmental entities. This work identified crucial Threat Events (TE) and showed that the system cannot serve as a suitable reference for electoral processes [15].

Furthermore, the Swiss federal structure leads to fragmented processes across jurisdictional barriers, from federal to cantonal, down to municipal authorities. The real-world deployment of the threat events identified requires a group of hostile individuals with specific knowledge. In small municipalities, authorities and citizens are intertwined and manipulations would either be not widely effective or detected rather swiftly. In large municipalities or large cities, processes are secured. Releasing an attack would require substantial effort from an attacker. Hence, an attack on the RPV is most likely to be successful in medium-sized municipalities, e.g., where processes have not yet adapted to the larger size of the formerly smaller municipality.

Apparently, federal laws are not complete yet in guiding the deployment of secure e-Counting tools [23]. Thus, the compilation of an open and transparent list of all the electronic tools in use in the current PV flow can help to identify further threat events and enable the design of mitigation measures to handle risks better. Further, the Risk Assessment (RA) needs to be extended and ultimately applied to full real-world processes of cantons. In turn, TEs identified can be assessed in more detail and improvements can be provided to act as a comparison to EV systems.

Acknowledgements. The authors would like to thank Anina Sax, Annina Zimmerli, Dr. Christian Folini, Marco Sandmeier, and Dr. Benedikt van Spyk for their valuable input. This paper was supported partially by (a) the University of Zurich UZH, Switzerland and (b) the European Union's Horizon 2020 Research and Innovation Program under Grant Agreement No. 830927, the Concordia project.

References

1. Andersen, K., Medaglia, R., Vatrapu, R., Zinner Henriksen, H., Gauld, R.: The forgotten promise of e-government maturity: assessing responsiveness in the digital public sector. Gov. Inf. Q. **28**(4), 439–445 (2011)
2. Berner Zeitung: Stimmzettel fehlen, Nachzählung über Motorfahrzeugsteuern ist gefährdet, August 2011. http://pvpf.ch/bz-pb. Accessed 9 July 2019
3. Bühlmann, M.: Schweiz am Sonntag, Aargauer Zeitung: Das Stimmcouvert per Post verschicken - ein Gratisangebot, das viele Aargauer ausschlagen, February 2016. http://pvpf.ch/az-ve. Accessed 9 July 2019
4. Bumbacher, B.: Neue Zürcher Zeitung: Hauswart fälscht aus Frust Stimmzettel bei Gemeindewahl, October 2005. http://pvpf.ch/nzzfraud. Accessed 9 July 2019

5. Computer Security Division, Information Technology Laboratory: Minimum Security Requirements for Federal Information and Information Systems. (FIPS PUB 200), US Department of Commerce, NIST, March 2006
6. Der Regierungsrat des Kantons Aargau: 101 -Bundesverfassung der Schweizerischen Eidgenossenschaft vom 18. April 1999 (Stand am 23. September 2018). http://pvpf.ch/bv. Accessed 9 July 2019
7. Der Regierungsrat des Kantons Aargau: 131.111 - Verordnung zum Gesetz über die politischen Rechte (VGPR) in Kraft seit 01.01.2013, Beschlussdatum: 30.05.2012). http://pvpf.ch/vgpr. Accessed 9 July 2019
8. Der Schweizerische Bundesrat: 161.1 Bundesgesetz über die politischen Rechte (BPR) (Stand am 1. November 2015). http://pvpf.ch/bpr. Accessed 9 July 2019
9. Der Schweizerische Bundesrat: 161.11 Verordnung über die politischen Rechte (VPR) (Stand am 15. Januar 2014). http://pvpf.ch/vpr. Accessed 9 July 2019
10. Die Schweizerische Bundeskanzlei: Anforderungskatalog Druckereien fur Vote électronique. http://pvpf.ch/bkreq. Accessed 9 July 2019
11. Die Schweizerische Bundeskanzlei: Vote électronique. http://pvpf.ch/ve. Accessed 9 July 2019
12. Die Schweizerische Bundeskanzlei: Änderung des Bundesgesetzes über die politischen Recht). Erläuternder Bericht zur Vernehmlassung, December 2018
13. Die Schweizerische Post AG: Das Briefrestmonopol - Finanzierungspfeiler für die Grundversorgung. http://pvpf.ch/spmon. Accessed 9 July 2019
14. Die Schweizerische Post AG: Factsheet, Briefe Wahl- und Abstimmungssendung. http://pvpf.ch/spfs. Accessed 9 July 2019
15. E-Voting-Moratorium: Initiativtext. http://pvpf.ch/evmor. Accessed 9 July 2019
16. Grühnenfelder, P.: Neue Zürcher Zeitung: Digitale Demokratie verlangt Pioniergeist, September 2015. http://pvpf.ch/nzzpio. Accessed 9 July 2019
17. Kantonales Wahlbüro Aargau: Wahlen und Abstimmungen, Checkliste Allgemeine Arbeiten (Rahmenorganisation), November 2017
18. Killer, C., Stiller, B.: A flow analysis of today's Swiss postal voting process and a respective security scrutiny. IfI Technical report No. 2019-02, Department of Informatics IfI, University of Zurich, April 2019
19. Krimmer, R., Triessnig, S., Volkamer, M.: The development of remote e-voting around the world: a review of roads and directions. In: First International Joint Conference on Electronic Voting and Identity (E-VOTE ID 2007), Bochum, Germany, October 2008, pp. 1–15 (2008)
20. Luechinger, S., Rosinger, M., Stutzer, A.: The impact of postal voting on participation: evidence for Switzerland. Swiss Polit. Sci. Rev. **13**, 167–202 (2007)
21. Milic, T., McArdle, M., Serdült, U.: Haltungen und Bedürfnisse der Schweizer Bevölkerung zu E-Voting = Attitudes of Swiss Citizens Towards the Generalisation of E-Voting. Studienbericht, Aarau, September 2016
22. Pammet, H.J., Goodman, N.: Consultation and evaluation practices in the implementation in the implementation of Internet Voting in Canada and Europe. Research Study, November 2013
23. Parlamentarische Verwaltungskontrolle (PVK): Elektronische Auszählung von Stimmen (E-Counting) Bericht der PVK zuhanden der Geschäftsprüfungskommission des Nationalrates, Februar 2017
24. Pauchard O., Swissinfo: Tausende beim Zählen der Wahlzettel, October 2003. http://pvpf.ch/swi. Accessed 9 July 2019
25. Regenscheid, A., Hastings, N.: A Threat Analysis on VOCAVA Voting Systems. Threat Analysis, US Department of Commerce, NIST, December 2008

26. Regenscheid, A., Hastings, N.: Guide for conducting risk assessments. NIST Special Publication 800-30, US Department of Commerce, NIST, September 2012
27. Sandmeier, M.: Stadtschreiber und Leiter Stadtkanzlei Baden, 22 February 2019. Personal Conversation, Stadtkanzlei, Baden (2019)
28. Sax, A.: Leiterin Wahlen und Abstimmungen, 20 February 2019. Personal Conversation. Staatskanzlei, Generalsekretariat, Kanton Aargau, Regierungsgebäude, Aarau
29. Serdült, U., Dubuis, E., Glaser, A.: Elektronischer versus brieflicher Stimmkanal im Vergleich. Überprüfbarkeit, Sicherheit und Qualität der Stimmabgabe. Jusletter IT, September 2017
30. Smith, R.: Implications of changes to voting channels in Australia. Research Report comm. by the Electoral Regulation Research Network, December 2018
31. van Spyk, B.: Vizestaatssekretär Kanton St. Gallen, 27 February 2019. Personal Conversation, Staatskanzlei, Recht und Legistik. Regierungsgebäude St, Gallen
32. Staatssekretariat für Wirtschaft SECO, Schweiz: Nationale E-Government Studie 2019. http://pvpf.ch/egov19. Accessed 9 July 2019, March 2019
33. Stine, K., Kissel, R., Barker, W.C., Fahlsing, J., Gulick, J.: Volume I: guide for mapping types of information and information systems to security categories. NIST Special Publication 800-60, vol. I, Rev. 1, US Department of Commerce, NIST, August 2008
34. Stine, K., Kissel, R., Barker, W.C., Lee, A., Fahlsing, J.: Volume II: appendices to guide for mapping types of information and information systems to security categories. NIST Special Publication 800-60, vol. II, Rev. 1, US Department of Commerce, NIST, August 2008
35. Verein eCH: eCH-Standards. http://pvpf.ch/ech. Accessed 9 July 2019

Auditing Indian Elections

Vishal Mohanty[1]([✉])[iD], Chris Culnane[2]([✉])[iD], Philip B. Stark[3]([✉])[iD],
and Vanessa Teague[2]([✉])[iD]

[1] Indian Institute of Technology Madras, Chennai, India
vishalmohanty97@gmail.com
[2] University of Melbourne, Melbourne, Australia
{christopher.culnane,vjteague}@unimelb.edu.au
[3] University of California, Berkeley, California, USA
stark@stat.berkeley.edu

Abstract. Electronic Voting Machines (EVMs) used in the 2019 General Elections in India were fitted with printers to produce Voter-Verifiable Paper Audit Trails (VVPATs). VVPATs allow voters to check whether their votes were recorded as they intended. However, confidence in election results requires more: VVPATs must be preserved inviolate and then actually used to check the reported election result in a trustworthy way that the public can verify. A full manual tally from the VVPATs could be prohibitively expensive and time-consuming; moreover, it is difficult for the public to determine whether a full hand count was conducted accurately. We show how *Risk-Limiting Audits* (RLAs) can provide high confidence in Indian election results. Compared to full hand recounts, RLAs typically require manually inspecting far fewer VVPATs when the outcome is correct, and are much easier for the electorate to observe in adequate detail to determine whether the result is trustworthy.

We show how to apply two RLA strategies, *ballot-level comparison* and *ballot polling*, to General Elections in India. Our main result is a novel method for combining RLAs in constituencies to obtain an RLA of the overall parliamentary election result.

Keywords: Risk-limiting audit · Ballot-polling audit ·
Ballot-level comparison audit · Transitive audit ·
Multi-level election audit · Fisher's combining function

1 Introduction

Since Electronic Voting Machines (EVMs) were introduced in India in the 1999 elections, there have been concerns about their transparency and trustworthiness; a number of security vulnerabilities have been documented [19]. In 2013, the Indian Supreme Court ruled that all EVMs in Indian General Elections must be equipped with printers providing Voter-Verifiable Paper Audit Trails (VVPATs, [17]). The Election Commission of India used VVPAT-equipped EVMs in the 2019 General Elections in all constituencies across the nation.

© Springer Nature Switzerland AG 2019
R. Krimmer et al. (Eds.): E-Vote-ID 2019, LNCS 11759, pp. 150–165, 2019.
https://doi.org/10.1007/978-3-030-30625-0_10

VVPATs allow each voter to verify that his or her intended selections are correctly printed on a paper record, collected in a separate container called the *VVPAT box*. VVPATs provide a way to check and correct election results, for instance, if there is a legal demand by a candidate, or for routine checks of election tabulation accuracy—audits. VVPATs could be manually recounted to check the electronic results, but that is labor-intensive and time-consuming. We show how auditing a random sample of VVPAT records can justify confidence in election results without a full manual tally. Auditing a VVPAT means manually inspecting the paper record to see the voter preferences it shows.

The Election Commission (EC) of India is increasing the transparency of the Indian elections. In a recent report,[1] the EC decided to tally the paper trail slips and compare them with the electronic result provided by the EVMs in 5% of the booths in each Assembly seat district, selected randomly. This effort, while well-intentioned, does not suffice to give strong evidence that election results are correct. In this paper, we show rigorous ways of attaining well-defined confidence levels.

Suitable post-election audits may justify confidence of voters, candidates, and parties that election results are correct. One type of post-election audit is a Risk-Limiting Audit (RLA), which either develops strong statistical evidence that the reported outcome is correct, or corrects the results (by conducting a full manual tally of a reliable paper trail). Here, "outcome" means the set of reported winners of the contests, not the exact vote tallies. To ensure that the tallies are correct to the last vote is prohibitively expensive, if not impossible; conversely, to ensure that the reported winners really won seems like the lowest reasonable standard for accuracy.

Before an RLA commences, the *risk limit* α must be chosen; ideally, it is set in legislation or regulation, so that auditors cannot manipulate the level of scrutiny a contest gets by adjusting the risk limit. The risk limit is the maximum probability that the audit will fail to correct the reported election outcome, on the assumption that the reported outcome is wrong. The risk limit is a worst-case probability that makes no assumption about *why* the outcome is wrong, *e.g.*, it could be because of accidental error, procedural lapse, bugs, misconfiguration, or malicious hacking by a strategic adversary who knows how the audit will be conducted. RLAs assume that the paper ballots reflect the correct outcome, *i.e.* that a full manual tally of the paper trail would show who really won. An RLA of an unreliable paper trail is "security theater." Hence, there need to be procedures (called *compliance audits* by [2,6,14,16]) to ensure that the paper trail is complete and intact before the RLA begins.

This paper shows how two types of RLAs can be used with Indian elections: transitive ballot-level comparison audits and ballot-polling audits. Ballot-level comparison audits are more efficient in the sense that they generally involve inspecting fewer ballots to attain the same risk limit when the reported outcome

---

[1] http://indianexpress.com/article/india/ec-to-tally-paper-trail-slips-with-evms-in-5-pc-booths-in-each-assembly-seat-4737936/.

is correct. However, they require more setup. As discussed in Sect. 3, they may require a voting system that can export its interpretation of individual ballots in a way that can be matched to the corresponding paper, or may require sorting the physical ballots or VVPATs before the audit, according to the votes they (reportedly) show.

Our main contribution is to develop RLAs for a new social choice function— Indian parliamentary majorities—with procedures suited to the logistics of Indian elections. To verify the overall election outcome we need to verify that the party/coalition reported to have been elected to form the government actually won. That generally requires less auditing than confirming the winner in every constituency. The method we develop splits the responsibility of the auditing among various constituencies in a way that the combined result gives higher confidence in the correctness of the overall parliamentary outcome than each constituency would have in its results alone. This procedure is discussed in Sect. 4. Our methods apply to any parliamentary democracy, but the computations are particularly simple when all constituencies have equal weight.

2 Background

RLAs are procedures that guarantee a minimum chance of conducting a full manual tally of the voter-verifiable records when the result of that tally would belie the reported outcome. They amount to a statistical test of the *null hypothesis* that the election outcome is wrong, at significance level α, the *risk limit*. An RLA continues to examine more ballots until the null hypothesis is rejected at significance level α, or until there has been a complete manual tally to set the record straight. The risk limit is the largest chance that the audit will *not* require a full manual tally of the paper records if the electoral outcome according that tally would differ from the reported electoral outcome.

2.1 Indian Elections

Indian General elections are held Quinquennially to elect the Lok Sabha (Lower House of the Parliament). The country is divided into 543 constituencies, each represented by one person elected to the Lok Sabha. Elections at the constituency level are *plurality* contests: the person who gets the most votes wins. Candidates at the constituency level typically belong to some political party, but can be unaffiliated with any party. At the parliamentary level, the party that gets the *majority* (at least 272) of the seats forms the government. If no party has a majority, parties may form coalitions to attain a majority. Coalitions can be formed before or after elections, although before is more common. Elections are conducted in phases spread over a month. Each phase consists of single-day elections in a subset of constituencies, typically grouped by geography.

2.2   Related Work on Election Auditing

RLAs were introduced by [11], but were not so named until [12]. The first RLAs were conducted in California in 2008 [4]. RLAs have been conducted in California, Colorado, Indiana, Michigan, New Jersey, Ohio, Rhode Island, Virginia, and Denmark. RLAs have been developed for a variety of social choice functions, a variety of sampling strategies (unstratified sampling of individual ballots or batches, with or without replacement, with or without weights; stratified sampling with and without replacement and with and without weights, Bernoulli sampling, weighted random sampling) and auditing strategies (*batch-level comparisons, ballot-level comparisons, ballot polling*, and mixtures of those strategies).

Ballot-polling audits [6–8] do not require knowing how the system interpreted individual ballots nor how it tallied the votes on subsets of ballots. They directly check whether the reported winner(s) received more votes than the reported loser(s) by sampling and manually interpreting individual ballots. To draw a random sample of ballots typically involves a *ballot manifest*, which describes how the physical ballots are organized: the number of bundles, the labels of the bundles, and the number of ballots in each bundle (however, see [8]).

The BRAVO ballot-polling method [7] uses Wald's sequential probability ratio test [18] to test the hypotheses that any loser in fact tied or beat any winner. The audit stops short of a full hand count if and only if there is sufficiently strong evidence that every winner beat every loser.

Comparison audits involve manually checking the voting system's interpretation of the votes on physically identifiable subsets of ballots. They require the voting system to export vote tallies for physically identifiable subsets of ballots, so that the votes on those ballots can be tallied by hand and compared to the voting system's tallies. They also require checking that the reported subtotals yield the reported contest results, and that the subtotals account for all ballots cast in the contest. They generally also require ballot manifests.

A comparison audit that checks the voting system's interpretation of individual ballots is a *ballot-level comparison* RLA. Ballot-level comparison RLAs are more efficient than batch-level comparison RLAs and ballot-polling RLAs in that they generally require examining fewer ballots when the reported outcome is correct. However, they have higher set-up costs and require more data export from the voting system: they need a *cast vote record* or *CVR* for each physical ballot, a way to locate the CVR for each physical ballot, and *vice versa*. (A CVR is the voting system's interpretation of voter intent for a given ballot.) Relying on more general results in [12] for batch-level comparison audits, [13] developed a sequential ballot-level comparison RLA method that results in particularly simple calculations.

Hybrid audits combine different approaches to using audit data in different strata, for instance, ballot-polling in some strata and ballot-level comparisons in other strata. See [9].

Transitive audits [3,6] involve auditing an unofficial system. If that system reports the same winner(s) as the official system, an audit that provides strong evidence that the unofficial system found the correct winner(s) transitively provides strong evidence that the official system did also; and if the audit of the unofficial system leads to a full manual tally, the outcome of that tally can be used to correct the official result. A transitive audit does not confirm that the official system tallied votes correctly: the two systems might disagree about the interpretation of every ballot, but still agree who won.

Indian EVMs do not create CVRs, but organizing VVPATs appropriately makes it possible to audit EVMs using a transitive ballot-level comparison audit. CVRs can be constructed for EVMs by sorting the VVPATs into bundles that (purportedly) show the same voter preferences, counting the number of VVPATs in each batch, and labeling each bundle with the number of ballots and the voter preferences it purports to contain. A report of the bundle labels, the number of VVPATs in each bundle, and the reported voter preference for the bundle amounts to a CVR for every VVPAT. Such a report in effect combines a *ballot manifest* [6] and a commitment to a cast vote record for every ballot, implied by the label of the bundle the ballot is in. We shall call such a report a *preference manifest*.

If ballots are sufficiently simple—*e.g.*, if each contains only one contest, as in India—sorting ballots by voter preference can be practical. Indeed, this is how ballots are tallied in Denmark: on election night, ballots are sorted within polling places according to the voter's party preference. The following day, ballots are sorted further according to the voter's candidate preference, to produce homogeneous bundles of ballots, each labeled with the number of ballots and the voters' preference.

Such sorting-based CVRs were the basis of an RLA in Denmark [10]. The sorting might be manual, as it is in Denmark, but it could be automated partly or entirely. (Sorting may also increase vote anonymity by breaking any link between voter and ballot.) When the official tallying process itself is based on creating and counting the homogeneous bundles, as it is in Denmark, the audit is a direct audit of the voting system. If the sorting is conducted independently of the tabulation, as it would be if India were to sort the paper ballots to produce a preference manifest, the resulting audit is a transitive audit.

The first step of a ballot-level comparison RLA is to verify that the CVRs produce the reported results: that applying the social choice function to the vote subtotals implied by the sizes of the bundles and the votes they purport to contain produces the same set of winners. If the preference manifest does not produce the reported set of winners, the audit should not continue: there is a serious problem. The audit should also check that the number of CVRs for each contest does not exceed the number of ballots cast in the contest, which should be determined without reliance on the voting system [1]. If the preference manifest passes these checks, the audit can check the accuracy of the CVRs implied by the preference manifest against a manual reading of voter intent from randomly selected paper ballots.

Kroll *et al.* [5] present a method for reducing the workload in auditing multi-level elections, inspired by the US Electoral College. They show that to achieve an overall confidence that a party or coalition secured the majority of seats, the individual constituencies can sometimes be audited to lower confidence levels. They provide a constrained optimization program describing the set of feasible solutions (*i.e.* those that constitute a sufficient audit) and a number of methods for finding the optimal solution. In India's electoral system, as in many other parliamentary democracies, every constituency has equal weight.

3   Auditing Individual Constituencies using Extant Methods

This section discusses how existing methods for RLAs apply to Indian elections. We consider auditing individual constituencies rather than the entire election; Sect. 4 shows how to combine audits of constituencies to audit an entire contest.

India's voting system currently does not support ballot-level comparison audits, but, as described above, if procedures were added to sort the paper ballots and produce a preference manifest, transitive ballot-level comparison audits would be possible. Because ballots in India are simple—a single selection in a single contest—such sorting is feasible.

Ballot-polling audits could be used in India without sorting the ballots or modifying the voting system, if ballot manifests were available (see Sect. 3.2). The calculations for BRAVO [7] and the ballot-polling method in [6] are simple enough to do with a pencil and paper or hand calculator, and are implemented in open-source online tools by Stark.[2]

When the election outcome is correct, ballot-level comparison audits generally require inspecting fewer ballots than ballot-polling audits. (Because they are RLAs, when the outcome is incorrect, both have a large chance of requiring a full manual tally.) The advantage grows as the margin shrinks: as a rule of thumb, workload increases inversely with the reported margin for ballot-level comparison audits, and increases inversely with the square of the actual margin for ballot-polling audits. However, preparing for a ballot-level comparison audit is harder, because it requires CVRs linked to the corresponding physical ballots. The simplicity of ballot-polling audits may offset the work of examining more paper ballots, unless the margin is very small.

3.1   Transitive Ballot-Level Comparison RLA

Ballot-level comparison RLAs were introduced by [13], who provides online tools[3]; see also [6]. Ballot-level comparison audits require a way to find the CVR corresponding to each paper ballot, and vice versa. The EVMs currently used in India do not provide CVRs at all.

However, as shown by [10], sorting ballots into groups according to the vote (if any) that they are reported to show in effect provides a CVR for each ballot

---

[2] https://www.stat.berkeley.edu/~stark/Vote/ballotPollTools.htm.
[3] https://www.stat.berkeley.edu/~stark/Vote/auditTools.htm.

through a preference manifest that lists the bundles of ballots, the number of ballots in each bundle, and the (single) preference that every ballot in the bundle is supposed to show. In Denmark, ballots are manually sorted into bundles with homogeneous voter intent, but sorting could be automated with relatively simple equipment, possibly something similar to the system used in South Korea.

Whether it is worth the effort to sort the ballots depends on the margin: if the margin is wide, it will be less expensive to use ballot polling, but if the margin is very narrow, the cost of sorting—whether manual or automated—may reduce the sample size required to confirm the outcome by orders of magnitude.

Classifying CVR Errors. Stark [12] reviews a number of methods to test the hypothesis that any loser received more votes than any winner by comparing hand counts of votes in randomly selected batches of ballots to the machine counts of the votes on the same ballots. The methods apply to arbitrarily small batches, including batches consisting of a single ballot; that is, to ballot-level comparison audits. [13] elaborated one of those methods, which relies on the Kaplan-Markov inequality. By introducing a taxonomy of discrepancies, the arithmetic can be simplified to the point that a pencil and paper suffice, while rigorously controlling the risk. That "super-simple simultaneous single-ballot" method was further simplified by [6], and is the basis of pilot audits in Denmark, California, Colorado, Indiana, Michigan, New Jersey, Rhode Island, and Virginia, and of the statutory risk-limiting audits in most Colorado counties.

Stark and Teague [15] presented a ballot-level comparison RLA method based on the Kaplan-Wald inequality, which has some advantages over the Kaplan-Markov inequality. In this paper, we use the method of [6], because it has been used more widely. We shall refer to it as the *LSKM method*. It is straightforward to modify the procedures below to use the method of [15] or any other ballot-comparison RLA method instead.

The LSKM method is *sequential*: it examines more and more ballots selected at random until either there is strong evidence that the reported winners really won, or until there has been a full hand count and the correct outcome is known. Conceptually, after examining one or more ballots, one calculates a sequentially valid[4] P-value of the hypothesis that the outcome is wrong. If that P-value is less than or equal to the risk limit α, the audit stops; otherwise, more ballots are audited and the sequential P-value is updated. The method presented in Sect. 4 to check the overall electoral outcome involves combining the P-values for individual constituencies.

---

[4] *Sequentially valid* means that the chance that the infimum of the P-value over all sample sizes is less than or equal to α is itself less than or equal to α if the null hypothesis is true. In contrast, standard hypothesis tests are designed for sample sizes that are fixed ahead of time: expanding the sample and re-calculating the P-value for such tests generally produces type I error rates far larger than the nominal significance level, because it does not account for multiplicity.

If the audit does lead to a full hand tally in a constituency, the reported results are replaced by the results according to that full hand tabulation. Election officials may elect to terminate the audit and conduct a full hand count at any time, for instance, if they estimate that the cost of additional sampling will exceed the cost of a full manual tally.

The LSKM method involves classifying discrepancies between the CVR and a manual reading of voter intent from the paper ballot:

- If correcting the CVR would reduce the margin between any (reported) winner and any (reported) loser by two votes, the discrepancy is a *2-vote overstatement* (the number of 2-vote overstatements is denoted o_2).
- If not, but if correcting the CVR would reduce the margin between any winner and any loser by one vote, the discrepancy is a *1-vote overstatement* (the number of 1-vote overstatements is denoted o_1).
- If not, but if correcting the CVR would not increase the margin between every winner and every loser, the discrepancy is a *neutral error*. (Neutral errors do not enter the stopping rule explicitly.)
- If not, but if correcting the CVR would increase the margin between every winner and every loser by at least one vote, and increase the margin between some winner and some loser by exactly one vote, the discrepancy is a *1-vote understatement* (the number of 1-vote understatements is denoted u_1).
- If correcting the CVR would increase the margin between every winner and every loser by two votes, it is a *2-vote understatement* (the number of 2-vote understatements is denoted u_2).

Two-vote overstatements should be rare if the voting system is working correctly: they involve mistaking a vote for a loser as a vote for a winner. Two-vote understatements should be even rarer—and are typically mathematically impossible. For instance, in a plurality, vote-for-one contest with three or more candidates, two-vote understatements are impossible, because they would require having mistaken a valid vote for the winner as a valid vote for every losing candidate.

We assume that there is a trustworthy upper bound on the total number of ballots cast, for instance, from pollbooks or from information about the number of eligible voters. A preliminary check should ensure that the preference manifest does not list more ballots than that upper bound: if there are more ballots listed than can exist, there is a serious problem that the audit cannot address by itself.[5]

In the sorted-ballot method described above,

- a *2-vote overstatement* occurs if we find a vote for a reported loser in the reported winner's pile;

---

[5] Prof. Sandeep Shukla of IIT Kanpur has pointed out that the current Indian VVPAT design does not protect against the EVM adding electronic votes and corresponding VVPATs when voters are not looking, because there is no publicly observable mechanism to ensure that at most one VVPAT is inserted into the box per voter. This needs to be addressed by improving the physical design in a way that is beyond the scope of this paper.

- a *1-vote overstatement* occurs if we find a vote for a different reported loser in a reported loser's pile;
- *neutral errors* don't occur;[6]
- a *1-vote understatement* occurs when there are at least three candidates and we find a vote for the reported winner in a reported loser's pile;
- a *2-vote understatement* occurs only when there are exactly two candidates, and we find a vote for the reported winner in the reported loser's pile;
- if a pile turns out to be *smaller* than reported, the discrepancy can be addressed using the "phantom to zombie" approach of [1].
- if a pile turns out to be *larger* than reported, then some other pile must be *smaller* than reported, and the "phantom to zombie" approach of [1] will still ensure that the risk is controlled conservatively.

There are sharper ways to treat discrepancies than to use these categories (in particular, keeping track of *which* margins are affected by each discrepancy can reduce the number of ballots the audit inspects; see [13]). However, the bookkeeping is more complex. Categorizing discrepancies this way makes the calculations simple enough to do with a pencil and paper (aside from calculating 5 constants involving logarithms, which can be done once and for all and verified by anyone).

Calculations. Let n denote the current sample size and α the risk limit. Fix $\gamma \geq 1$. The LSKM method stops auditing (and concludes that the reported winners really won) if

$$
\begin{aligned}
n \geq \frac{2\gamma}{\mu} \Bigg(& o_1 \log \left(\frac{1}{1 - \frac{1}{2\gamma}} \right) + o_2 \log \left(\frac{1}{1 - \frac{1}{\gamma}} \right) \\
& - u_1 \log \left(1 + \frac{1}{2\gamma} \right) - u_2 \log \left(1 + \frac{1}{\gamma} \right) - \log(\alpha) \Bigg).
\end{aligned}
\tag{1}
$$

In this expression, μ is the *diluted margin*, the smallest difference in votes between any winner and any loser, divided by the total number of ballots in the population from which the sample is to be drawn, including ballots with invalid votes. The constant $\gamma \geq 1$ is the *error inflation factor*, which controls the operating characteristics of the LSKM method: the larger γ is, the fewer additional ballots need to be audited if a 2-vote overstatement is observed, but the smaller γ is, the fewer ballots need to be audited if no 2-vote overstatements are observed. Because two-vote overstatements should be rare, taking γ slightly larger than

---

[6] Indian EVMs (as far as we know) do not produce blank votes. However, if they did they could be accommodated easily. A 1-vote overstatement occurs if we find a blank vote in the reported winner's pile. A neutral error would occur when there were at least three candidates and we found a blank vote in a reported loser's pile. A one-vote understatement would occur when there were exactly two candidates and we found a blank vote in the reported loser's pile.

1 should suffice. For γ exactly equal to 1, then if the audit finds even one 2-vote overstatement, the audit will not terminate without a full hand count. [6] suggest using $\gamma = 1.03905$, which makes the "cost" of a 2-vote overstatement 5 times larger than the "cost" of a 1-vote overstatement, where "cost" means the number of additional ballots that must be audited to attain the risk limit. Any value of $\gamma \geq 1$ gives a risk-limiting audit, but γ must be chosen before inspecting any ballots.

3.2   Ballot-Polling RLA Using BRAVO

The BRAVO ballot-polling RLA by [7] can be applied immediately to constituencies in India. In the Indian scenario, we have only one winner per constituency and one candidate per ballot. For each loser ℓ, the null hypothesis $H_{0w\ell}$ states that w did not get more votes than ℓ, that is, that ℓ actually tied or beat w. BRAVO uses the Sequential Probability Ratio Test by [18] to test all the null hypotheses simultaneously.

The audit begins by choosing the risk limit α. It also requires the reported vote totals for each candidate,[7] but no other data from the voting system.

For every apparent loser ℓ, define the *conditional vote share* $s_{w\ell}$

$$s_{w\ell} \equiv \frac{v_w}{v_w + v_\ell} \qquad (2)$$

Here, v_w and v_ℓ are the reported vote totals for the winner w and the loser ℓ respectively. If the reported vote tally is correct, the chance that a randomly selected ballot shows a vote for w, given that it shows a vote for either w or ℓ, is $s_{w\ell}$.

BRAVO maintains a test statistic $T_{w\ell}$ for each reported (winner, loser) pair. In Indian elections, there is only one reported winner w per constituency, so this amounts to a test statistic for each reported loser ℓ. Null hypothesis $H_{0w\ell}$ is rejected if

$$T_{w\ell} \geqslant \frac{1}{\alpha}. \qquad (3)$$

If the null hypotheses $\{H_{0w\ell}\}$ for all apparent losers $\ell \in L$ are rejected, the audit stops and the reported outcome becomes final.

At any time, for example if the audit is expected to take more time than simply counting the ballots, auditors can stop sampling and perform a full manual recount. The algorithm runs as follows:

---

[7] There are other ballot-polling methods that do not use the reported results at all.

Algorithm 1. BRAVO with protection against manifest errors. This is a simplified version of BRAVO that assumes the contest has only one winner, and that there can be at most one valid vote per ballot. It incorporates the "phantom to zombie" method of [1] for dealing with errors in the ballot manifest.

Input: Risk Limit α; ballot manifest, announced winner w, losers set L and corresponding weighted vote shares $s_{w\ell}$ for each $\ell \in L$. Upper bound N on the number of ballots, where N is at least as large as the number of ballots listed in the manifest. Work threshold $K \leq N$.

1: Initialize probability ratios: $\forall \ell \in L : T_{w\ell} \leftarrow 1$
2: Number of audited ballots: $n \leftarrow 0$
3: $\mathcal{L} \leftarrow L$
4: **while** $\mathcal{L} \neq \emptyset$ **do**
5:     Generate a random number i between 1 and N
6:     Look up the ith ballot in the ballot manifest and (attempt to) retrieve it
7:     **if** Ballot i is not in the ballot manifest or cannot be found **then**
8:         For every $\ell \in \mathcal{L}$, $T_{w\ell} \leftarrow T_{w\ell} * 2(1 - s_{w\ell})$
9:     **else if** Ballot i shows a vote for the winner w **then**
10:        For each $\ell \in \mathcal{L}$, $T_{w\ell} \leftarrow T_{w\ell} * 2s_{w\ell}$
11:     **else if** Ballot i shows a vote for loser $\ell \in \mathcal{L}$ **then**
12:        $T_{w\ell} \leftarrow T_{w\ell} * 2(1 - s_{w\ell})$
13:     **if** $T_{w\ell} \geq \frac{1}{\alpha}$ for any loser $\ell \in \mathcal{L}$ **then**
14:        $\mathcal{L} \leftarrow \mathcal{L} \setminus \{\ell\}$
15:     **if** the number of ballots inspected exceeds K, or optionally at any time **then**
16:        **STOP** the audit and perform a full manual recount.
17: Declare election outcome correct—since all null hypotheses have been rejected.

At any stage, $P = \max_{\ell \in L} 1/T_{w\ell}$ is a conservative sequential P-value for the hypothesis that the reported winner w did not actually win the constituency.

Number of Votes to Be Audited. Consider an example of a 3-candidate contest with a single plurality winner. The candidates are Ram, Shyam and Janani. Their respective shares are recorded in the following table:

Ram	Shyam	Janani
20,000	30,000	50,000

In this case, the winner is Janani. Let us denote the winner-loser pairs as (j, r) for Janani and Ram and (j, s) for Janani and Shyam. The weighted vote shares are:

$$s_{jr} = \frac{v_j}{v_j + v_r} = \frac{50000}{50000 + 20000} = 0.714$$

$$s_{js} = \frac{v_j}{v_j + v_s} = \frac{50000}{50000 + 30000} = 0.625$$

We set the risk limit α at 5%. Every time the audit selects a ballot that shows a vote for Janani we multiply T_{jr} by $\frac{0.714}{0.5} = 1.428$ and T_{js} by $\frac{0.625}{0.5} = 1.25$.

Therefore, the minimum sample size n to attain a risk limit $\alpha = 0.05$ satisfies

$$1.428^n \geq 20$$

and

$$1.25^n \geq 20$$

The smallest such n is $n = 14$. Hence, we need to audit at least 14 ballots—if they all show up votes for Janani, BRAVO will confirm the election outcome at risk limit 5%.

If the reported election results were accurate, on average we would see 50% of ballots for Janani, 30% for Shyam and 20% for Ram. [7] describe how to find the *Average sample number (ASN)*, the expected sample size necessary to reject all the null hypotheses, assuming the reported results are indeed correct. Stark's online ballot-polling tool shows an ASN of 123 for this example. There have been numerous improvements to the efficiency of Risk-Limiting Audits, any of which could easily apply to India's simple electoral system.[8]

The next section explains how to audit the overall parliamentary winner by an efficient combination of single-constituency audits. It requires independent, sequentially valid P-values $\{P_i\}$ for the hypotheses that the reported outcome in constituency i is incorrect. It does not require the P-values to be obtained using the same method. For instance, some constituencies could use ballot polling and others could use transitive ballot-level comparison audits.

4   Auditing the Overall Parliamentary Winner

A party or a coalition needs a majority of the seats in the Lower House of Parliament to form a new government. The total number of seats is 543, so to win, a party or coalition needs at least 272 seats. The audit needs to confirm that the reported winning party or coalition truly won at least 272 seats. (The particular seats the reported winner won is immaterial to whether they won overall.) If party w supposedly won $M \geq 272$ constituencies, then for a different party to have won in fact, the reported outcome must be wrong in at least $m = M - 271$ of the constituencies that w supposedly won. This condition is necessary but not sufficient for the parliamentary outcome to be wrong: if w in fact won some constituencies it was reported to have lost, the outcome could be wrong in m constituencies w supposedly won and yet w could still be the overall winner.

Let W denote the set of constituencies w reportedly won. Then $|W| \geq 272$ and $m = |W| - 271$, where $|W|$ denotes the cardinality of the set W. If there is no set of constituencies $C \subset W$ with $|C| = m$ for which w lost in *every* $c \subset C$, w must have won overall.

---

[8] See for example https://github.com/pbstark/S157F17/blob/master/kaplanWald. ipynb and https://github.com/pbstark/S157F17/blob/master/pSPRTnoReplace- ment.ipynb.

Let α denote the overall risk limit, and let P_c denote a P-value for the hypothesis that the reported outcome in constituency c is wrong. We suppose that the audits in different constituencies rely on independently selected random samples of ballots, so the P-values $\{P_c\}$ are independent random variables. If the reported outcome in constituency c is incorrect, the probability distribution of P_c is stochastically dominated by a uniform distribution. That is, $\Pr\{P_c \le p\} \le p$ if the reported outcome in constituency c is wrong.

Let C denote a set of constituencies. *Fisher's combining function* for a set of P-values $\{P_c\}_{c \in C}$ is

$$\chi^2(C) \equiv -2 \sum_{c \in C} \ln P_c. \tag{4}$$

If the P-values $\{P_c\}$ are independent and all the null hypotheses are true, the probability distribution of $\chi^2(C)$ is stochastically smaller than a chi-square distribution with $2|C|$ degrees of freedom.[9] That is, if the reported outcome in every constituency $c \in C$ is wrong,

$$\Pr\{\chi^2(C) \ge \chi^2_{2|C|}(1 - \alpha)\} \le \alpha, \tag{5}$$

where $\chi^2_{2|C|}(1 - \alpha)$ is the $1 - \alpha$ quantile of the chi-square distribution with $2|C|$ degrees of freedom.

Let W denote the set of constituencies the reported winning party allegedly won, and let $m \equiv |W| - 271$. Then m is the parliamentary "margin" in constituencies: the reported winner really won overall unless there are at least m constituencies where the overall winner reportedly won, but in fact lost. For any set C of constituencies, let C_m denote the set of all subsets of C with cardinality m. The overall auditing strategy is to test whether there is any subset of m constituencies in W where the reported parliamentary winner actually lost. If there is no such subset, the reported winner must actually have won overall. We test that hypothesis by examining all such subsets. For each such subset, we use the separate audits of the constituencies to construct, via Fisher's combining function, a test of the hypothesis that the reported winner lost in all m constituencies.

If the audit of some constituency c leads to a full hand count that confirms the result, then all subsets of size m that contain c can be eliminated from further consideration: the reported winner cannot have lost in all m constituencies in such a subset, because it actually won in c.

For any collection $\mathcal{U}$ of sets of constituencies, define $\mathcal{U}(c) \equiv \{U \in \mathcal{U} : U \ni c\}$, all sets of constituencies in $\mathcal{U}$ that contain c. (These will be the collections eliminated from further consideration if a full count of c confirms the result in c.)

BRAVO and LSKM produce sequentially valid P-values. That is, the chance that the infimum of the P-value for constituency c over all sample sizes is less than or equal to p is itself less than or equal to p, if the outcome is incorrect in constituency c. For that reason, every rule for increasing sample sizes in constituency c results in a valid P-value for constituency c. Because the samples

---

[9] See, e.g., [9].

are selected independently in different constituencies (although sample *sizes* are dependent), the composite P-value from Fisher's combining function remains valid. Thus, the rule for increasing sample sizes when the risk limit has not been attained could be as simple as "increase every n_c by 1 ballot," or it could be designed to minimize the expected total amount of auditing required, for instance, by preferentially increasing the sample size in constituencies with large margins and taking into account differences in auditing methods in different jurisdictions (ballot polling versus transitive ballot-level comparison). All else equal, when the outcome is correct, auditing an additional ballot is expected to decrease the P-value more, the larger the true margin is. Similarly, all else equal, auditing an additional ballot in a jurisdiction conducting a transitive ballot-level comparison RLA is expected to decrease the P-value more than auditing an additional ballot in a jurisdiction conducting a ballot-polling RLA. It is always permissible to perform a full hand count in any constituency rather than increase the sample size incrementally: anything that increases the chance of a full count cannot increase the risk.

With these definitions, our audit procedure is as follows:

1. Select an overall risk limit α for the parliamentary outcome and select an auditing method for each constituency $c \in W$, e.g., BRAVO or LSKM.
2. Perform the following audit.

Algorithm 2. Audit of overall election result.

Input: W, the constituencies reportedly won by w; α, the risk limit; a sequential auditing method for each $c \in W$

1: Set $\mathcal{U} = \mathcal{W}_m$, the collection of all subsets of W of cardinality $m = |W| - 271$.
2: **while** $\mathcal{U} \neq \emptyset$ **do**
3:     Augment the sample in one or more constituencies c
4:     Find the constituency-level P-values $\{P_c\}$ using the auditing method pre-specified for each c
5:     **if** $\exists C \in \mathcal{U}$ such that $\forall c \in C$ a full hand count revealed a different winner **then**
6:         Perform a full hand count of the entire election; report the resulting outcome, and stop.
7:     **for all** constituencies $c \in \cup \mathcal{U}$ **do**
8:         **if** c has been fully counted by hand, and the count confirmed the reported outcome in c **then**
9:             $\mathcal{U} \leftarrow \mathcal{U} \setminus \mathcal{U}(c)$
10:    $\mathcal{U} \leftarrow \mathcal{U} \setminus \{C \in \mathcal{U} : \chi^2(C) \geq \chi^2_{2|C|}(1 - \alpha)\}$

---

3. If the loop terminates with $\mathcal{U} = \emptyset$, the audit has confirmed the parliamentary outcome at risk limit α.

Proof that the algorithm above is a RLA of the parliamentary outcome. We show that if the parliamentary outcome is wrong, the chance that the audit stops without a full manual tally of every constituency is at most α. If the parliamentary outcome is wrong, the reported winner is wrong in every $c \in C$ for some $C \in \mathcal{W}_m$. Suppose there is such a C. If the audit leads to hand counting every $c \in C$, step (5) ensures that there will be a full manual tally of the entire election. Therefore, there will be a full manual tally unless C is removed from $\mathcal{U}$. There are two places that sets of constituencies can be removed from $\mathcal{U}$: step (9) and step (10). Step (9) cannot remove C from $\mathcal{U}$, because, by assumption, hand-counting any $c \in C$ would belie the reported outcome in c. Therefore, the chance that C is *not* fully hand counted is at most the chance that step (10) removes C from $\mathcal{U}$. But, by construction (through Fisher's combining function applied to the independent constituency-level P-values), that chance is not larger than α. If there is more than one $C \in \mathcal{W}_m$ for which every reported outcome is wrong, the audit must erroneously remove *all* of them at step (10). But the chance of erroneously removing all of them cannot be larger than chance of removing any one of them individually, which is in turn at most α.

5   Conclusion and Future Work

We have presented an approach to conduct risk-limiting audits of the national outcome of Indian elections by combining audits conducted in different constituencies using independent samples. Within a given constituency, the audit could use ballot polling, or—with an initial step of sorting VVPATs—transitive ballot-level comparisons. The sets of constituencies are constructed in such a way that for the reported parliamentary outcome to be wrong, the reported outcome must be wrong in *every* constituency in at least one of the sets. If there is strong statistical evidence that there is no set of constituencies in the collection for which every reported outcome is wrong, that confirms the national parliamentary outcome. In future research we will address how to schedule increases in sample sizes in different constituencies to minimize the total expected workload, taking into account the reported margins in different constituencies and the auditing methods used in different constituencies.

Acknowledgments. Many thanks to Andrew Conway, Archanaa Krishnan, Chittaranjan Mandal, Sandeep Shukla, Nicholas Akinyokun, Peter Stuckey and Poorvi Vora for valuable suggestions on this work.

References

1. Bañuelos, J., Stark, P.: Limiting risk by turning manifest phantoms into evil zombies. arXiv preprint arXiv:1207.3413 (2012)
2. Benaloh, J., Jones, D., Lazarus, E., Lindeman, M., Stark, P.: SOBA: secrecy-preserving observable ballot-level audit. EVT/WOTE 11 (2011)
3. Calandrino, J., Halderman, J., Felten, E.: Machine-assisted election auditing. EVT **7**, 9 (2007)
4. Hall, J., et al.: Implementing risk-limiting audits in California. EVT/WOTE (2009)
5. Kroll, J.A., Halderman, A., Felten, E.: Efficiently auditing multi-level elections. Ann Arbor **1001**, 48109 (2014)

6. Lindeman, M., Stark, P.: A gentle introduction to risk-limiting audits. EEE Secur. Priv. **10**(5), 42–49 (2012)
7. Lindeman, M., Stark, P., Yates, V.: BRAVO: ballot-polling risk-limiting audits to verify outcomes (2012)
8. Ottoboni, K., Bernhard, M., Halderman, A., Rivest, R., Stark, P.: Bernoulli ballot polling: a manifest improvement for risk- limiting audits. In: Voting 2019 (2019)
9. Ottoboni, K., Stark, P.B., Lindeman, M., McBurnett, N.: Risk-limiting audits by stratified union-intersection tests of elections (SUITE). In: Krimmer, R., et al. (eds.) E-Vote-ID 2018. LNCS, vol. 11143, pp. 174–188. Springer, Cham (2018). https://doi.org/10.1007/978-3-030-00419-4_12
10. Schürmann, C.: A risk-limiting audit in Denmark: a pilot. In: Krimmer, R., et al. (eds.) E-Vote-ID 2016. LNCS, vol. 10141, pp. 192–202. Springer, Cham (2017). https://doi.org/10.1007/978-3-319-52240-1_12
11. Stark, P.: Conservative statistical post-election audits. Ann. Appl. Stat. **2**(2), 550–581 (2008)
12. Stark, P.: Risk-limiting post-election audits: P-values from common probability inequalities. IEEE Trans. Inf. Forensics Secur. **4**, 1005–1014 (2009)
13. Stark, P.: Super-simple simultaneous single-ballot risk-limiting audits. USENIX Association Berkeley, CA, USA ©2010 (2010)
14. Stark, P.: An introduction to risk-limiting audits and evidence-based elections: testimony to the Little Hoover Commission (2018)
15. Stark, P., Teague, V.: Verifiable European elections: risk-limiting audits for d'hondt and its relatives. USENIX J. Election Technol. Syst. (JETS) **1**(3), 18–39 (2014)
16. Stark, P., Wagner, D.: Evidence-based elections. IEEE Secur. Priv. **10**(5), 33–41 (2012)
17. Supreme Court of India: Civil appeal no. 9093 of 2013–Dr. Subramanian Swamy vs. Election Commission of India, October 2013
18. Wald, A.: Sequential tests of statistical hypotheses. Ann. Appl. Stat. **16**(2), 117–186 (1945)
19. Wolchok, S., et al.: Security analysis of India's electronic voting machines. In: Proceedings of the 17th ACM Conference on Computer and Communications Security, pp. 1–14. ACM (2010)

Election Integrity and Electronic Voting Machines in 2018 Georgia, USA

Kellie Ottoboni$^{(\boxtimes)}$ [iD] and Philip B. Stark$^{(\boxtimes)}$ [iD]

Department of Statistics, University of California, Berkeley, CA, USA
kellieotto@berkeley.edu, stark@stat.berkeley.edu

Abstract. Direct recording electronic (DRE) voting systems have been shown time and time again to be vulnerable to hacking and malfunctioning. Despite mounting evidence that DREs are unfit for use, some states in the U.S. continue to use them for local, state, and federal elections. Georgia uses DREs exclusively, among many practices that have made its elections unfair and insecure. We give a brief history of election security and integrity in Georgia from the early 2000s to the 2018 election. Nonparametric permutation tests give strong evidence that something caused DREs not to record a substantial number of votes in this election. The undervote rate in the Lieutenant Governor's race was far higher for voters who used DREs than for voters who used paper ballots. Undervote rates were strongly associated with ethnicity, with higher undervote rates in precincts where the percentage of Black voters was higher. There is specific evidence of DRE malfunction, too: one of the seven DREs in the Winterville Train Depot polling place had results that appear to be "flipped" along party lines. None of these associations or anomalies can reasonably be ascribed to chance.

Keywords: Permutation testing · Anomaly detection · DREs

1 Introduction

The state of Georgia was a focal point in the civil rights movement of the twentieth century. It also has a history of election problems: systematic voter suppression, voting machines that are vulnerable to undetectable security breaches, and serious security breaches of their data systems.

The 2018 midterm election returned Georgia to the national spotlight. Civil rights groups alleged that then Secretary of State Brian Kemp—who was running for Governor against Stacey Abrams, a Black woman—closed polling places, deleted voters from the rolls, and challenged voter signatures—disproportionately in Black neighborhoods [9,18,22]. A federal lawsuit against the Secretary of State demanded that Georgia replace paperless direct recording electronic (DRE) voting machines with optically scanned voter-marked paper ballot (opscan) voting systems [34]. While the judge accepted the plaintiffs' argument that DREs (and Georgia's election management) have serious security

© Springer Nature Switzerland AG 2019
R. Krimmer et al. (Eds.): E-Vote-ID 2019, LNCS 11759, pp. 166–182, 2019.
https://doi.org/10.1007/978-3-030-30625-0_11

problems, defendants successfully argued that they were unable to replace their equipment in time for the election. Ultimately, in-person voting in Georgia's 2018 election was on DREs.

The 2018 election produced anomalous results that could have been caused by malfunctioning, misprogrammed, or hacked election technology, including DREs. The accuracy of DRE results cannot be checked (for instance by a risk-limiting audit) because the DREs used in Georgia do not produce a voter-verifiable paper record. There has been no forensic investigation of the DREs used in the 2018 election, although the (continuing) suit seeks to conduct one.

This paper begins with a short history of recent election integrity issues in Georgia. We summarize known security flaws of DRE voting systems and what took place in the months leading up the 2018 election. We analyze public election results and poll tapes photographed by a volunteer, finding strong statistical evidence that DREs were the source of these anomalies: that something caused DREs to miss votes in the Lieutenant Governor's contest and to "flip" votes for one party into votes for another.

2 DRE Voting Machines

Congress passed the Help America Vote Act (HAVA) in 2002 after the problems in Florida in the 2000 presidential election. HAVA requires states to allow provisional voting and to build statewide voter registration databases, and provided funds for states to upgrade voting systems for accessibility. To receive funding, states were required to replace punchcard and lever voting systems and to provide at least one accessible voting machine per polling place [14].

Two types of systems were on the market: optical scanners (opscan), which primarily used hand-marked paper ballots, and DREs. DREs eliminate the need to print and store paper ballots, can present ballots in multiple languages, and satisfied the accessibility requirement [14].[1] DREs and in-precinct opscan systems also make it easier to report results faster than central opscan systems. While HAVA only required one accessible machine per polling place, some states opted to use DREs exclusively [43]. In 2002, four voting machine manufacturers offered DREs: Diebold Election Systems, Election Systems and Software (ES&S), Hart InterCivic, and Sequoia Voting Systems. This paper focuses on Diebold (now Premier), the lone DRE provider in Georgia.

In the following year, newly-adopted DREs caused serious problems. In the 2002 Florida primaries, some machines in Miami-Dade county failed to turn on, creating long lines that prevented some would-be voters from voting. In New Mexico, faulty programming caused machines to drop a quarter of the votes. In Virginia, the software on 10 machines caused one vote to be subtracted for every 100 votes cast for a particular candidate [40].

---

[1] There is ample evidence that the systems are not very usable in practice by voters with disabilities [33], yet they satisfy the legal requirement.

In 2007, studies sponsored by the Secretaries of State of California (the Top-to-Bottom Review, TTBR) and Ohio (the EVEREST study) gave conclusive evidence that the DREs on the market had fundamental security flaws. The TTBR found physical and technological security flaws with Premier Election Systems' (formerly Diebold) DREs, including vulnerabilities that would allow someone to install malicious software that records votes incorrectly or miscounts them; susceptibility to viruses that propagate from machine to machine; unprotected information linked to individual votes that could compromise ballot anonymity; access to the voting system server software, allowing an attacker to corrupt the election management system database; "root access" to the voting system, allowing attackers to change the settings of any device on the network; and numerous physical security holes that would allow an attacker to disable parts of the device using standard office tools [5]. EVEREST found that the software for Premier DREs was "unstable" and lacked "sound software and security engineering practices" [17]. California decertified DREs from Premier, Hart InterCivic, and Sequoia, and the EVEREST study prompted Ohio to move to optical scanners.

White-hat hackers have found even more security flaws. In 2005 and 2006, Finnish computer scientist Harri Hursti demonstrated that Diebold's optical scanners could be hacked to change vote totals, and uncovered security flaws with Diebold's AccuVote-TSx machines that render "the voting terminal incurably compromised" [12,13]. In 2017, the annual DEF CON hacker conference held a "Voting Village" and supplied participating hackers with over 25 pieces of election equipment used in the United States. While EVEREST restricted the types of hacks that could be deployed against the machines, there were no such restrictions at DEF CON. Within minutes, hackers with little prior knowledge of voting systems penetrated several DREs, including the Premier AccuVote-TSx used in Georgia. They uncovered serious hardware vulnerabilities, including chips installed in sockets instead of being soldered in place to prevent removal and tampering [2]. The Voting Village has become a regular part of DEF CON as voting system vulnerabilities persist: the organizers reported in 2018, "while, on average, it takes about six minutes to vote, machines in at least 15 states can be hacked with a pen in two minutes" [3].

Security experts recommend that jurisdictions using DREs conduct forensic audits both before and after every election. An examination of the software and machines done by an independent, neutral party might detect tampering, bugs, or hacking, and would help discourage malicious attacks [35]. (However, forensic investigation is not guaranteed to detect all hacking: for instance, malware can be programmed to erase itself after doing its damage.) But historically, it has been illegal to examine voting machine software because it is considered proprietary information [24]. Without a forensic audit or a reliable paper trail against which to check reported results, there is no way to know whether a DRE accurately captured and tallied votes.

To make DREs more secure, printers can be added to create a "voter-verifiable paper audit trail" (VVPAT) displayed behind glass, so the voter can check whether their vote was cast as intended. The paper record can be used in a post-election audit, and serves as a back-up in case the device's electronic memory fails. The NIST Auditability Working Group found that the only satisfactory way to audit DREs is with a trustworthy paper record such as a VVPAT [20].

However, VVPATs can be compromised. If the printer malfunctions, the paper record is incomplete. VVPATs are difficult to audit: they are typically printed on continuous, flimsy, uncut rolls of paper, which need to be unrolled and segmented to count votes. Most VVPATs are thermal paper, which degrades quickly when exposed to heat, light, human touch [20], or household chemicals [5].

Verifiable does not imply *verified*: voters might not check a VVPAT effectively or at all. Research has shown that voters don't review their selections effectively. Voters often walk away from DREs before an electronic review screen is displayed. Errors in votes occur at the same rate whether a review screen is shown or not. In experiments where the wrong candidate was marked on an electronic review screen, only 37% of study participants noticed the error on the review screen, though 95% reported that they had checked their ballot either somewhat or very carefully [7]. A report by the Pennsylvania State Department found that when voters were shown VVPATs displayed behind glass, the glare and edges of the glass cage obstructed their selections [33]. VVPATs may not reflect voter intent, even if voters claim to review them.

Many states have been phasing out paperless DREs. In 2006, nearly 40% of voters used DREs to cast their vote. In 2016, 28 states used DREs in some capacity, but most jurisdictions had some paper record, either opscan or an electronic method with a paper backup [40]. Only five states still use paperless DREs exclusively: Delaware, Georgia, Louisiana, New Jersey, and South Carolina.

3   Voter Suppression in Georgia

Georgia faced heightened scrutiny under the Voting Rights Act of 1965 due to a history of discrimination in elections. Sections 4(b) and 5 of the 1965 Voting Rights Act required jurisdictions with prior evidence of racial discrimination to get "preclearance" from the federal government before changing their election policies. In 2013, the Supreme Court ruled in *Shelby County v. Holder* that these sections were unconstitutional because they placed undue burden on some states based on outdated evidence of discrimination against minority voters [30].

The ruling revitalized efforts to disenfranchise minority voters: without federal oversight, some states that were previously subject to the preclearance rule of the Voting Rights Act reinstated some discriminatory policies. States began to close polling places and create stricter voter registration laws. Previously, counties and states would have had to show that these changes would not differentially disenfranchise minority voters. After *Shelby County v. Holder*, Arizona, Louisiana, and Texas made changes that affect a large number of registered voters, disproportionately Black and Latino [36].

Strategically closing polling places can reduce voter turnout for specific demographic groups. It can force voters to travel farther to vote and create long lines in remaining polling places. Since the ruling, nearly a thousand polling places in the United States have been closed, many which served African American communities [36]. Since 2012, election officials in Georgia have closed 214 precincts—nearly 8% of the state's polling places [22]. Officials claim that consolidating low-turnout polling places is purely a cost-saving measure [38]. However, 39 of the 159 counties in Georgia where polling places were closed have poverty rates above the state average and 30 of them served significant African American populations [22]. These closures would not have been permissible prior to 2013 under the Voting Rights Act's preclearance rule.

Under Secretary of State Kemp, over 1.4 million voter registrations were cancelled in "routine maintenance" of the voter rolls, eliminating those marked inactive according to the law. Kemp implemented the first "exact match" law in 2010 with preclearance from the federal government, requiring a name on a registration application to exactly match the voter's legal name. The law made it harder for voters whose registrations were removed to get back on the voter rolls. The law was dismantled after it was found unconstitutional in 2016 [32]. It was replaced in 2017 by a new exact match law. Any discrepancy between the name on the application and legal name—as innocuous as a missing hyphen—renders the registration "pending." Civil rights groups argue that, though they are eligible, having a pending application discourages people from voting. Over 53,000 voter registration applications were pending leading up to November 2018. Nearly 70% of pending applications were from Black voters, more than double the 32% Black population percentage in the state [18].

Kemp denies he has attempted to suppress minority voting, claiming that the decision to close a precinct is up to county election officials. However, in 2015 his office provided a document giving county officials guidance on why and how to close polling places [22]. Kemp blames the racial disparity in pending voter registration applications is on sloppy voter registration efforts and poorly trained canvassers, in particular the New Georgia Project, a voter registration group (founded by Kemp's gubernatorial opponent Stacey Abrams) that targeted African American voters and used primarily paper registration forms [18].

4   Georgia After HAVA

Georgia was the first state to adopt DREs statewide in the wake of HAVA: in November 2002, just days after HAVA was passed, the state signed a $54 million contract with Diebold Election Systems to use the AccuVote-TS/TSx DREs [43].

During the summer of 2002, Diebold began preparing more than 20,000 DREs to be used in Georgia for the November election. A former Diebold employee alleged that during this time, before the machines had been delivered to counties, employees were asked to install three software patches on all of the DREs that would be used statewide that year. These patches did not undergo the federal certification process for voting equipment [41]. Another former Diebold employee reported that the president of Diebold's election unit, Bob Urosevich, came to the warehouse himself to order the installation of uncertified software patches on about 5,000 machines used in DeKalb and Fulton, two historically Democratic counties [15].

This raised eyebrows when key contests in Georgia's 2002 election defied poll predictions. Longtime Democratic Senator Max Cleland was predicted to beat Republican opponent Saxby Chambliss by 3%, but in fact lost his seat by a 7% margin. Democratic incumbent Governor Roy Barnes was predicted to win 51% to 40%, but in fact lost to Republican candidate Sonny Perdue by 6% [8,24]. These Republican victories were a surprise in a historically Democratic state: Perdue was Georgia's first Republican governor in 130 years. There is no way to tell whether the outcome resulted from faulty programming or hacking, because the DREs left no paper trail.

Diebold has used political connections to ensure they remained the sole voting machine provider in Georgia. Former Secretary of State Cathy Cox, who signed the 2002 contract with Diebold, had strong ties to the company. The election director she appointed, Kathy Rogers, helped kill house bills that would have required paper records. In 2006, she resigned and took a job as Government Liaison at Diebold [6]. Cox's successor as Secretary of State, Karen Handel, started as a vocal supporter of paper trails and acknowledged publicly that she would not interact with Rogers as Diebold's liaison due to the conflict of interest. Later, Handel reversed her position on paper ballots, and the media revealed that she had received $25,000 in campaign contributions from employees connected with Diebold's lobbying firm, Massey and Bowers [37]. Members of the state government have ignored security experts who pointed out problems with Diebold's touchscreen machines.

Georgia's election security issues reach beyond voting machines. In 2016, a cybersecurity researcher at Oak Ridge National Laboratory, Logan Lamb, discovered that he could download files from the state's "secure" election server. Among these files were the entire voter registration database for the state of Georgia, including sensitive personal information, instructional PDFs with passwords for poll workers to sign into a central server on Election Day, and software files for the state's ExpressPoll pollbooks that are used to verify voters' eligibility [44]. This intrusion would have allowed Lamb to alter entries in the voter registration database or the pollbooks, preventing some voters from casting their ballots. Lamb's concern about malicious hacking was not a purely theoretical: an NSA investigation found that Russian hackers targeted 39 states in the summer and fall leading up to the 2016 presidential election [26].

These were not the only security concerns at the state's Center for Election Services (CES), housed at Kennesaw State University under a long-standing contract with the Secretary of State. For instance, CES was using an outdated version of their content management software, Drupal, which would allow hackers to seize control of their websites. A software patch had been available since 2014, but CES had not installed it. Lamb notified the executive director of CES, Merle King, of the problems; King agreed to fix them and allegedly pressed Lamb not to talk to the media or other officials about the security issues [42].

CES did not secure their server, nor did they inform anyone about Lamb's breach. In March 2017, another cybersecurity researcher found that CES still had not secured its files properly. The issue was elevated to authorities above King, and it was the first time that the Secretary of State's office heard about the breach. In response to this poor management, the Secretary of State office signed a new agreement with Kennesaw State University to transfer CES to its own offices [42].

In July 2017, state voters and The Coalition for Good Governance filed a lawsuit against Georgia Secretary of State Kemp, alleging that he had ignored evidence that the state's electoral system is vulnerable to fraud and hacking. The plaintiffs demanded that the state use paper ballots in future elections to guard against interference [34,35]. They requested to examine the CES servers at Kennesaw State University for evidence. Four days after the group filed the lawsuit, IT employees at CES wiped their servers of all prior election data. They later degaussed two remaining servers: key evidence was permanently erased. There is no proof that CES deliberately destroyed evidence, and the Secretary of State's office claims that the servers were wiped before they were officially served with the lawsuit in late July. However, Kemp's office was alerted about the lawsuit and declined to comment in the days between when the suit was filed and when the CES wiped its servers [27].

4.1 The November 2018 Election

The lawsuit, *Curling v. Kemp*, continued into September 2018, just before the midterm elections (and is ongoing at the time of writing). Testimony from the plaintiffs centered on two issues: security issues with DREs and the state's procedures and data handling before and after Election Day. The current director of CES testified that the server that each county uses to construct its ballots is "air-gapped" from the Internet, but that he uses thumb drives, email, and an online repository to store and move data—all of which expose voting systems to malware. A county official testified that they use analog phone lines to transmit results to the Secretary of State. Computer scientists have testified that these are all vulnerable channels [19].

The state's rebuttal did not seriously address the security concerns, but argued that there was not enough time before the election to switch to paper ballots. Kemp had convened the Secure, Accessible, & Fair Elections (SAFE) Commission in 2017 to select a new voting system in time for the 2020 election. Ultimately, U.S. District Judge Amy Totenberg ruled that the trade-off between election integrity and the feasibility of making changes before the impending election tipped in favor of continued use of DREs for the 2018 election. Judge Totenberg ruled that the plaintiffs provided sufficient evidence that DRE voting has the potential to cause irreparable harm to voters, but that the burden of switching to paper ballots so close to the election could cause even more harm to voters by causing bureaucratic confusion.

Ultimately, any chaos or problems that arise in connection with a sudden rollout of a paper ballot system with accompanying scanning equipment may swamp the polls with work and voters—and result in voter frustration and disaffection from the voting process. There is nothing like bureaucratic confusion and long lines to sour a citizen. And that description does not even touch on whether voters themselves, many of whom may never have cast a paper ballot before, will have been provided reasonable materials to prepare them for properly executing the paper ballots.

Judge Totenberg also noted that the evidence and testimony "indicated that the Defendants and State election officials had buried their heads in the sand" [34].

Secretary of State Kemp refused to recuse himself from overseeing the election in which he ran for Governor, a clear conflict of interest [39]. Election Day voting in November 2018 was conducted on paperless DREs. Machines in four polling places in Gwinnett County malfunctioned, forcing voters to use paper ballots, which caused some voters to wait four hours to cast their vote [16]. Reported vote totals were anomalous: the rate of undervotes in the Lieutenant Governor (LG) contest was unusually high compared to historical LG races and compared to other statewide contests on the ballot, and the undervote rate was far higher for DREs than for paper ballots. The Coalition for Good Governance brought another lawsuit against the Georgia Secretary of State, calling for a redo of the LG contest [29]. Statistical evidence of anomalies in this election, presented in that lawsuit, is discussed below in Sect. 5.

After the election, Kemp's office planned to certify the election results six days before state law required it, omitting nearly 27,000 provisional ballots. Provisional ballots are cast by voters whose registration or identification is in question; deliberately omitting provisional ballots is one way to disenfranchise voters. It would have ensured that the margin between Kemp and his opponent Stacey Abrams remained large enough to avoid a runoff election [4]. A civil rights group sued to delay the certification, and Judge Totenberg ruled against Kemp, ordering election officials to review the provisional ballots.

The SAFE Commission was scheduled to recommend a new voting system in January, 2019. In early January, the Democratic Party of Georgia called on Kemp to delay any decision to purchase new voting systems as more misbehavior came to light: now-Governor Kemp appointed Charles "Chuck" Harper, chief lobbyist for ES&S (the voting machine company that eventually acquired Diebold), as Deputy Chief of Staff in the Governor's office [23].

5   Evidence of Malfunctioning DREs in 2018

While the results of the controversial governor's race did not have obvious anomalies, the results of the LG race did. Shortly after the November 2018 election, The Coalition for Good Governance filed another lawsuit against the new Secretary of State, demanding a redo of the LG vote. The plaintiffs blamed malfunctioning DREs for an unusually high number of undervotes in the LG race, but not in others [29]. The judge overseeing the case initially agreed to let the plaintiffs examine the memory, but not the programming, of machines in three counties. She eventually dissolved this agreement and dismissed the case [45].

The plaintiffs did not specify the cause of the malfunction—faulty programming, poor electronic ballot design, hacking, or something else [29]. Numerous voters reported irregularities when attempting to cast their vote for LG on DREs, including many who reported that the race did not appear on their ballot until they were shown the review screen. Without forensic evidence, it is impossible to determine exactly what happened.

This section gives three lines of statistical evidence that DREs did not record every vote properly in this election. First, in 101 of Georgia's 159 counties, the rate of undervotes in the LG race was much higher among DRE votes (those cast on Election Day and advance in-person) than on (paper) absentee ballots. (For other statewide contests, the undervote rates are similar across modes of voting in nearly all counties.) Second, in Fulton County, higher differential undervote rates tended to occur in precincts where a larger percentage of registered voters were Black. Third, on six of seven machines in the Winterville Train Depot polling place in Clarke County, Democrats got the majority of votes in every statewide contest, matching the overall results at the polling place. On the seventh machine, Republican candidates got a majority in every statewide contest.

Permutation tests show that these three anomalies are implausible unless something went wrong. Permutation tests require a minimum of assumptions, which can make them appropriate and convincing in situations where standard parametric tests require unrealistic or counterfactual assumptions, for instance, assumptions that voter preferences follow a parametric model, such as multinomial logistic. In contrast, the permutation tests we use treat one characteristic, such as the mode by which a ballot containing an undervote was cast or the machine on which a ballot was cast, as an arbitrary label that might as well have been assigned at random. Software implementing the tests reported here can be found at https://github.com/pbstark/EvoteID19-GA.

5.1   Undervotes for Lieutenant Governor

Undervotes occur when a voter selects fewer candidates in a contest than the contest rules allow, for instance, not voting for any candidate in a winner-take-all contest. The rate of undervotes tends to increase for "down-ticket" contests compared to major contests such as presidential and gubernatorial contests. In Georgia in 2018, the LG race had a 4% undervote rate, while the next contest on the ballot had an undervote rate of 1.4%. Moreover, this pattern appeared only in votes cast on DREs—Election Day votes and advance in-person votes.

Data were downloaded from Clarity Elections, the private sector vendor that reports official election results on behalf of the Georgia Secretary of State.[2,3] Data included the total number of ballots cast in each county and the number cast by each mode of voting (e.g. by mail) for each candidate by county. The file

---

[2] The fact that this crucial election function is outsourced without oversight might give the reader pause.
[3] https://results.enr.clarityelections.com/GA/91639/222278/reports/detailxml.zip, downloaded in January 2019.

did not report ballots cast in each county by mode of voting. In order to calculate the number of undervotes, we assumed that the total number of ballots cast by county and mode of voting equalled the maximum number of votes cast in *any* contest for that county and mode of voting.

While political preferences might differ systematically between voters who vote by mail (on paper) and those who vote in person (on DREs), there is no reason to think that interest in a *contest* should differ across those groups. The usability literature suggests that DREs ought to help people of disparate education and ethnicities vote correctly, in which case, the undervote rate on DREs should be *lower* than the rate for paper ballots [31]. If so, then it is reasonable to treat the mode of voting as a label assigned randomly to ballots in such a way that the number of ballots cast on DREs and the number cast on paper is fixed (conditioned to be equal to the actual numbers). The number of undervotes in a contest among DRE votes then has a hypergeometric distribution. Under the alternative that undervotes are more likely on DREs, we would expect to see more undervotes on DREs (and fewer on paper ballots) than the hypergeometric distribution predicts.

In 101 of 159 Georgia counties, the difference in undervote rates between mail votes and DRE votes in the LG race is statistically significant at level 0.01%. In contrast, in the 8 statewide contests further down the ballot, the difference is statistically significant in no more than 5 counties. Table 1 shows the counts.

Table 1. Counties with statistically significant ($p < 0.0001$) disparities in undervote rates between paper ballots and DREs.

Contest	Counties with significant undervote rate disparities
Lt. Governor	101
Secretary of State	4
Attorney General	4
Commissioner of Agriculture	5
Commissioner of Insurance	4
State School Superintendent	5
Commissioner of Labor	2
Public Service Commission District 3	4
Public Service Commission District 5	4

5.2   Undervotes and Race in Fulton County

Undervote rates on touchscreen voting machines were reported to be higher in predominantly Black precincts across the state [10]. If so, that is evidence that security and usability issues with DREs disparately impact historically disadvantaged groups. We investigated this issue in Fulton County, which includes most of the capital, Atlanta, and had over 424,000 voters in November 2018.

Precinct-level reported vote totals were downloaded from the Clarity Election site that reports official results for the Georgia Secretary of State.[4] Data included total votes cast for each candidate by each mode of voting, in each precinct within Fulton County. As with the statewide data, we estimated the number of undervotes by subtracting the votes from the maximum number of votes in any contest, by mode of voting and precinct.

Voter turnout data were downloaded from the Secretary of State's website.[5] From these data, we computed the percentage of registered voters who were Black in each precinct.

A permutation test was used to assess the correlation between the difference in undervote rates between voters who used paper ballots and voters who voted electronically and the percentage of registered voters who were Black. Of the 373 precincts in Fulton County, we restricted analysis to the 302 precincts in which at least 10 people voted electronically and at least 10 voted on paper.

The undervote rate was substantially lower for voters who used paper ballots than for voters who voted electronically, by an amount that—on average—was larger in precincts with a larger percentage of Black registered voters. Table 2 shows the correlation between the difference in undervote rates and the percentage of registered voters who are Black. p-values are for randomized permutation tests with 10,000 replications, carried out using the Python **permute** package.[6] Small p-values for multiple statewide contests could explained by voter behavior; prior research suggests that Black voters may intentionally undervote at a higher rate than other voters, and may cast valid votes at a rate that is lower than the rate for the general electorate [11,31]. However, it is notable that the correlation for the Lieutenant Governor's contest is more than twice what it is for any other contest.

5.3 Party Preferences in Winterville Train Depot Polling Place

A citizen photographed printed poll tapes from the seven DRE machines in the Winterville Train Depot polling place in Clarke County. The photographs were transcribed to CSV and double checked by a second person.[7]

The Winterville Train Depot polling place is just one polling place in Georgia where a member of the public photographed poll tapes posted at the precinct after the polls closed. It was not selected at random, but neither was there particular reason to suspect problems there. There is no reason to believe that problems are confined to this polling place—where then-Secretary of State Kemp himself voted—but even if they were, any anomaly is of concern.

The DREs in the precinct recorded comparable numbers of voters (117, 135, 131, 133, 135, 144, 135). In this polling place, Democratic candidates won a

[4] https://results.enr.clarityelections.com/GA/Fulton/91700/221530/reports/detailxml.zip, downloaded in January 2019.
[5] http://sos.ga.gov/admin/uploads/PRECINCT_Nov_2018.zip, downloaded in January 2019.
[6] http://statlab.github.io/permute.
[7] The data were submitted as evidence in [29].

Table 2. Correlation between the difference in undervote rates and percentage of registered voters who are Black, for the 10 statewide contests in Georgia in November 2018, in Fulton County.

Contest	Correlation	p-value
Governor	−0.134	0.9903
Lt. Governor	0.557	0.0001
Secretary of State	0.092	0.0582
Attorney General	0.078	0.0902
Commissioner of Agriculture	0.207	0.0003
Commissioner of Insurance	0.246	0.0001
State School Superintendent	0.154	0.0050
Commissioner of Labor	0.041	0.2376
Public Service Commission District 3	0.042	0.2329
Public Service Commission District 5	0.125	0.0145

majority in all ten statewide contests. Every DRE reported a majority of votes for the Democratic candidate in every statewide contest except machine 3, which reported a majority for the Republican candidate in every statewide contest.

If voters were directed to DREs as if at random, then the number of voters who used different machines should be roughly equal, as should the percentage of votes for each candidate. Conditional on the number of ballots on each machine and the total number of votes for each candidate across machines, all permutations of votes across machines are equally likely under the null hypothesis. We performed a two-sided permutation test using the difference between the expected and actual fraction of Republican votes in each contest as the test statistic. Permutations were done using the `cryptorandom` pseudo-random number generator for Python[8]. The p-values for different contests were combined using Fisher's combination function to obtain a global p-value on the assumption that the distribution of Fisher's combining function under the null hypothesis is chi-square. That would be true if votes in different contests were independent; however, voters tend to vote along party lines. If ballot-level data were available, Fisher's combining function could be calibrated to take that correlation into account. However, the poll tapes give only totals by contest. Hence, while p-values for individual contests are on a firm statistical footing, the global p-value should be viewed as suggestive rather than precise.

On the assumption that voters were directed to DREs as if at random, the chance any of the seven machines would show disparities as large as machine 3 did in individual contests ranges from less than 1% to approximately 15%.

---

[8] http://statlab.github.io/cryptorandom.

Seven of the ten values are significant at level 5% or below; see Table 3. The global p-value for the ten tests is 0.00009%.[9]

Table 3. Consistency of results across DREs in Winterville Train Station Polling Place and consistency of results if D and R were flipped on machine 3.

Contest	p-value	p-value if machine 3 were flipped
Governor	0.114	0.464
Lt. Governor	0.025	0.795
Secretary of State	0.018	0.450
Attorney General	0.151	0.543
Commissioner of Agriculture	0.026	0.734
Commissioner of Insurance	0.030	0.604
State School Superintendent	0.097	0.807
Commissioner of Labor	0.008	0.797
Public Service Commission District 3	0.046	0.280
Public Service Commission District 5	0.025	0.939

These results are entirely driven by the results on machine 3. If the Democratic and Republican party labels were flipped on that machine, the anomaly disappears, and the global p-value for the ten contests becomes 97%. For individual contests, no p-value is then below 0.280, compared with values as small as 0.008 (and seven values below 5%) for the actual poll tapes. See Table 3.

These tests strongly suggest that machine 3 had some software or hardware problem: misconfiguration, error, defect, hack, or malfunction. The most plausible explanation is that misconfiguration caused votes for Republican candidates to be recorded as votes for Democratic candidates, and vice versa.

6   Conclusion

The 2018 midterms demonstrated that election integrity in Georgia remains fraught. In the weeks leading up to the election and for weeks after, citizens challenged the Secretary of State's treatment of provisional ballots and voter registrations, alleging that these practices were intended to disenfranchise minority voters. Touchscreen DRE voting machines were used statewide, even after security experts voiced their concerns and a nonprofit organization sued the state to replace DREs with hand-marked paper ballots. There is evidence that some DREs malfunctioned in the election; statistical anomalies suggest that DREs

---

[9] As mentioned above, the assumptions under which Fisher's combining function has a chi-square distribution may not hold, so the global p-value should be viewed as suggestive.

failed to record a large percentage of votes cast in the Lieutenant Governor's race, and that "missing votes" were more frequent in jurisdictions with large African American populations [10]. The Secretary of State has refused to investigate these issues. Some particular anomalies (i.e., the Winterville Train Depot data) are most easily explained by "vote flipping," in which the DRE recorded votes for one candidate as votes for the candidate's opponent.

Lawmakers are poised to replace the state's DREs with a new system: either hand-marked paper ballots with optical scanners, using touchscreen ballot-marking devices (BMDs) for accessibility, or BMDs for all voters. In February 2019, the state legislature voted to purchase BMDs statewide [21]. While BMDs do produce a paper record, they are more expensive than opscan systems,[10] and they are neither as reliable nor as secure as hand-marked paper ballots and opscan systems. Among other issues, BMD malfunctions can prevent voting on Election Day; inadequate provisioning of equipment can produce long lines; there is evidence that voters cannot and do not reliably verify their BMD selections; and BMDs require the same trust in software as DREs, with no practical recourse if machines malfunction and little possibility that outcome-changing errors will be detected [1,28]. The SAFE Commission's only security expert, Prof. Wenke Lee, warned against BMDs.

House Minority Leader Bob Trammell expressed his stance on the evidence for hand-marked paper ballots [21]:

> It's unequivocally clear that cybersecurity experts have expressed concerns about the ballot-marking devices. It comes down to whether you think the opinion of election officials ... is more important than the issue of credentialed experts in the field talking about a material risk to the voting process.

Acknowledgements. We are grateful to Marilyn Marks and Jordan Wilkie for helpful conversations and suggestions.

References

1. Appel, A., DeMillo, R., Stark, P.B.: Ballot-marking devices (BMDs) cannot assure the will of the voters. Social Science Research Network (2019)
2. Blaze, M., Braun, J., Hursti, H., Hall, J.L., MacAlpine, M., Moss, J.: DEFCON 25 voting village report. Technical report, DEFCON (2017). https://www.defcon.org/images/defcon-25/DEFCON%2025%20voting%20village%20report.pdf
3. Blaze, M., Braun, J., Hursti, H., Jefferson, D., MacAlpine, M., Moss, J.: DEFCON 26 voting village report. Technical report, DEFCON (2018). https://www.defcon.org/images/defcon-26/DEF%20CON%2026%20voting%20village%20report.pdf
4. Blinder, A.: Federal judge delays certification of Georgia election results. The New York Times (2018). https://nyti.ms/2DiWDzx

---

[10] The State of Georgia has claimed otherwise, but their analysis was deeply flawed, omitting costs associated with BMDs and overstating the cost of printing ballots, among other things. See [25].

5. Bowen, D.: Top-to-bottom review of voting machines certified for use in California. Technical report, California Secretary of State (2007). https://www.sos.ca.gov/elections/voting-systems/oversight/top-bottom-review/
6. Chronicle, T.A.: Voting machine maker hires former state election chief. The Augusta Chronicle (2006). https://www.augustachronicle.com/article/20061224/NEWS/312249946
7. Everett, S.P.: The usability of electronic voting machines and how votes can be changed without detection. Ph.D. thesis, Rice University, Houston, Texas (2007). https://scholarship.rice.edu/handle/1911/20601
8. Freeman, S.F., Bleifuss, J.: Was the 2004 Presidental Election Stolen?: Exit Polls, Election Fraud, and the Official Count. Seven Stories Press, New York (2006)
9. Harnik, A., Press, A.: Officials scrap plan to cut most polling places in majority black GA County. WABE (2018). https://www.wabe.org/officials-scrap-plan-to-cut-most-polling-places-in-majority-black-ga-county/
10. Harriot, M.: Thousands of black votes in Georgia disappeared. The Root (2019). https://www.theroot.com/exclusive-thousands-of-black-votes-in-georgia-disappea-1832472558
11. Herron, M.C., Sekhon, J.S.: Overvoting and representation: an examination of over-voted presidential ballots in Broward and Miami-Dade counties. Electoral. Stud. **22**(1), 21–47 (2003)
12. Hursti, H.: Critical security issues with Diebold optical scan design. Technical report, Black Box Voting (2005)
13. Hursti, H.: Critical security issues with Diebold TSx. Technical report, Black Box Voting (2006)
14. Jones, D.W., Simons, B.: Broken Ballots: Will Your Vote Count? CSLI Publications, Stanford (2012)
15. Kennedy, R.J.: Will the next election be hacked? electronic voting machines can't be trusted. Rolling Stone (2006). https://www.organicconsumers.org/news/robert-kennedy-jr-will-next-election-be-hacked-electronic-voting-machines-cant-be-trusted
16. Lockhart, P.R.: Voting hours in parts of Georgia extended after technical errors create long lines. Vox (2018). https://www.vox.com/policy-and-politics/2018/11/6/18068492/georgia-voting-gwinnett-fulton-county-machine-problems-midterm-election-extension
17. McDaniel, P., Blaze, M., Vigna, G.: EVEREST: evaluation and validation of election-related equipment, standards and testing. Technical report, Ohio Secretary of State (2007). http://siis.cse.psu.edu/everest.html
18. Nadler, B.: Voting rights become a flashpoint in Georgia governor's race. AP News (2018). https://apnews.com/fb011f39af3b40518b572c8cce6e906c
19. Nakashima, E.. In Georgia, a legal battle over electronic vs. paper voting. The Washington Post (2018). https://wapo.st/2QADbm8
20. National Institute of Standards and Technology Auditability Working Group: Report of the auditability working group. Technical report, NIST (2015). https://www.eac.gov/assets/1/28/AuditabilityReport_final_January_2011.pdf
21. Niesse, M.: Bill to buy new Georgia voting machines clears committees. The Atlanta Journal-Constitution (2019). https://www.myajc.com/news/state-regional-govt-politics/new-georgia-voting-machines-approved-house-committee/avz21tiapWPwM1Qx4bq3AP/

22. Niesse, M., Prabhu, M.T., Elias, J.: Voting precincts closed across Georgia since election oversight lifted. The Atlanta Journal-Constitution (2018). https://www. myajc.com/news/state-regional-govt-politics/voting-precincts-closed-across-georgia-since-election-oversight-lifted/bBkHxptlim0Gp9pKu7dfrN/
23. Party, G.D.: Breaking: democratic party of Georgia calls on SAFE commission to delay vote following news that voting machine Lobbyist is Longtime Kemp Crony (2019). https://www.georgiademocrat.org/2019/01/breaking-democratic-party-of-georgia-calls-on-safe-commission-to-delay-vote-following-news-that-voting-machine-lobbyist-is-longtime-kemp-crony/
24. Peha, J.: Touch-and-go elections: the perils of electronic voting. The Nation (2006). https://www.thenation.com/article/touch-and-go-elections-perils-electronic-voting/
25. Perez, E., Miller, G.A.: Georgia state election technology acquisition: a reality check. Technical report, OSET Institute (2018)
26. Riley, M., Robertson, J.: Russian hacks on U.S. voting system wider than previously known. Bloomberg (2017). https://www.bloomberg.com/news/articles/2017-06-13/russian-breach-of-39-states-threatens-future-u-s-elections
27. Stahl, J.: Georgia destroyed election data right after a lawsuit alleged its voting system was a mess. Why? Slate Magazine (2017). https://slate.com/technology/2017/10/georgia-destroyed-election-data-right-after-a-lawsuit-alleged-the-system-was-vulnerable.html
28. Stark, P.B.: Ballot-marking devices (BMDs) are not secure election technology (2019). https://www.stat.berkeley.edu/~stark/Preprints/bmd19.pdf
29. Superior Court of Fulton County, State of Georgia: Coalition for Good Governance, Martin, Duval, and Dufort v. Crittenden, 2018-CV-3134-18 (2019)
30. Supreme Court of the United States: Shelby County v. Holder, pp. 12–96 (2013)
31. Tomz, M., van Houweling, R.P.: How does voting equipment affect the racial gap in voided ballots? Am. J. Polit. Sci. **47**(1), 46–60 (2003)
32. Torres, K.: Federal lawsuit alleges Georgia blocked thousands of minority voters. The Atlanta Journal-Constitution (2016). https://www.myajc.com/news/state-regional-govt-politics/federal-lawsuit-alleges-georgia-blocked-thousands-minority-voters/EKb979oRoBe4yJ3Uo1nDfP/
33. Torres, R.: Report concerning the examination results of election systems and software EVS 6021 with DS200 precinct scanner, DS450 and DS850 central scanners, ExpressVote HW 2.1 marker and tabulator, ExpressVote XL tabulator and electionware EMS. Technical report, Commonwealth of Pennsylvania Department of State (2018)
34. United States District Court for the Northern District of Georgia, Atlanta Division: Curling v. Kemp, 1:17-CV-2989-AT (Order Denying Motion to Dismiss) (2018)
35. United States District Court for the Northern District of Georgia, Atlanta Division: Curling v. Kemp (2018)
36. Vasilogambros, M.: Polling places remain a target ahead of November elections. Stateline (2018). https://pew.org/2MCsiBT
37. Voters organized for trusted election results in Georgia: Georgia unverifiable voting system chronology. VOTER GA (2014). https://voterga.org/history/
38. Whitesides, J.: Polling places become battleground in U.S. voting rights fight. Reuters (2016). http://reut.rs/2cKzOaZ
39. Williams, V.: Georgia groups call on GOP gubernatorial nominee Brian Kemp to step down as the state's elections chief. The Washington Post (2018). https://wapo.st/2MrHZHP

40. Wofford, B.: How to Hack an Election in 7 minutes. POLITICO magazine (2016). https://politi.co/2K2OGOv
41. Zetter, K.: Did e-vote firm patch election? Wired (2003). https://www.wired.com/2003/10/did-e-vote-firm-patch-election/
42. Zetter, K.: Will the Georgia special election get hacked? POLITICO magazine (2017). http://politi.co/2heBRW2
43. Zetter, K.: The crisis of election security. The New York Times (2018). https://nyti.ms/2N3hoAh
44. Zetter, K.: Was Georgia's election system hacked in 2016? POLITICO magazine (2018). https://politi.co/2moAWUS
45. Zetter, K.: Georgia voting irregularities raise more troubling questions about the state's elections. POLITICO (2019). https://politi.co/2SOlvas

Risk-Limiting Tallies

Wojciech Jamroga[1,2], Peter B. Roenne[1], Peter Y. A. Ryan[1(✉)],
and Philip B. Stark[3]

[1] Interdisciplinary Centre for Security, Reliability, and Trust, SnT,
University of Luxembourg, Luxembourg, Luxembourg
{wojciech.jamroga,peter.roenne,peter.ryan}@uni.lu
[2] Institute of Computer Science, Polish Academy of Sciences, Warsaw, Poland
[3] Department of Statistics, University of California, Berkeley, California, USA
stark@stat.berkeley.edu

Abstract. Many voter-verifiable, coercion-resistant schemes have been
proposed, but even the most carefully designed systems necessarily leak
information via the announced result. In corner cases, this may be problematic. For example, if all the votes go to one candidate then all vote
privacy evaporates. The mere possibility of candidates getting no or
few votes could have implications for security in practice: if a coercer
demands that a voter cast a vote for such an unpopular candidate, then
the voter may feel obliged to obey, even if she is confident that the voting system satisfies the standard coercion resistance definitions. With
complex ballots, there may also be a danger of "Italian" style (aka "signature") attacks: the coercer demands the voter cast a ballot with a
specific, identifying pattern.

Here we propose an approach to tallying end-to-end verifiable schemes
that avoids revealing all the votes but still achieves whatever confidence
level in the announced result is desired. Now a coerced voter can claim
that the required vote must be amongst those that remained shrouded.
Our approach is based on the well-established notion of Risk-Limiting
Audits, but here applied to the tally rather than to the audit. We show
that this approach counters coercion threats arising in extreme tallies
and "Italian" attacks. We illustrate our approach by applying it to the
Selene scheme, and we extend the approach to Risk-Limiting Verification,
where not all vote trackers are revealed, thereby enhancing the coercion
mitigation properties of Selene.

Keywords: End-to-end verifiability · Risk-limiting audits ·
Plausible deniability · Coercion resistance

1 Introduction

Many verifiable voting schemes have been proposed that are designed to give a
high level of resistance against coercion or vote buying [4,8,12,20,22]. However,
it is typically assumed that little can be done about coercion threats in case

© Springer Nature Switzerland AG 2019
R. Krimmer et al. (Eds.): E-Vote-ID 2019, LNCS 11759, pp. 183–199, 2019.
https://doi.org/10.1007/978-3-030-30625-0_12

of extreme outcomes, e.g., no or few votes for some candidates. Unfortunately, such situations do happen in real elections. If there is a (perceived) risk that candidate X will get no votes, and the coercer tells the voter to vote for X, then the voter may feel obliged to comply even if the voting scheme satisfies the standard definitions of coercion resistance. The possibility is more dangerous than it seems at the first glance. True, coercing for the low support candidate X is unlikely to get him or her win. However, the coercer can use X to construct what is effectively an abstention attack, and take away the votes from the main opponent of his preferred candidate. If the coercer prefers candidate A, he can help him win by coercing supporters of B to vote for X.

Another difficulty that may arise is that of so-called "Italian"-style attacks, also known as "signature" attacks: if the voting method allows for a large number of distinct ways of filling out the ballot, a coercer may require the voter to fill out the ballot with a distinctive pattern allowing it to be uniquely identified with high probability in the final tally. This is especially an issue with long, complex ballots and with preferential voting schemes. It can be countered by, for example, using homomorphic tallying techniques to compute the overall result without revealing the individual ballots, but this is computationally intensive and even then may leak some critical information [27].

Here, we show that risk-limiting audit techniques [16] can be adapted to achieve whatever level of confidence in the outcome is required while ensuring that a proportion of the ballots remain shrouded. This allows us to significantly enhance the coercion resistance of verifiable schemes. The Risk Limiting Tally (RLT) approach that we present here provides a simple way to guarantee voters plausible deniability against the above attacks: a coerced voter, who did not cast the ballot the way the coercer had demanded, can simply claim that the required ballot is amongst those unrevealed.

We also present a variant of the idea, *Risk Limiting Verification* (RLV), where we ensure that a proportion of verification tokens remain unrevealed. The basic version of the Selene scheme [20] has the drawback that the coercer can claim that the fake tracker provided by a voter is his own. We describe how RLV mitigates this.

A possible objection to RLT is that it is "undemocractic" not to count all votes. However, the method allows the electoral outcome (i.e. the winner or winners) to be ascertained to any desired level of statistical certainty. Moreover, the sample of ballots will be drawn in such a way that every cast vote has an equal chance of being in the revealed sample, so there is no lack of fairness. RLTs are related to *random sample voting* (RSV), due to Chaum [7], except that there the sample is drawn from the set of eligible voters, rather than from the cast votes. If anything, RLTs seem to be more democratic in that in RSV voters who are not chosen might well feel excluded. Furthermore, in RLTs we are able to adjust the sample size after voting to achieve the desired confidence level. We note also that some tally algorithms, e.g. some forms of STV, intrinsically involve a probabilistic element.

The outline of this paper is as follows. In Sect. 2 we discuss coercion-resistant and verifiable voting schemes in general, and Selene in particular. Section 3 briefly recalls Risk-Limiting Audits, and Sect. 4 introduces the techniques for RLTs. We present the actual protocol in Sect. 5, and a brief security discussion in Sect. 6. Section 7 discusses the risk-limiting verification. Related work is presented in Sect. 8, and we conclude in Sect. 9.

1.1 Contribution

In this paper we present several contributions:

1. The use of using risk-limiting techniques to shroud a proportion of votes, improving coercion resistance while achieving whatever confidence level is required.
2. A novel extension of Risk-Limiting Audit (RLA) techniques to handle the situation in which we do not have an initial null hypothesis (reported outcome).
3. A new test statistic for RLAs with operating characteristics that do not depend on the reported votes, only on the reported winner(s).
4. Protocols to enable RLT for most end-to-end verifiable schemes, including strategies to ensure plausible deniability whatever the vote distribution is.
5. Extension of the approach to Risk-Limiting Verification: the shrouding of a randomly selected subset of verification tokens to improve coercion resistance, in particular for the Selene scheme.

2 Coercion-Resistant and Verifiable Voting

We set the scene by recalling the concepts of End-to-End Verifiability [21] and coercion-resistance [4,12], and showing an example scheme designed to balance the two requirements.

2.1 An Outline of End-to-End Verifiable Voting

The use of digital technologies to record and process votes might provide efficiency and convenience, but it can also bring serious new threats, in particular, virtually undetectable ways to manipulate votes on a large scale. These concerns motivated the development of *End-to-End Verifiable* (E2E V) voting schemes. Such schemes provide the voters with means to confirm that their vote is accurately included in the tally, without opening up possibilities of coercion or vote-buying. This is usually accomplished by creating an encryption of the vote at the time of casting, and posting this to a public *Bulletin Board* (*BB*). Voters can then confirm that their "receipt," i.e., the encrypted vote, appears correctly on the *BB*.

Once we have consensus on the correct set of encrypted votes, these can be processed in a verifiable fashion to calculate the outcome in a way that does not compromise the privacy of the votes. For instance, the encrypted votes might be put through a sequence of verifiable re-encryption mixes and then verifiably decrypted, allowing anyone to compute the result. Alternatively, the encrypted votes might be tallied under encryption, exploiting the homomorphic properties of the encryption algorithm, and the final result decrypted. To complete the assurance argument we need some additional ingredients:

- The voter needs to be confident that her intended vote is correctly encrypted in her receipt.
- We need to prevent ballot stuffing, i.e., we need to ensure that only legitimately cast votes appear in the list of receipts on the *BB*, and only one per voter.
- We need to know that "enough" voters check that their intended votes are correctly encrypted, and that their encrypted votes appear on *BB*.
- We need dispute-resolution mechanisms in place to ensure that if voters detect (or claim to detect) problems, the culprit can be identified and appropriate action taken.

Typically the first point is addressed by some form of cut-and-chose protocol, e.g. *Benaloh Challenge* [5], or a more sophisticated approach such as Neff's *MarkPledge* scheme [2]. Ballot stuffing is usually countered either by procedural measures in the polling station, or by requiring that receipts be digitally signed by the voters. The former does not provide *universal eligibility verifiability* while the latter can but requires infrastructure to equip voters with signing keys.

We will not delve deeper into how the various E2E V schemes work but rather assume that the correct set of encrypted votes is posted to the *Bulletin Board*.

2.2   Ballot Privacy, Receipt-Freeness and Coercion Resistance

Ballot privacy is often defined using anonymity style definitions as originally proposed in [23]. Informally, consider two instances of the system, one in which A votes for X and B for Y, and the other in which the votes are swapped. If the attacker is unable to distinguish these two instances then the system is deemed to satisfy *ballot privacy*. More formal definitions can be found, for example, in [10]. Note that even in extreme cases, for example when all voters vote for X, such a system will satisfy the above definition, even though in that case the attacker knows precisely how each voter voted.

It was later realised that simple notions of ballot privacy in the presence of a passive attacker are not enough. For E2E V schemes we have to worry about ways that the voter might be able to prove her vote to a third party. This motivates the requirement for *receipt-freeness* [4]: the voter cannot acquire evidence that would enable her to construct a proof to a third party as to how she voted.

In the face of a yet more active attacker who might interact with the voter before, during and after voting, potentially issuing detailed instructions and requiring the voter to reveal credentials, ephemeral random values etc, we need even stronger notions. This threat model motivates the property of *coercion resistance* for which many different definitions have been proposed [12], reflecting various subtle distinctions. We will adopt the following definition, informally stated:

> A voting system S is coercion resistant if, for all $c \in C$ there exists a voter strategy ψ such that for all attacker strategies ϕ, the voter can cast her intended vote c and the attacker cannot tell that she did not obey his instructions.

Such a style of definition appears to be the most powerful in that it captures the privacy failure in the case of unanimous votes, forced abstention and randomisation attacks.

2.3 Selene

We now give a sketch of how voter-verification is achieved in the Selene voting protocol. Full details can be found in [20]. In Selene, the verification is much more direct and intuitive than is the case for conventional E2E V systems: rather than checking for the presence of her encrypted vote on the BB, the voter checks her vote in cleartext in the tally on the BB identified by a secret, deniable tracker.

During the setup phase the set of distinct trackers are posted on the BB, verifiably encrypted and mixed and then assigned to the voters according the resulting secret permutation. This ensures that each voter is assigned a unique, secret tracker.

For each encrypted tracker, a trapdoor commitment is created for which the voter holds the secret trapdoor key. In essence this is the "β" term of an El Gamal encryption of the tracker, where the "α" term is kept secret for the moment.

Voting is as usual: an encryption of the vote is created, and sent to the server for posting to the BB against the voter (pseudo)Id. Once we are happy that we have the correct set of validly cast, encrypted votes, we can proceed to tabulation: the (encrypted vote, tracker) pairs are put through verifiable, parallel re-encryption mixes and decrypted, revealing the vote/tracker pairs in plaintext.

Later, the α terms are sent via an untappable channel to the voters to enable them to open the commitment using their secret, trapdoor key. If coerced, the voter can generate a fake α that will open her commitment to an alternative tracker pointing to the coercer's choice. With the trapdoor, creating such a fake α is computationally straightforward. On the other hand, computing a fake α that will open the commitment to a given, valid tracker is intractable without the trapdoor. Thus, assuming that the voter's trapdoor is not compromised, the α term is implicitly authenticated by the fact that it opens to a valid tracker.

3 Risk-Limiting Audits

A *risk-limiting audit* (RLA) [16] of a reported election outcome is any procedure that has a known minimum chance of correcting the reported outcome if the outcome is wrong (and that cannot render a correct outcome incorrect).

In this case, the *outcome* means the winner or winners, not the precise tally. The reported outcome is *correct* if it is the outcome that an accurate manual tally of the underlying voter-verified records would show.[1] The maximal chance that the procedure will fail to correct an outcome that is wrong is the *risk limit*.

RLAs generally pose auditing as a sequential test of the hypothesis that the reported outcome is incorrect. The audit continues to examine more ballots until either the hypothesis is rejected or the audit has conducted a full manual tally. The use of sequential tests enables RLAs to stop as soon as there is convincing evidence that the reported outcome is correct, reducing the number of ballots the audit inspects.

RLAs check reported outcomes while RLTs determine what outcomes to report. However, similar sequential testing methods can allow RLTs to stop the tally (of a random permutation of the ballots) as soon as there is convincing statistical evidence of the electoral outcome, which the RLT then reports. A RLT declares "either this is the correct outcome, or an event occurred that had probability no larger than α," where $\alpha \in (0,1)$ is any pre-specified risk limit. Minimizing the number of ballots that must be tallied maximizes the number of ballots kept shrouded, improving privacy and coercion-resistance.

There are two general strategies for RLAs: *ballot-polling* and *comparison*. Ballot-polling manually examines randomly selected ballots for evidence of who won. A comparison audit has three steps: first, the voting system must commit to its interpretation of physically identifiable individual ballots or groups of ballots comprising all ballots validly cast in the election. Second, auditors check that the exported data reproduces the reported results. Third, auditors compare the manual interpretation of a random sample of ballots or groups of ballots to the voting system's interpretation. Further, "hybrid" methods combine ballot-polling for some groups of ballots and comparisons for other groups; see [18].

Comparison audits require auditors to know how the equipment interpreted the ballots, so they are not suitable for RLTs, where we seek evidence about who won just from a subset of the shrouded votes. Below, we show how a new procedure for ballot-polling RLAs can be adapted for RLTs.

4   Risk-Limiting Tallies

We propose a simple modification of the way that votes are tallied to address the issues outlined in the introduction. Rather than tallying all votes straight-off, the election authority reveals the votes for a random sequence of encrypted ballots, continuing until the sample gives the acceptable level of risk in the outcome (i.e., who won). If the true margin of victory is not too small, the outcome can be determined with high confidence (i.e., low risk) while leaving a substantial number of ballots unopened, thus allowing a voter to claim that they cast the ballot required by the coercer even if such a ballot was not revealed during

---

[1] The trustworthiness of the underlying records should be assessed by a *compliance audit* [25]. A RLA that relies on an untrustworthy record cannot reliably assess whether outcomes reflect how voters voted.

the partial tally. The approach is thus inspired by the idea of Risk-Limiting Audits (RLAs), [16,24], but here we apply the approach to determining the correct outcome rather than checking whether a reported outcome is correct. That difference turns out to have surprising statistical implications; in particular, larger sample sizes are generally required to control the risk to the same level.

RLAs test the null hypothesis that the reported winner(s) did not actually win, rather than determine the correct outcome *ab initio*. Moreover, the operating characteristics of existing RLAs depend on the reported results. For instance, *comparison audits* test whether the reported margin overstated the true margin by enough to cause the reported winners to be incorrect. Previous methods for *ballot-polling* audits, such as BRAVO [15] test the hypothesis that the reported outcome is wrong against the alternative that the reported vote shares are nearly correct.

For RLTs, we do not have reported results to leverage, so we need a new approach. Section 4.1 presents a probability inequality; Sect. 4.2 applies it to produce a new sequential ballot-polling test, the engine for the RLT scheme presented in Sect. 5 based on the Selene E2E V protocol.

4.1   Tests for the Mean of a Non-negative Population

Extant methods for RLAs generally involve the reported results in some way. Here, we present a new sequential method to determine with high confidence who won, without specifying a particular alternative hypothesis. The method applies to plurality (including vote-for-k), majority, and super-majority social choice functions, but we present the method in detail only for plurality contests.

Our RLT method is based on tests about the mean of a non-negative population. Consider a population of N items, each labeled with a non-negative number.[2] Let $x_i \geq 0$ be the label of item i, $i = 1, \ldots, N$. Let $\mu \equiv \frac{1}{N} \sum_{i=1}^{N} x_i$ be the mean of the labels. Moreover, let t denote the hypothesized value of the population mean μ.

We sample items at random, sequentially, without replacement, such that the (conditional) probability that item k is selected in the jth draw is $\frac{1}{N-j+1}$, given that item k was not selected before the jth draw. X_j denotes the number on the label of the item selected on the jth draw. Define $S_j \equiv \sum_{k=1}^{j} X_k$, $\tilde{S}_j \equiv S_j/N$, and $\tilde{j} \equiv 1 - (j-1)/N$. Let

$$Y_n \equiv \int_0^1 \prod_{j=1}^{n} \left(\gamma \left[X_j \frac{\tilde{j}}{t - \tilde{S}_{j-1}} - 1 \right] + 1 \right) d\gamma. \tag{1}$$

It has been shown in [11] that if $\mu = t$ (i.e., if the null hypothesis is true), then $(Y_j)_{j=1}^{N}$ is a nonnegative closed martingale with expected value 1. Kolmogorov's inequality then implies that for any $J \in \{1, \ldots, N\}$ and any $p \in (0,1)$,

$$\Pr \left(\max_{1 \leq j \leq J} Y_j(t) > 1/p \right) \leq p.$$

---

[2] In our case, the items will be ballots, and their labels will represent votes; see Sect. 4.2.

This can be used as the basis of a ballot-polling RLA that does not require a reference tally, as we show below. The same result holds for sequential sampling *with* replacement, re-defining $\tilde{S}_j \equiv 0$ and $\tilde{j} \equiv 1$ (the limit of the finite-population result as $N \to \infty$). We also note that [11] provides a recursive algorithm for computing the integral (1).

4.2 Risk-Limiting Tallies

Consider plurality contests that allow each voter to vote for $k \geq 1$ of C candidates. The winner(s) are the k candidates who receive the most votes. We ignore the possibility of ties; they are an easy extension. Majority and super-majority are straightforward generalizations; see [24].

Candidate w is one of the winners if w received more votes than at least $C - k$ other candidates. In general, some ballots will have invalid votes or votes for other candidates. Consider a single pair of candidates, w and ℓ. Let N_w denote the number of ballots in the population that show a vote for w but not for ℓ; let N_ℓ denote the number of ballots in the population that show a vote for ℓ but not for w, and let $N_u \equiv N - N_w - N_\ell$ denote the number of ballots that show a vote for neither w nor ℓ or show votes for both w and ℓ.

Let W_j be the number of items labeled with w selected on or before draw j; and define L_j analogously. The probability distributions of those variables depend on N_w, N_ℓ, and N_u, even though we only care about one parameter, $N_w - N_\ell$. Now $N_w \leq N_\ell$ if and only if $N_w + N_u/2 \leq N_\ell + N_u/2$. Since $N_\ell + N_u/2 = N - (N_w + N_u/2)$, we have $N_w + N_u/2 \leq N - (N_w + N_u/2)$. We can now divide by N to obtain $\frac{N_w + N_u/2}{N} \leq 1 - \frac{N_w + N_u/2}{N}$ from which we get

$$\frac{N_w + N_u/2}{N} \leq \frac{1}{2}. \tag{2}$$

Let

$$\mu_{w\ell} \equiv \frac{1 \times N_w + \frac{1}{2} \times N_u + 0 \times N_\ell}{N}.$$

This is the mean of a population derived from re-labeling each vote for w as 1, each vote for ℓ as 0, and the rest as 1/2. The mean of this population is greater than 1/2 iff w received more votes than ℓ. We can test the hypothesis $\mu_{w\ell} \leq 1/2$ (i.e., w did not beat ℓ) using the martingale-based test above by simply treating the sampled ballots that way: every ballot with a vote for w (but not ℓ) counts as 1, every ballot with a vote for ℓ (but not for w) counts as 0, and invalid ballots, ballots with votes for other candidates, and ballots with votes for both w and ℓ count as 1/2.

To determine the set of winners, we sequentially test the collection of $C(C-1)$ hypotheses

$$\{H_{w\ell} : \mu_{w\ell} \leq 1/2, w = 1, \dots, C; \ell = 1, \dots, C; w \neq \ell\}, \tag{3}$$

stopping when either

- there is a set $\mathcal{W}$ of cardinality k such that we have rejected the hypothesis $\mu_{w\ell} \leq 1/2$ for every (w, ℓ) with $w \in \mathcal{W}$ and $\ell \notin \mathcal{W}$, or
- we have examined a too high percentage of votes from the privacy point of view, in which case the sampling strategy is abandoned and different means are used to determine with certainty who won, see Sect. 5.1 for details.

Proposition 1. *If every hypothesis is tested at level α, the probability that this algorithm misidentifies the set of winner(s) is at most $k(C - k)\alpha$.*

Proof. The approach misidentifies one or more winners iff it terminates in the first branch, but $\mathcal{W}$ is not the set of winners: $\exists w \in \mathcal{W}, \ell \notin \mathcal{W}$ s.t. $\mu_{w\ell} \leq 1/2$. In a RLA, a wrong outcome can only be confirmed if *every* true null hypothesis is erroneously rejected. In contrast, in a RLT, a wrong outcome can be confirmed if just one particular true null hypothesis is rejected: the hypothesis that the candidate with the $k + 1$st highest vote share got fewer votes than the candidate with the kth highest vote share.

There are $C(C - 1)$ hypotheses $\{H_{w,\ell}\}$ in all, of which $C(C - 1)/2$ are true. Of the true null hypotheses, those whose erroneous rejection would make the reported outcome wrong are the $k(C - k)$ that compare the vote share of a candidate in $\mathcal{W}$ to the vote share of a candidate in $\mathcal{W}^c$: if none of those is erroneously rejected, the set of winners is correct. Observe that if we used the logical implications of the statistical rejections to entail rejections of other hypotheses—for instance, $H_{w\ell} \cap H_{\ell k} \rightarrow H_{wk}$—this would not be true. Therefore, a Bonferroni multiplicity adjustment of $k(C - k)$ certainly suffices. Note that this may be conservative as an estimate, because there are logical dependencies among the hypotheses. □

The aim of the sampling is to test the hypothesis "$\mu_{w\ell} \leq 1/2$." Rejecting $\mu_{w\ell} \leq 1/2$ means proving with risk at most α that w won the pairwise contest with ℓ.

Proposition 2. *If we reject $\mu_{w\ell} \leq 1/2$ at significance level α and reject $\mu_{\ell m} \leq 1/2$ at significance level α, then we reject $\mu_{wm} \leq 1/2$ at significance level α.*

Proof (sketch). This transitivity property follows from the monotonicity of the P-values in the number of votes for each candidate, at each sample size j. □

4.3 Sample Sizes

Because the underlying statistical test is sequential, the audit can start by looking at a single ballot selected at random, calculate the p-values for all not-yet-rejected null hypotheses, and continue to increase the sample one ballot at a time until the risk limit has been met. However, depending on the desired risk limit, the RLT will not be able to terminate until some minimum number of ballots has been tallied.

The minimum sample sizes required to identify the winner with a maximum error rate of α are given in Table 1, for sampling without replacement, for a plurality contest with 2 candidates and a plurality contest with 10 candidates. The sample sizes listed are exactly those that would be required if the votes were unanimously for one candidate; if more than one candidate receives votes, the sample size becomes random and becomes stochastically larger.

Similarly, if a fraction u of ballots do not have a valid vote for any candidate, the sample size will also be random, and the expected sample size will grow by a factor of $1/(1-u)$. For instance, if 10% of ballots have no vote and 90% of ballots have a vote for candidate A in a 10-candidate plurality election, the expected sample size to identify the winner with risk limit 0.1% is $17/0.9 = 18.9$ ballots.

The closer the vote is to unanimous, the fewer ballots need to be revealed (the distribution is stochastically smaller the more nearly unanimous the vote). I.e., the protection a RLT offers is greatest when the risk is greatest.

For a two-candidate plurality election, only one of the two null hypotheses $\mu_{\ell m} \leq 1/2$ can be true; thus, no multiplicity adjustment is needed. (This is consistent with the formula $k(C - k) = 1 \times (2 - 1) = 1$). For a 10-candidate plurality election, the Bonferroni adjustment factor is $1 \times (10 - 1) = 9$. As the table shows, if the vote is (nearly) unanimous, the number of ballots required to identify the winner with negligible error probability is small: 35 suffices to have an error probability less than 10^{-9} for a two-candidate contest, and 38 suffices for a 10-candidate contest. Because the risk drops by an order of magnitude with an increase in sample size of about 4 ballots when the vote is (nearly) unanimous, the penalty for multiplicity is low in absolute terms. If the RLT sample is drawn *without* replacement, the expected sample sizes required to attain a given risk are smaller—but not by much unless the total number of ballots is small.

Table 1. Minimum sample sizes to identify the winner of a two-candidate plurality contest and a 10-candidate plurality contest at risk limit α, for sampling with replacement. Actual sample sizes approach these minima (with high probability) as voter preferences approach unanimity.

Candidates	α								
	10^{-1}	10^{-2}	10^{-3}	10^{-4}	10^{-5}	10^{-6}	10^{-7}	10^{-8}	10^{-9}
2	5	9	13	17	21	24	28	31	35
10	9	13	17	20	24	27	31	34	38

5   Incorporating RLT in E2E V Voting Protocols

RLTs can be used in a straightforward way with any E2E V scheme in which the set of encrypted votes appears on a Bulletin Board (BB) and is applicable to either remote or in-person voting. The encryption should be homomorphic and probabilistic: for instance, ElGamal can be used. Helios [1], Prêt à Voter [8], Selene [20], etc., would all be amenable.

Conceptually, we can start with a random permutations of the encrypted votes and take samples from left to right, opening more ballots as required.

The verifiable shuffles used in many schemes naturally give us a random permutation. However, we must be careful about simply taking the permutation output of the underlying scheme's shuffles, as there may be opportunities to manipulate this and bias the sampling. The sampling must be truly random and demonstrably outwith the control of any entity. This brings us to the challenge of *certifiable randomness*, which arises in many contexts: lotteries, voting, auctions, public ledgers etc. A number of approaches have been proposed, for example using a seed derived from a hash of prices of previously agreed stock market options at an agreed future time. Alternative approaches involve combining random values previously committed by a number of independent entities. Algorand [17] adopts such an approach combined with the use of verifiable random functions. Another possibility is to derive the seed from a cryptographic hash of suitable data posted to the BB. RLAs have employed seeds generated in a public ceremony of dice rolling. We might rely on a trusted third party such as the NIST random beacon service. For the purposes of this paper do not specify a particular approach but leave it for the stakeholders to select.

Sampling with replacement can be implemented straightforwardly by performing further mixes between samplings.

5.1 Guaranteeing Plausible Deniability

For most elections, the RLT approach will naturally leave a good proportion of unrevealed votes. However, there will be cases where the winning margins are narrow, and thus the RLT might result in all or almost all votes being revealed. It is not enough for a system to be (objectively) coercion resistant, it must also be seen as coercion resistant. Thus, for the RLT approach to be effective, we must ensure that the voters will never be, nor expect to be, in a situation in which plausible deniability fails. In this section we identify such situations, and describe some strategies to deal with the potential vulnerability.

Of course, a close run referendum will not be a problem, but a problematic scenario is a close margin between candidates X and Y, along with a low-support candidate Z. This could result in a full count where the low score Z opens up the possibility of coercion. We have already indicated that coercion for Z is possibly harmful for the outcome of the election, as it can be used to decrease the number of votes that either X or Y gets. Note also, again, that this kind of coercion is feasible not only when the voter *knows* (e.g., from polls) the a close run will occur. In many cases, it suffices that the voter thinks it *might* happen to get her worried and vulnerable to threats. We propose that, in such circumstances, the system should switch to a *fallback strategy* that works in all cases. Example fallback strategies are sketched below.

PET Testing. In the event of a close race between X and Y, start Plaintext Equivalence Testing of randomly selected, unrevealed ballots against $\{X\}_{PK}$ and $\{Y\}_{PK}$, until we reach the required confidence for the winner.

Tally Hiding. One can also fall back to computationally heavy methods e.g. MPC for only disclosing the winner, see e.g. [6,9,26,27]. Note that the revealed votes and reduced number of possible winners will make these methods more efficient than if used from the onset.

A possibility is to have the tellers perform a secret computation of the tally, and announce the winner(s), but not the numerical tally, on which to base a null hypothesis. This allows the RLT to be computed much more efficiently, and the secretly computed tallies can guide the appropriate strategy to adopt in the event of narrow margins.

6   Security Assumptions

In this section we briefly state the security guarantees and give some arguments for their validity. For the exposition below, we introduce the following three authorities besides the voters: The Tally Tellers TT holding the secret election key in a threshold manner, the Mixnet Tellers MT mixing the encrypted votes before doing the risk-limiting tally, and a random sampling authority RSA organising the random sampling of votes for the tally.

For simplicity let us also assume that the underlying voting scheme that we build on is mixnet-based, i.e., the main difference between the RLT version and the original version is that not all ciphertexts output from the mixnet are decrypted, but only a proportion of them.

In general, if RSA is acting honestly, or bound to do so e.g. via a verifiable proof based on a computational assumption, then the security reduces to that of the underlying scheme. For privacy, we normally have to trust that a threshold set of TT is not colluding and at least one server in MT is honest. For verifiability most schemes will not impose verifiable trust in TT or MT but might rely on computational assumptions and the RO-model or a CRS setup.

Verifiability. When random sampling procedure is corrupted, the adversary could possibly adjust the outcome in his favour. However, note that in this situation we can still achieve verifiability by having RSA committing to the sampling order before mixing, and assuming the last mix node is honest (or assuming one arbitrary mix node is honest and no threshold set of TT is corrupted). This will ensure that the final sampling is random.

Ballot-Privacy. Obviously, a necessary assumption for ballot-privacy is that a threshold set of TT are not colluding, and at least one mix node is honest. If the random sampling is also honest, we get strictly less information from the tally than in the original scheme, and we thus achieve better privacy in an information theoretic sense. When using standard ballot-privacy definitions on the scheme it should also be possible to reduce the ballot-privacy to that of the underlying scheme, the only subtlety being that tally functions differ in the two schemes.

It might seem that a corruption of the random sampling procedure should not influence ballot-privacy. However, there is one assumption to make: the random sampling should, in the computational view of the adversary, be uncorrelated with the cast votes. Having input from the voters to the random sampling could indeed make sense from a verifiability viewpoint, like in Demos [13], but should not depend on the vote choice unless this is computationally hidden.

Coercion-Resistance and Vote-Buying Resistance. As we have discussed above, the RLT protocol in general improves the coercion-resistance especially when candidates are expected to have a low vote count. It would be interesting to relate this to the coercion-resistance level δ in Kusters et al. [14]. On the other hand, the security against vote-buying is not increased in the same way since the voter here has an intent to obtain a receipt. The vote buyer could indeed follow the Italian attack method and the marked ballot would often appear.

The above is reminiscent of a distinguishing example between vote-buying and coercion resistance due to Rivest:[3] the system chooses at random whether or not to provide the voter with a plaintext receipt. Such a system is, arguably, coercion resistant (the voter can claim to have received no receipt) but is vulnerable to vote buying (the voter might comply in the hope of getting the pay-off).

7   Risk-Limiting Verification

The idea of using risk-limiting techniques to improve coercion resistance can also be applied to verification of votes. Here, we apply the idea to Selene, allowing us to ensure that a proportion of the trackers remain unrevealed. In consequence, the coerced voter can always claim that her tracker was amongst those that remained shrouded. Some subtleties have to be handled in the case of an obnoxious coercer who demands the voter divulge their tracker; we describe those below. Indeed, these consideration require some modifications of the way Selene works.

7.1   Risk-Limiting Verification in Selene

A drawback of Selene, as noted in the original paper, is that when a coerced voter claims a fake tracker, the coercer (who is also a voter) could maintain that this is in fact his tracker. By construction, the coercer cannot prove this to the voter, but the voter is now in a difficult position: she knows that the claim might be true. Elaborations of the basic scheme are proposed, but they complicate things and render the verification less transparent: the final tally contains dummy votes that must be subtracted out to get the true result.

The RLT idea can be extended to avoiding revealing all the trackers in a run of a Selene election. The natural step is to apply the RLT mechanisms described above to reveal as many votes as necessary and then reveal the corresponding trackers. There would seem to be little point in revealing trackers for which the corresponding vote has not been revealed. There may, however, be some merit in revealing a subset of the trackers for which the votes have been revealed, as we discuss below.

Risk Limiting Verification (RLV), as applied to Selene, can ensure that not all trackers are revealed, thus allowing a coerced voter to simply claim that their tracker did not appear. There is still a problem, however, if we use Selene in its

---

[3] Private communication.

original form: the full set of trackers is published, so the coercer could require the voter to reveal her tracker anyway, and still claim that it is his.

We can fix this fairly easily: one purpose of revealing all the trackers in the setup phase is to demonstrate that they are all distinct, so the EA could publish a list of encrypted trackers for which the trustees run pairwise PETs to show that all the plaintexts differ. This would be computationally heavy and does not scale well, but is no worse than, e.g., JCJ [12]. Moreover, we can use some of the approaches to linearising the JCJ-style checks, for example by raising the tracker ciphertexts to the same, secret exponent and then verifiably decrypting.

We note that we get a form of partial random checking anyway when we reveal a random sample of the trackers: if all the revealed trackers in say a 90% random sample are distinct then we have very high confidence that they all are distinct. The drawback of this approach is that if the EA has cheated and included collisions then we will not discover this until rather late. Note, however, that we could reveal the trackers first, before revealing the votes. Now, if we find collisions, we can abort the election before any tally results have been revealed.

Still, one problem remains: another reason to publish the set of trackers is to allow voters to confirm that the α term sent to them is authentic: it opens the commitment to a valid tracker, i.e., a member the published set. If we do not publish the set of trackers then we need another mechanism for voters to confirm that their notified tracker is "valid." We can achieve this by requiring that valid trackers are drawn from a negligible subset of the full space, e.g., numbers with say six digits. Now it is still intractable to produce fake α terms that will open a given commitment to a member of this set, but, by adjusting the number of digits we can ensure that the chance that a fake tracker will collide with the coercer's is greatly reduced, so improving the plausible deniability.

If this reduced probability of tracker collision is deemed unacceptable, then we could allow the voter to request a fake tracker from the Notification Authority. This authority knows which valid trackers have not been assigned and so can provide an unassigned tracker to the coerced voter. This requires a level of trust in this entity, to keep tracker-related information secret but such trust is needed anyway.

There remains the question of whether all the voters should be notified of their tracker, even when their tracker has not been revealed on the BB. The immediate thought is not to notify unrevealed trackers, but this introduces possibilities of the authorities exploiting this: leading many voters to think that their tracker was not revealed and so denying them the possibility to verify their vote. It is not clear how we could verify that all the voters whose trackers are revealed are notified, so it seems wiser to notify each voter of their tracker.

8   Related Work

A number of papers [6,9,26,27] try to achieve tally hiding, either by only calculating the winner(s), or via multi-party computation and other cryptographic means. An idea closer to RLTs is that of Random Sample Voting (RSV) by

Chaum [7]. A scheme that seeks to implement RSV in a fully verifiable fashion is Alethea [3]. RSV typically samples a small and predetermined number of voters, regardless of the margins. In contrast, RLTs adjust the sample size to obtain the desired level of confidence in the reported outcome.

The idea of Risk-Limiting Verification is somewhat analogous to Rivest's ThreeBallot protocol [19]. Recall that, in ThreeBallot, each voter can verify a random 1/3 of her cast ballot. Thus, RLV gives "vote handles" to a fraction of voters, whereas in ThreeBallot each voter gets a handle to a fraction of her vote.

9 Conclusions

This paper presents two simple methods, RLT and RLV, for reducing the amount of information provided in the tally and verification stages. In consequence, we enhance the coercion-resistance by giving coerced voters plausible deniability, while achieving whatever confidence level in the outcome is required. An important future step will be to understand how well this method protects coerced voters in practice. It would be good also to understand better the trade-off between confidence in the outcome and plausible deniability levels.

There exist other methods that leak less information in the tally process, e.g., by using multi-party computation to only reveal the winner of the election. Such methods might be better suited to avoid strategic voting in runoff elections, and may provide somewhat better deniability. However, those methods require more elaborate and computationally expensive cryptography; arguably, our methods are more efficient and transparent.

The novel Risk-Limiting techniques introduced here should be of independent interest and have applications beyond the RLTs and RLVs described here.

Acknowledgements. WJ and PYAR acknowledge the support of the Luxembourg National Research Fund (FNR) and the National Centre for Research and Development (NCBiR Poland) under the INTER/PolLux project VoteVerif (POLLUX-IV/1/2016). PBR was supported by the EU Horizon 2020 research and innovation programme under grant agreement No. 779391 (FutureTPM).

References

1. Adida, B., de Marneffe, O., Pereira, O., Quisquater, J.-J.: Electing a university president using open-audit voting: analysis of real-world use of Helios. In: Proceedings of EVT/WOTE (2009)
2. Adida, B., Neff, C.A.: Ballot casting assurance. In: Proceedings of the USENIX/Accurate Electronic Voting Technology Workshop 2006 on Electronic Voting Technology Workshop, EVT 2006, p. 7 (2006)
3. Basin, D.A., Radomirovic, S., Schmid, L.: Alethea: a provably secure random sample voting protocol. In: 31st IEEE Computer Security Foundations Symposium, CSF 2018, pp. 283–297 (2018)
4. Benaloh, J., Tuinstra, D.: Receipt-free secret-ballot elections. In: Proceedings of the Twenty-Sixth Annual ACM Symposium on Theory of Computing, pp. 544–553. ACM (1994)

5. Benaloh, J.: Simple verifiable elections. In: Proceedings of the USENIX/Accurate Electronic Voting Technology Workshop 2006 on Electronic Voting Technology Workshop, EVT 2006, p. 5 (2006)
6. Canard, S., Pointcheval, D., Santos, Q., Traoré, J.: Practical strategy-resistant privacy-preserving elections. In: Lopez, J., Zhou, J., Soriano, M. (eds.) ESORICS 2018. LNCS, vol. 11099, pp. 331–349. Springer, Cham (2018). https://doi.org/10.1007/978-3-319-98989-1_17
7. Chaum, D.: Random-sample voting. http://rsvoting.org/whitepaper/white_paper.pdf
8. Chaum, D., Ryan, P.Y.A., Schneider, S.: A practical voter-verifiable election scheme. In: di Vimercati, S.C., Syverson, P., Gollmann, D. (eds.) ESORICS 2005. LNCS, vol. 3679, pp. 118–139. Springer, Heidelberg (2005). https://doi.org/10.1007/11555827_8
9. Cohen, J.: Improving privacy in cryptographic elections. Technical report (1986)
10. Delaune, S., Kremer, S., Ryan, M.: Verifying privacy-type properties of electronic voting protocols: a taster. In: Chaum, D., et al. (eds.) Towards Trustworthy Elections. LNCS, vol. 6000, pp. 289–309. Springer, Heidelberg (2010). https://doi.org/10.1007/978-3-642-12980-3_18
11. Evans, S.N., Stark, P.B.: Confidence bounds for the mean of a non-negative population (2019, in press)
12. Juels, A., Catalano, D., Jakobsson, M.: Coercion-resistant electronic elections. In: Proceedings of the 2005 ACM Workshop on Privacy in the Electronic Society, pp. 61–70. ACM (2005)
13. Kiayias, A., Zacharias, T., Zhang, B.: DEMOS-2: scalable E2E verifiable elections without random oracles. In: Proceedings of CCS, pp. 352–363 (2015)
14. Küsters, R., Truderung, T., Vogt, A.: A game-based definition of coercion-resistance and its applications. In: Proceedings of IEEE Computer Security Foundations Symposium (CSF), pp. 122–136 (2010)
15. Lindeman, M., Stark, P.B., Yates, V.: BRAVO: ballot-polling risk-limiting audits to verify outcomes. In: Proceedings of EVT/WOTE 2011 (2012)
16. Lindeman, M., Stark, P.B.: A gentle introduction to risk-limiting audits. IEEE Secur. Priv. 10, 42–49 (2012)
17. Micali, S.: ALGORAND: the efficient and democratic ledger. CoRR, abs/1607.01341 (2016)
18. Ottoboni, K., Stark, P.B., Lindeman, M., McBurnett, N.: Risk-limiting audits by stratified union-intersection tests of elections (SUITE). In: Krimmer, R., et al. (eds.) E-Vote-ID 2018. LNCS, vol. 11143, pp. 174–188. Springer, Cham (2018). https://doi.org/10.1007/978-3-030-00419-4_12
19. Rivest, R.L.: The ThreeBallot voting system. https://people.csail.mit.edu/rivest/Rivest-TheThreeBallotVotingSystem.pdf
20. Ryan, P.Y.A., Rønne, P.B., Iovino, V.: Selene: voting with transparent verifiability and coercion-mitigation. In: Financial Cryptography and Data Security: Workshops, pp. 176–192 (2016)
21. Ryan, P.Y.A., Schneider, S.A., Teague, V.: End-to-end verifiability in voting systems, from theory to practice. IEEE Secur. Priv. 13(3), 59–62 (2015)
22. Christianson, B.: Introduction: brief encounters. In: Christianson, B., Malcolm, J.A., Matyáš, V., Roe, M. (eds.) Security Protocols 2009. LNCS, vol. 7028, pp. 1–2. Springer, Heidelberg (2013). https://doi.org/10.1007/978-3-642-36213-2_1
23. Schneider, S., Sidiropoulos, A.: CSP and anonymity. In: Bertino, E., Kurth, H., Martella, G., Montolivo, E. (eds.) ESORICS 1996. LNCS, vol. 1146, pp. 198–218. Springer, Heidelberg (1996). https://doi.org/10.1007/3-540-61770-1_38

24. Stark, P.B.: Conservative statistical post-election audits. Ann. Appl. Stat. **2**, 550–581 (2008)
25. Stark, P.B., Wagner, D.A.: Evidence-based elections. IEEE Secur. Priv. **10**, 33–41 (2012)
26. Szepieniec, A., Preneel, B.: New techniques for electronic voting. USENIX J. Election Technol. Syst. (JETS) **3**(2), 46–69 (2015)
27. Teague, V., Ramchen, K., Naish, L.: Coercion-resistant tallying for STV voting. In: 2008 USENIX/ACCURATE Electronic Voting Workshop, EVT 2008, Proceedings (2008)

Technical and Socio-Technical Attacks on the Danish Party Endorsement System

Carsten Schürmann[✉] and Alessandro Bruni

Center for Information Security and Trust, IT University of Copenhagen,
Copenhagen, Denmark
{carsten,brun}@itu.dk

Abstract. In this paper we analyze the security of the online Danish party endorsement system (DVE) and present two attacks: one technical, which we discovered during our study of the system in 2016 and which compromises the integrity of the endorsements stored in the DVE-database and another socio-technical, which allows parties to circumvent mechanisms to protect voters against abuse. To understand these attacks, we introduce the legal and technical frameworks of the DVE-system, analyze its problems, and describe a sequence of events that has led to endorsing three new parties that stood in the 2019 Danish Parliament election.

1 Introduction

Collecting signatures to endorse parties running for parliament is an important part of the democratic process, and for Denmark it is no exception. Prior to March 29, 2014, all endorsements were done on paper. Prospective parties had to go out to shopping malls and libraries, talk to people, and collect hand-written signatures. These signatures were subsequently checked by the municipalities for eligibility and correctness, i.e. that each endorser had the right to endorse and had not already endorsed another party. This was tedious work.

On March 29, 2014, the law governing party endorsements was changed to allow a digital solution to be used for collecting endorsements. The Ministry for Social Affairs and the Interior (in Danish "Social- og Indenrigsministeriet" or SIM, as it was known at the time) would become responsible for providing, running, and maintaining the solution. The prospective parties would be responsible for collecting endorsements using the solution. Prior to the law change, SIM was not involved in the operational aspects of collecting and checking endorsements, but with the new law in place the ministry had to provide a digital solution assisting parties to collect endorsements.

The law requires that to stand for Danish Parliament election, a prospective party must collect at least a number of endorsements equal to 1/175 of all valid votes cast in the previous Danish Parliament election, which corresponds to 20.109 endorsements in 2019. In comparison, to be admitted to the European Parliament election, a prospective party must collect more than 2% of all valid

© Springer Nature Switzerland AG 2019
R. Krimmer et al. (Eds.): E-Vote-ID 2019, LNCS 11759, pp. 200–215, 2019.
https://doi.org/10.1007/978-3-030-30625-0_13

votes cast in the previous Danish Parliament election, which corresponds to 70.380 endorsements in 2019.[1]

Not long after the law changed, SIM released the corresponding administrative regulation and commenced with the procurement of the Danish party endorsement system (DVE). A feasibility study was conducted, requirement documents were drafted, and the Danish company KMD was tasked with developing the system.[2] Eventually, the DVE-system was deployed after some delay, and voters were invited to endorse prospective parties.

From an operational point of view, the DVE-system works as follows: any new prospective party that strives to be recognized collects email addresses of potential endorsers and then forwards invitations to endorse the party through the DVE-system. Eligibility is checked using Denmark's national digital identity system, which allows the DVE-system to verify information about the endorser, such as nationality and age. Moreover, the DVE-system allows endorsers to withdraw their endorsements at a later point in time. The system also supports the collection of paper-based endorsements.

In this paper, we discuss some challenges that accompanied the introduction of the DVE systems in the Danish electoral process. We first describe the legal and technical framework of the DVE-system in Sect. 2, then present best practices following recommendations of international and non-governmental organizations in Sect. 3. In Sect. 4, we show two attacks against the 2016 version of the DVE-system, one technical and one socio-technical. In Sect. 5, we present our reflections and unsolicited recommendations, which we consider important for a future DVE-system. Finally, in Sect. 6, we conclude and discuss briefly the impact of the DVE-system on the 2019 Danish Parliament election.

2   The DVE Framework

2.1   The Legal Framework

In Denmark, every resident has a digital ID, called NemID[3], a personal identification number, which is called CPR[4], and access to an authenticated email service, called e-Boks[5] (Digitale Post). With the availability of these technologies, Denmark's Parliament passed a law in March 2014 that would allow the collection of party endorsements using a digital online system.[6] SIM, which changed its name to Ministry of Economic Affairs and the Interior (Økonomi- og Indenrigsministeriet, ØIM) in 2016, was ordered to develop the appropriate administrative regulation, which was published in January 2016.[7]

---

[1] See European Parliament election law §11, Sect. 1.
[2] Neither the authors nor their affiliations were involved in this project, neither during procurement, nor development, nor quality assurance.
[3] See https://www.nemid.nu.
[4] See https://cpr.dk/.
[5] See https://www.e-boks.com/danmark/da.
[6] See https://www.ft.dk/samling/20131/lovforslag/l124/index.htm.
[7] See Vælgererklæringsbekendtgørelsen, https://www.retsinformation.dk/Forms/R07-10.aspx?id=176933.

Compared to the early versions of the legal framework, this administrative regulation focused on the usability of the digital solution. To this end, the authority to check the validity of the endorsements and the eligibility of the endorser was transferred away from the municipalities to the DVE-system, relieving the municipalities of the need to procure their own local systems.

The new regulation defines necessary roles in connection with the digital solution, among them the "party administrator", who works on behalf of the prospective party to drive the endorsement collection activity. The regulation also uses several technical terms, such as "granting access to the digital solution", "is contacted by email", "the email contains a link", "a voter declaration", "voter's declaration's key", "archive key" etc. which are underspecified and can be interpreted in many different ways. In addition, the new regulation explicitly requires that seven days must pass between the time of registration to the time of endorsement, granting the prospective endorser time to reflect upon whether or not to endorse the prospective party. The new regulation also prescribes what must happen in case the digital solution is not functional or ceases to work.

We observe that the new regulation does not make any reference to the verifiability of the operation of the DVE-system, the accuracy of the endorsements, the integrity of the database, the confidentiality of the endorser, nor the availability of the DVE-system.

2.2   The Technical Framework

The steps to endorse a party using the DVE-system are depicted in Fig. 1. The process is driven by the prospective party. In a first step, the party has to apply with ØIM to initiate the endorsement collection process, and ØIM configures the DVE-system accordingly. Prospective voters can be asked to endorse a new party either by email or by regular mail. As nearly all of the Danish residents have a digital ID, only few will endorse parties by regular mail (this case will not be considered any further in this paper).

The legal framework requires that the party should initiate the process (Init) by sending the email address of the prospective voter to ØIM through the online interface of the DVE-system. Once received, the email address will be stored for seven days (which is referred to as the "period to reflect") before sending an invitation (Invitation) email to the endorser containing the link to finalize the endorsement and the token to identify it.

After receiving the email, the endorser can follow the link to log into the DVE-system through the website vælgererklæring.dk using the digital ID NemID. By confirming the information on the screen, the endorsement is then given (Endorsement). The DVE-system will subsequently send a receipt (Receipt) to the endorser via the authenticated email service e-Boks including a link that give the endorser the possibility to withdraw the endorsement (Revocation).

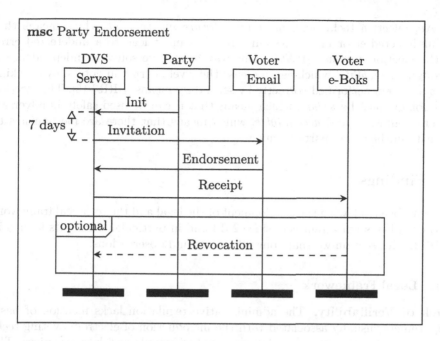

Fig. 1. Process of endorsing a party

The DVE-system was implemented in 2016 by the Danish company KMD, and since then has been used by more than 100 prospective parties, four of which applied for recognition, with the result that three applications were granted and one was rejected.

3 Best Practices

In this section we describe our reflections on best practices, before analyzing the legal and technical framework of the DVE-system in the subsequent sections.

Although party endorsement is usually considered secondary to electronic voting, it exhibits all defining characteristics of an Internet voting system: all endorsements are submitted through the Internet; there is no paper trail; the integrity of the database (of all endorsements) is instrumental for creating public confidence in the decisions that follow from it; all voters who are eligible to vote in the election are also eligible to endorse upcoming parties; finally, voters can only endorse one party. Newly approved parties will appear on the ballot and there is likely extensive media coverage of such new parties. Therefore, the DVE-system qualifies as an election technology that should live up to best practices and standards of any election technology.[8]

---

[8] See Recommendation CM/Rec(2017)5[1] of the Committee of Ministers to member States on standards for e-voting (Adopted by the Committee of Ministers on 14 June 2017 at the 1289th meeting of the Ministers' Deputies).

Any election technology must be *software independent*, which means that an undetected error in the system software cannot lead to a undetected error in the election outcome [RW06]. One way to achieve software independence is through *verifiability*, which can increase the level of trust in voters, by checking that a system performed correctly by secondary means [BRR+15]. The election technology must be *secure*, which means that it can be used safely in adversarial environments, and *accountable*, which means that there are mechanisms to identify misbehaving participants.

4   Findings

We have been following the development of the legal and the technical framework of the DVE-system attentively since 2014 and in particular during its launch in 2016. In this section we share our reflections and observations.

4.1   Legal Framework

Lack of Verifiability. The administrative regulation lacks mention of basic requirements usually associated with the introduction of electronic voting technologies, which is contrary to international standards and best practices. The regulation does not mention requirements regarding security, accountability, software independence, or verifiability. Consequently, it is impossible to judge whether a DVE-system is compliant with the regulation, which is particularly worrisome.

A grave oversight of the regulation is that essential elements of the DVE-system are not adequately defined, including what constitutes a *binding endorsement*. The regulation fails to specify how endorsements should be linked to the voter (if at all), and how they are secured. The regulation also omits which mechanisms must be put in place to guarantee the authenticity of an endorsement, and to protect them against copying, tampering, and deletion.

Absence of Endorsement Privacy. It is also noteworthy that the regulation fails to take advantage of new opportunities to guarantee higher levels of endorsement privacy. The role of vote privacy in Internet voting systems is well understood as are the mechanisms and the challenges to protect it. We believe that the reason why endorsement privacy is not considered in the regulation is most likely because prior versions of the legal framework did not require it either. Operationally speaking it is not clear how to collect party endorsements on paper, while at the same time verifying the eligibility of the endorser and guaranteeing their privacy.

The Impossibility to Revert. Before the law was changed and the administrative regulation was released, the municipalities had the authority and responsibility to verify the validity of endorsements and the eligibility of the endorser.

By transferring this responsibility to the digital solution run by ØIM, the legal framework has forfeit the possibility to revert to a manual process, which would have to be, presumably, carried out by the ministry, which simply does not have the resources to do so. The legal framework therefore did not only create the legal foundation for the use of a digital solution, it made its use mandatory.

Transparency. The legal framework refers to the digital solution, as if it was already constructed and as if under no circumstances it could negatively affect the public confidence of endorsers and voters. The administrative regulation does not explicitly require any quality assurance processes (for example software reviews or penetration tests) nor certification with respect to applicable standards (e.g. ISO). It also does not require the source code of the system nor any evaluation or penetration testing reports to be public [EBB+15].

4.2   Technical Framework

The protocol depicted in Fig. 1 is implemented in the DVE-system. As, apparently, there is no concern to run the DVE-system in a highly contested adversarial environment, it is perhaps not surprising that the implementation that we studied in 2016 did little to defend against cyberattacks and socio-technical attacks, which we discuss next.

Cyberattacks. The design documentation and the source code of the DVE-system is closed source, contrary to best practice and international recommendations [CKN+14]. It is therefore impossible for any outsider to conduct a security analysis of the DVE-system, in its entirety, i.e. review of requirement documents, design documents, implementation, and deployment plans. Collaborating closely with officials at ØIM, we were asked to endorse a fictional test party (which in our eyes required a limited security analysis, pretending to be an ineligible adversary who was invited by a party administrator to endorse). We submitted our email-address to our contact at ØIM, who set up a test party, and invited us to endorse. By they time we tried to endorse, we observed that the invitation had already expired. Upon request, our contact in the ministry forwarded a second invitation, this time not for the test party but for a real and non-fictional party "De Visionære". The invitation message is depicted in Fig. 1.

Architecture. The outward facing interface of the DVE-system is a website that runs a Java application server and is connected to NemID for the purpose of authentication. Once authenticated, a set of JavaScript files are uploaded to the client computer and the application is then executed client-side.

Following the exchange of messages described in Fig. 1, the party owner sends an invitation to the endorser by the way of the DVE-system, who receives a link and a token (a random looking string of characters) that initiates the endorsement procedure. To endorse, the recipient of the mail follows the link, authenticates via NemID and confirms the party endorsement.

The website follows a three-step process. The first step checks whether the endorser has the proper rights to endorse the party: endorsers can only endorse one party and they must have the right to vote in the election the prospective party stands for; the second step requires confirmation from the voter, showing the party details and the voter identity; finally, the third step returns feedback on the success or failure of the process. Because endorsement invitations and endorsers are not linked, the requirement that seven days must have passed between the initiation of the process and the actual endorsement ("reflection period") is not checked by the DVE-system.

Adversary Model. An election is a contest, where different stakeholder groups, often with conflicting interests, stand as candidates before an eligible voting population to determine who will go in power. Public confidence in the election outcome is paramount.

The party approval process is similar, except perhaps that there is not one but many winners. The adversary model is therefore relatively well defined. It includes every individual who tries on behalf of a party to influence the approval process in any form. Any individual can get an invitation to endorse a party, by contacting the party administrator directly, and therefore any user of the DVE-system must be considered an adversary, which is exactly the adversary group that we focus on in this paper.

In the bigger picture, there are of course other adversaries that must be taken under consideration, including insider attackers (working for example for ØIM or the system vendor), generating spurious endorsements or removing them to influence the result. There are also Nation States who aim to influence the approval process, for example, with the objective to destabilize a country or influence the public discussion on media. Unfortunately, because of ØIM's policy to keep all information confidential, our security analysis is restricted to an individual attempting to endorse a party by breaking client-side security.

Client-side security refers to the capability of the end-points of a larger distributed system to defend against cyberattacks by keeping adversaries out, protecting the integrity of the data, the confidentiality of sensitive information, and the overall availability of the system. ØIM should be concerned with client-side security because it grants endorsers direct access to sensitive data by the way of end-points, such as laptops, mobile phones, or tablet computers. Weak or no client-side security allows adversaries to gain access to sensitive data, i.e. party endorsement, corrupt the integrity of the databases, or, in the worst case, disrupt service altogether.

Objective of the Security Analysis. According to Danish law, citizens are permitted to endorse parties for the Danish Parliament, EU-citizens are permitted to endorse parties for the European Parliament elections, and every individual is only allowed to endorse one and only one party. The DVE-system should enforce this policy and the objective of the security analysis is to determine if it really does. Unfortunately, this was not the case.

Detailed Description of an Identified Vulnerability. On August 12th 2016, 9:00 the authors of this paper commenced the security analysis of the DVE-system by studying the client-side security of the website vælgererklæring.dk. Figure 2 depicts the redacted version of the Invitation email that was forwarded to us on August 11, 2016, 15:20, only three hours after our initial request on August 11, 12:10. It is also noteworthy, that this email was not sent to the email address we provided, but to the email of an employee at ØIM (redacted), which means that the ØIM staff was aware that tokens are not bound to the identity of the endorser, but can be forwarded to anyone, effectively circumventing the seven day "reflection period". The token is clearly displayed as the last argument to the clickable link in the email.

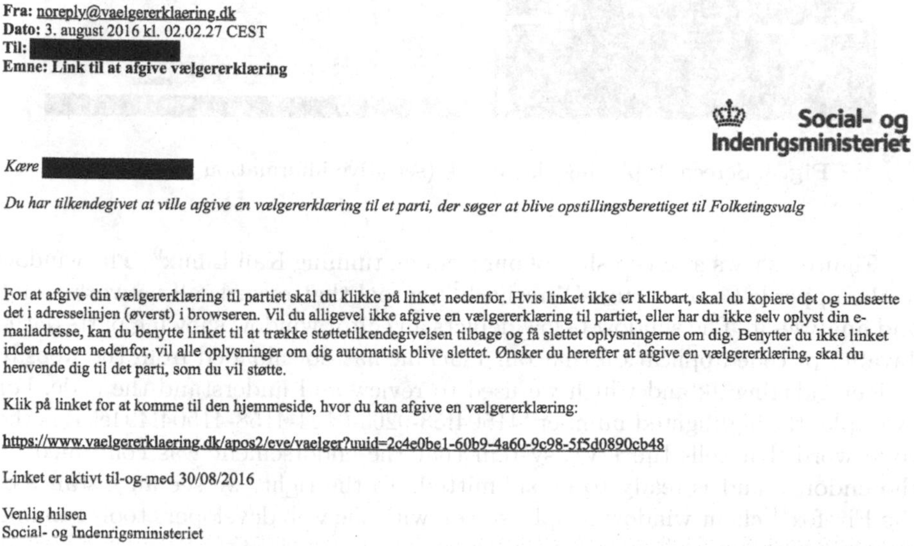

Fra: noreply@vaelgererklaering.dk
Dato: 3. august 2016 kl. 02.02.27 CEST
Til:
Emne: **Link til at afgive vælgererklæring**

♔   **Social- og**
     Indenrigsministeriet

Kære

Du har tilkendegivet at ville afgive en vælgererklæring til et parti, der søger at blive opstillingsberettiget til Folketingsvalg

For at afgive din vælgererklæring til partiet skal du klikke på linket nedenfor. Hvis linket ikke er klikbart, skal du kopiere det og indsætte det i adresselinjen (øverst) i browseren. Vil du alligevel ikke afgive en vælgererklæring til partiet, eller har du ikke selv oplyst din e-mailadresse, kan du benytte linket til at trække støttetilkendegivelsen tilbage og få slettet oplysningerne om dig. Benytter du ikke linket inden datoen nedenfor, vil alle oplysninger om dig automatisk blive slettet. Ønsker du herefter at afgive en vælgererklæring, skal du henvende dig til det parti, som du vil støtte.

Klik på linket for at komme til den hjemmeside, hvor du kan afgive en vælgererklæring:

https://www.vaelgererklaering.dk/apos2/eve/vaelger?uuid=2c4e0be1-60b9-4a60-9c98-5f5d0890cb48

Linket er aktivt til-og-med 30/08/2016

Venlig hilsen
Social- og Indenrigsministeriet

Fig. 2. Invitation Email with token (sensitive information redacted)

Upon receiving this token by email, we followed the link, and were prompted with the NemID login procedure, which we used to authenticate the first author of this paper. At this point, it was time to launch the tools that any security expert and hacker would use.

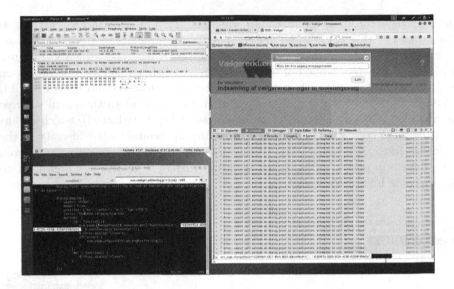

Fig. 3. Screen displaying the attack (sensitive information redacted)

Figure 3 shows a screen shot of our system, running Kali Linux[9]. The window in the upper left corner runs Wireshark[10], a tool that records all network traffic and analyzes it. The window below depicts an editor window showing parts of the JavaScript code application that our machine has downloaded from the website vælgererklæring.dk and which we used to review and understand the code. For example, the highlighted number '41504f53-0203-0124-4158-41504f494e54' is the code word that tells the DVE-system that the endorsement was confirmed by the endorser and is ready to be submitted. To the right, we see an instance of the Firefox[11] client window in split screen with the web developers tools running in the lower part.

Our first step was to collect information on how the DVE-system works, so we logged into the website using the first author's credentials, and proceeded to try to endorse the party "De Visionære". We observed that the system worked according to specification: as the first author is not a Danish citizen, the system rightly rejected his attempt to endorse the party, which was acknowledged by an "access denied" message on screen. With this information at hand, we started to study the JavaScript code that was running on our computer to learn as much as we could about the implementation.

```
1  page.find('a.button').bind('click', function(e){
2    e.preventDefault();
3    $.ajax({
4      type: 'GET',
```

---

[9] See https://www.kali.org/.
[10] See https://www.wireshark.org/.
[11] See https://www.mozilla.org/en-US/firefox/new/.

```
5      url: '!checkVoterRightsProxy',
6      dataType: 'xml',
7      async: false,
8      cache: false,
9      data: {
10      cpr: $.session.get('personCpr'),
11      type: $.session.get('indsamlingsType')
12     },
13     success: function(xml){
14      if($(xml).find('responseMessage').attr('response')
15          == "success"){
16        eve.page.confirmAfgivErklaering();
17      }else if($(xml).find('responseMessage').attr('response')
18               == "dobbelterklaering"){
19        $.session.set('afvistGrund', 'dobbelt');
20        eve.page.afvistErklaeringKvittering();
21      }else if($(xml).find('responseMessage').attr('response')
22               == "valgret"){
23        $.session.set('afvistGrund', 'mangledeValgret');
24        eve.page.afvistErklaeringKvittering();
25      }else{
26        eve.core.confirmationsDialog(
27          $(xml).find('responseMessage').attr('response'));
28      }
29     }
30   });
31 });
```

This piece of code contacts the `!checkVoterRightsProxy` to check if the user has the proper rights to vote. On line 13 we can see how the client reacts to possible responses by the server. There are three cases:

1. all the checks succeed (`response == 'success'`), so the user is allowed to endorse the party; in this case `eve.page.confirmAfgivErklaering()` is called by the client;
2. the user has already endorsed a party (`response == 'dobbelterklaering'`), hence the user is hence denied the option to cast an endorsement;
3. or the user does not have the right to vote at all, (`response == 'valgret'`), and is similarly denied to cast an endorsement for the party.

Since the first author is not Danish, the request is clearly is handled by case 3. and so we inspected the code for implementing the necessary functionality. First, the following function is called:

```
1 afvistErklaeringKvittering: function(){ //V9
2   eve.core.clean($('#vContent'));
3   eve.core.clean($('#vInfo'));
4   eve.page.renderAfvistErklaeringKvittering();
5   eve.page.configHelpButton('V9');
6 },
```

which then in turn calls:

```
1  renderAfvistErklaeringKvittering: function(){
2    var page = $('#vContent'), information = $('#vInfo');
3
4    $.ajax({
5      type: 'GET',
6      url: '!rejectVoterProxy',
7      dataType: 'xml',
8      async: false,
9      cache: false,
10     data: {
11       uuid: $.session.get('functionUuid'),
12       cpr: $.session.get('personCpr')
13     }
14   });
15
16   page.append(eve.page.breadcrumbs(3, 3);)
17
18   var insdsamlingsNavn =
19     $.session.get('indsamlingsType') == "FV" ?
20     "folketingsvalg" : "Europa-Parlamentsvalg" ;
21   var partyNameLink = $.session.get('www') != "" ?
22     '<a href="' + $.session.get('www') + '" target="_blank">'
23     + 'Link til ' + $.session.get('navn') + ' hjemmeside</a>' :
         "" ;
24
25   [...]
26
27   page.find('a.button').bind('click', function(e){
28     e.preventDefault();
29     eve.page.logout();
30   });
31 },
```

This function contacts the server calling !rejectVoterProxy, then constructs a
return HTML message using a sequence of appends, which we have abbreviated
under [...] on line 25. Now we understood and could reconstruct the behavior
of the DVE-system. The next step therefore was to try to trick the DVE-system
into accepting the first author's endorsement despite him not being a Danish
citizen. We traced the code to determine what would have happened if all checks
succeeded and inspected the confirmAfgivErklaering function, which displays the
confirmation of a vote, and it looked as follows:

```
1  confirmAfgivErklaering: function(){
2    var dialog = $('#confirm_dialog');
3
4    dialog.find('span.handling').text('Du er ved at bekræfte' +
5      ' din vælgererklæring. Er du sikker?');
6
7    dialog.dialog({
8      width: '450px',
9      modal: true,
10     position: {"my":"center", "at": "top +200"},
11     title: "Godkend vælgererklæring",
12     buttons: {
13       "Ja": function(){
14         eve.page.changeState($.session.get('functionUuid'),
15           '41504f53-0203-0124-4158-41504f494e54',
16           $.session.get('personCpr'));
17         $(this).dialog("close");
18         if(!error) {
19           eve.page.afgivetErklaeringKvittering();
20         }
21       },
22       "Nej": function() {
23         $(this).dialog("close");
24       }
25     }
26   });
27 },
```

Line 13 displays the function call that gets executed once the endorsement is confirmed, which is triggered by the user pressing the "Ja" button as the last step. In particular, the following function call is interesting:

```
1  eve.page.changeState($.session.get('functionUuid'),
2    '41504f53-0203-0124-4158-41504f494e54',
3    $.session.get('personCpr'));
```

Digging deeper into the JavaScript code, we observe that the function being called is the following:

```
1  changeState: function(funktionUuid, stateUuid, cpr){
2    var data = {functionUuid: funktionUuid,
3                stillingsbetegnelseUuid: stateUuid}
4
5    $.ajax({
6      type: 'GET',
7      url: '!changeVoterStateProxy',
8      dataType: 'xml',
9      async: false,
10     cache: false,
11     data: data,
12     success: function (xml) {
13       if($(xml).find('responseMessage').attr('response')
14         != "success") {
15         eve.core.confirmationsDialog($(xml).find('
             responseMessage')
```

```
16              .attr('response'));
17          error = true;
18        } else {
19          error = false;
20        }
21      }
22    });
23  },
```

The function contacts the server on !changeVoterStateProxy to change the record of the voter.

Returning to the preceding code snippet, we notice that there are two parameters missing from the function call that have to be provided, which are functionUuid and personCpr. After finding the right functionUuid (see Fig. 3) in the browser's cookie store, and knowing the first author's civil registration number (CPR) we were able to construct and place a request to the DVE-system through the vælgererklæring.dk website that would allow us to submit a fraudulent endorsement for the party De Visionære (which we later removed to return the database to an "uncorrupted state").

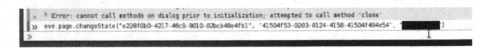

Fig. 4. The attack line (sensitive information redacted)

Figure 4 depicts the problematic command with the CPR number redacted that we issued through the Firefox console, while Fig. 5 shows the letter sent to the first author's authenticated e-Boks, confirming a successful attack.

In summary, we have shown that even the simple client-side security objective was violated. After this shocking revelation, we did not attempt further attacks, but many, similar in nature, come to mind. For example: would it be be possible to submit or withdraw endorsements impersonating other voters? or to circumvent other restrictions imposed by the law? We concluded at the time that this attack demonstrates a complete lack of integrity in the endorsements database, which also questions the decisions that have been drawn from it.

4.3   Socio-Technical Vulnerabilities

Another grave vulnerability of the DVE-system was pointed out by ØIM, when they sent us the invitation depicted in Fig. 2: the tokens for submitting endorsements are not bound to the identity of the endorser. This observation can certainly be turned into another serious attack. A party administrator could, just as our contact at ØIM has done, generate many tokens by specifying a party email. These tokens will arrive in the mailbox after seven days, which can then be forwarded to potential endorsers, effectively bypassing the seven day "reflection period" required by administrative regulation. Endorsements can happen

Social- og Indenrigsministeriet
Holmens Kanal 22
1060 København

Carsten Elmar Schürmann

 **Social- og Indenrigsministeriet**

Journalnøgle
2c4e0be1-60b9-4a60-9c98-5f5d0890cb48

Dato
12. august 2016

Kvittering for afgivelse af vælgererklæring

Du har nu afgivet vælgererklæring til partiet:

> De Visionære
> Prins Jørgens Gård 1
> 1218 København K
> Tlf.: 22460608
> Www.Visionaer.dk

Din vælgererklæring er gyldig i 18 måneder fra datoen for afgivelsen. Du kan ikke afgive vælgererklæring til støtte for et andet partis opstilling til folketingsvalg, så længe vælgererklæringen er gyldig. Når gyldigheden udløber, slettes din vælgererklæring og alle øvrige oplysninger om din afgivelse af vælgererklæring automatisk i den digitale løsning. Du kan dog trække din vælgererklæring tilbage via nedenstående link, hvis du ikke længere ønsker at deltage i anmeldelse af partiet, eller hvis du ønsker at afgive vælgererklæring til et andet parti. Har partiet allerede anmeldt sig for social- og indenrigsministeren, kan du dog ikke trække din vælgererklæring tilbage. Anmeldelsen af et parti er gyldig indtil førstkommende folketingsvalg, dog mindst 18 måneder. Herefter kan du igen frit afgive vælgererklæring til et parti.

Klik på linket for at komme til vælgererklæring.dk, hvis du ønker at trække din vælgererklæring tilbage:

https://www.vaelgererklaering.dk/apos2/eve/vaelger?
uuid=2c4e0be1-60b9-4a60-9c98-5f5d0890cb48

Linket er aktivt til og med 3. februar 2018.

Venlig hilsen
Social- og Indenrigsministeriet

Fig. 5. The receipt (sensitive information redacted)

right in front of party representatives, exposing voters to social engineering and coercion attacks.

The only argument that softens the severity of the attack is that endorsers receive a final receipt to their personal e-Boks, and therefore they will always be able to withdraw an endorsement that they may not feel comfortable with.

5   Reflections and Recommendations

The legal framework and the technical framework do not match. The legal framework is weak, because it does not require the digital solution to be software independent or at the very least verifiable. The administrative regulation permits technical solutions that do little to strengthen public confidence in endorsement integrity. The technical framework (that we studied in this paper) is weak, because it is not made to be used in an adversarial environment.

We recommend that the ØIM strengthens the administrative regulation and involves experts in designing a new generation DVE-system as soon as possible, to ensure that the system lives up to best practices and follows international recommendations. ØIM should also consider to strengthen the privacy of endorsers and require coercion resistance beyond just the ability to withdraw endorsements at a later stage.

6   Conclusions

In this paper, we present an analysis of an early and unpatched version of the Danish party endorsement (DVE)-system and argue that the design of the law and the DVE-system are fundamentally flawed. We show that even non-eligible endorsers in possession of an invitation email and a valid NemID could have endorsed the prospective party. According to ØIM this was the only successfully executed attack using this particular vulnerability before the system was fixed in December 2016. A consequence of our demonstration is that the DVE-database of endorsements may lack integrity, and consequently so do all decisions based on it.

Responsible Disclosure. After discovering the flaw on August 12th 2016, we informed the ministry of our findings by email. On August 25th the ministry asked the first author to present a detailed document with all our findings. On September 14th 2016 we were invited to present our findings to ØIM and the software vendor, which we did on September 27th and offered our help to fix the fundamental design issues in the protocol. Finally, on October 25th, 2016, we organized a meeting with the vendor at the IT University of Copenhagen, screening a video recording of the attack, and on December 19th we received notification that the specific issue was resolved. Since then, ØIM has neither invited us to look at the security of the DVE-system again, nor have they invited us to bid or participate in a commissioned security review, nor have they shared with us the results of the security review conducted by an unknown third party.

The Aftermath. In 2016, a new party called the "Nye Borgelige"[12] was introduced on the ballot based on the endorsements stored in the database. Another prospective party "Nationalpartiet"[13] also applied to become a party in 2016, but did not succeed, citing unavailability of paper endorsements and problems with the DVE-system. Their application was eventually rejected. Both decisions were made using the version of the DVE-system discussed in this paper. In 2019, two new parties were added to the ballot, "Klaus Riskær Pedersen"[14] and "Stram Kurs"[15]. Both parties stand accused of having exploited the socio-technical vulnerability described in Sect. 4.3.

---

[12] See https://nyeborgerlige.dk/.
[13] See http://www.nationalpartiet.dk/.
[14] See https://www.klausriskaerpedersen.dk/.
[15] See https://stramkurs.dk/.

In the the light of the recent accusations, representative of all parties represented in the parliament have voted that a new DVE-system should be built/procured, citing lack of usability and usable security. The new system should be in place as soon as possible. We pledge our support to ØIM to assist with improving both the regulatory framework and the technology.

Acknowledgements. We would like to thank Christine Boeskov and Søren Stauning from ØIM for their comments on earlier versions of this paper.

References

[BRR+15] Benaloh, J., Rivest, R.L., Ryan, P.Y.A., Stark, P.B., Teague, V., Vora, P.L.: End-to-end verifiability. CoRR, abs/1504.03778 (2015)
[CKN+14] Clouser, M., Krimmer, R., Nore, H., Schürmann, C., Wolf, P.: The use of open source technology in elections. Resources on electoral processes. International IDEA, Stockholm (2014). ISBN 978-91-87729-68-3
[EBB+15] Esteve, J.B., et al.: Certification of ICTs in Elections. International Institute for Democracy and Electoral Assistance (IDEA), Stockholm (2015)
[RW06] Rivest, R.L., Wack, J.P.: On the notion of 'software independence' in voting systems, July 2006. http://vote.nist.gov/SI-in-voting.pdf

On Practical Aspects of Coercion-Resistant Remote Voting Systems

Kristjan Krips[1,3] and Jan Willemson[1,2(✉)]

[1] Cybernetica AS, Ülikooli 2, 51003 Tartu, Estonia
{krisjan.krips,jan.willemson}@cyber.ee
[2] STACC, Ülikooli 2, 51003 Tartu, Estonia
[3] Institute of Computer Science, University of Tartu, J. Liivi 2, Tartu, Estonia

Abstract. Coercive behaviour is hard to control in the remote electronic voting setting. This is why a number of protocols have been proposed that aim at mitigating this threat. However, these proposals have remained largely academic. This paper takes the practical viewpoint and analyses the most common assumptions that are required by the various schemes, together with the exact level of coercion-resistance they provide.

1 Introduction

With introduction of Australian secret ballot into the voting process in mid-19th century, the threat of voter coercion was significantly reduced. Voting in a private booth surrounded by a controlled environment became the "gold standard" which has served democratic societies around the world well for over a 100 years.

However, several developments in recent decades have undermined the effect of Australian ballot as a coercion-resistance measure. First, technology of recording the private events within the voting booth (both with the voter cooperation and stealthily) has become readily available [3,17,18]. And second, human mobility has increased to an extent where expecting all the voters to come to a controlled environment on a particular day is less and less of an option [32].

These problems have motivated research and development in the field of coercion-resistant (remote) voting solutions. However, only a few of these solutions have actually been implemented in practice, leaving practical considerations such as usability or technical complexity of satisfying necessary assumptions often out of scope.

Another issue with the notion of coercion resistance is that it does not have a single clear interpretation. Thus it is not always immediately clear which levels of coercion resistance are achieved by various proposals.

The current paper aims at narrowing these gaps. We have selected seven different schemes from recent proposals and analyse them from two viewpoints. First, we identify common technical and organisational assumptions that these schemes rely on and assess their practical satisfiability. Second, we gather different interpretations of coercion resistance and analyse to what extent each one of the considered schemes achieves them.

© Springer Nature Switzerland AG 2019
R. Krimmer et al. (Eds.): E-Vote-ID 2019, LNCS 11759, pp. 216–232, 2019.
https://doi.org/10.1007/978-3-030-30625-0_14

We do not claim full coverage of all coercion-resistant schemes that have ever been proposed, but we have made an attempt to put together a representative selection of different approaches used for remote voting. Also, voting schemes often come in families. In this case we have selected members of such families for which coercion resistance and/or usability issues have been addressed the most.

2 Notions of Voting Freedom

One of the fundamental requirements of democratic elections is that the voter should be able to express her true preference freely, i.e. without being coerced. This broad statement has several possible interpretations, leading to more fine-grained requirements. E.g. following [4], we can identify the following properties.

- Basic *ballot privacy* guarantees that no one can learn how a voter voted (if she is not coerced and is willing to keep her vote secret). All the voting schemes studied in this paper satisfy this requirement.
- *Receipt-freeness* ensures that a malicious voter is unable to produce a proof for the value of her vote, making coercion essentially inefficient.
- *Coercion resistance* means intuitively that the voter should be able to cast a vote reflecting her true preference even if being monitored by the coercer for (most of) the voting period. To distinguish this property from the generic term, we will also call it *over-the-shoulder coercion resistance* in this paper.

Juels *et al.* [16] go even further and state three additional requirements that a fully coercion-free voting system should correspond to.

- The coercer should not be able to force the voter to abstain from elections.
- The coercer should not be able to force the voter to cast an invalid vote.
- The coercer should not be able to cast a valid vote if he gets access to the voter's credentials.

3 Coercion-Resistant Schemes and Their Assumptions

The threat of coercion depends on many aspects: type of elections, properties of the voting protocol, assumptions on the voting system and environment, awareness and coercibility of the voters, capabilities of the attacker, etc.

Typically, voting protocols aiming at some form of coercion resistance must make trade-offs between different goals. In the following, we describe and classify existing coercion resistant voting protocol proposals according to their assumptions, usability and applicability for different types of elections.

3.1 Re-voting Based Schemes/Estonian Scheme

Re-voting is a metatechnique that can be used on top of other voting systems to provide voter with an option of changing her vote in case she was coerced during the first attempts(s). An example of a pure re-voting-based protocol is the Estonian scheme, where this is the only anti-coercion measure in use [22].

The biggest problem with such schemes is that the coercer might stay with the voter until the end of the voting period (either physically or virtually [3]) to make sure that she does not cast a re-vote. To mitigate this threat (and also some other risks of remote voting), Estonia has chosen to end the Internet vote submission two hours before the polling stations are closed on the last day of advance voting period. The rationale is that if the voter feels coerced, she still has some time to submit her vote on paper and the paper vote cancels the e-vote. However, if the voter resides far from any of the polling stations (and enabling this scenario is one motivation of Internet voting), she can not submit an un-coerced vote. The whole system operates under the assumption that the share of such events is insignificant.

In addition, the re-voting functionality can affect integrity of the cast vote as an active attacker may use it to overwrite the previous vote.

On the positive side, enabling re-voting does not need extra setup on the client side, and the process is easy to understand for an average voter.

Aside from that, the Estonian system relies on significant technical assumptions, most notably voter credential pre-distribution. This is implemented via the national digital identity mechanisms (ID-card and mobile-ID), with the corresponding public keys being available via national PKI. Thus, even though the Estonian scheme relies on special client-side hardware, these devices are already very widely in use.

3.2 JCJ/Civitas Family

Formal study of coercion resistance in voting systems was initiated in 2002 by Juels, Catalano and Jakobsson [15]. They gave a definition of coercion resistance and proposed the first scheme satisfying it, later becoming known as the JCJ scheme [16]. This research introduced fake credentials which the voter can use under coercion, but the coercer is unable to distinguish from the genuine ones.

In 2008, the JCJ scheme was extended by Clarkson, Chong and Myers by introducing distributed trust assumptions and improving the performance. The resulting protocol was called Civitas [8].

Neither of the JCJ and Civitas proposals specified how exactly the voter should select the appropriate credentials. Neumann and Volkamer noted in 2012 that this action is non-trivial, and may lead to both usability and security issues when implemented carelessly. Improving the specification of Civitas, they proposed an implementation based on smart cards and readers with PIN-pads and trusted displays [28]. Selection between a fake and a real credential would be accomplished by entering either a real or a fake PIN into the reader.

Essentially, Neumann-Volkamer proposal encapsulates all the critical voter-side operations into special hardware, which has to be trusted. While in principle such an approach can make credential handling more secure, it does not really move us much closer to a practical implementation. Smart card readers with trusted preview are not commonplace on the market, and the smart cards would require a lot of non-standard functionality.

In a later research Neumann *et al.* have shown that, in principle, modern smart cards have sufficient performance required to implement such functions [27]. However, performance is not the only bottleneck in the practical deployment. The software implementing the protocol functionality needs to somehow get onto the cards.

Roughly speaking, election organisers have two approaches to tackle this problem. First, they can approach a large smart card vendor and convince it to implement the required functionality as part of the card firmware. Our interview with a representative of Gemalto (previous supplier of Estonian ID-cards) revealed that smart card vendors are quite reluctant to include limited-use applications on their products, and prefer implementing only general-purpose cryptographic primitives like standardised asymmetric signatures. One reason for this is that in many applications (likely including voting as well) the customers require certification, testing and validation of the security features of smart cards (for example, according to Common Criteria standard or FIPS-140-2). Such processes are expensive and time-consuming, and the vendor cannot earn this investment back selling limited-use cards.

Another option would be using programmable cards and implementing the functionality oneself in the spirit of [27]. The drawback of this approach is the need to support the whole software development life cycle locally. While it may give better control over the implementation, the risks are also higher. In case a bug is discovered, updating applications on the cards that have been distributed to numerous remote voters is a nightmare. Also, the whole expense of certification (in case it is desired) needs to be carried locally.

We conclude that while special-purpose smart cards provide an appealing option for a "poor man's HSM", their deployment has problems that are not necessarily easier to solve than the original challenge they were designed to meet.

As a part of the registration procedure, the Neumann-Volkamer protocol also depends on availability of anonymous channels (e.g. Tor is suggested by the authors). We refer to Sect. 3.4 for a more elaborate discussion on difficulties of achieving anonymous channels (using Tor) in practice.

Another branch of JCJ was developed by Araújo *et al.* in 2010 [2]. They introduced shorter credentials and provided a formal proof of coercion-resistance, although their proof relied on a non-standard number-theoretic assumption. In 2018, Neto *et al.* conducted usability studies for the CIVIS system [26], which is an implementation of the protocol proposed by Araújo *et al.* [2]. The study revealed that more than 90% of the test participants did not understand the functionality of casting fake votes. Also, they did not feel comfortable with the result, being unable to distinguish whether their submitted vote was real or fake. This brings the whole concept of using fake credentials under question.

3.3   Helios Family

The original proposal of Helios by Adida [1] was explicitly targeted towards low-coercion environments. During later research, several extensions have been developed to enhance its coercion resistance.

KTV-Helios. Kulyk, Teague and Volkamer have extended the Helios voting system to provide private eligibility verifiability, i.e. the property that anyone can verify that only votes from eligible voters are included in the tally, without revealing who actually submitted them [19,20]. As a by-product, they achieve receipt-freeness in the sense that the voter can not prove how she voted as she can undetectably re-vote. However, the authors stated that the protocol is susceptible to forced abstention and randomisation attacks. Following the authors' initials, the scheme is known as KTV-Helios.

The core idea of Kulyk *et al.* is to hide the true votes among dummy ones. Receipt-freeness is achieved allowing the voter to cast differential vote updates, so that the final vote would be a combination (e.g. product) of the votes cast. A similar approach was independently developed by Locher and Haenni [21].

Even though the dummy votes can be cast by any voter, most of them would probably not bother to do so. Hence a specific party called posting proxy or posting trustee is introduced by Kulyk *et al.*, and its task is to submit the dummy votes. In order to prevent timing side channels (see Sect. 3.4), posting trustee must operate in a randomised fashion.

Regarding the practical implementation aspects, the authors of KTV-Helios admit themselves that the understandability and usability issues remain largely unsolved [20]. Seeing many votes submitted onto the bulletin board on her behalf probably makes an average voter quite anxious. We add here a potential legal problem of voter impersonation, even if there are cryptographic proofs certifying that the extra votes do not change the final tally.

BeleniosRF. In the original version of Helios, the voter can present encryption randomness as a receipt for the coercer. BeleniosRF uses re-randomisable ciphertexts and signatures, with part of the randomness being out of the voter's control, making it impossible for a voter to produce such a receipt [4].

The ballot is signed by the voter and re-randomisation of the ballot by the server does not invalidate the corresponding signature. Thus, the voter can verify the signature to make sure that the vote has not been changed. However, this applies only when re-voting is not enabled. The authors of BeleniosRF state that in case of re-voting the voters would not be able to check which of their ballots were re-randomised by the server. Therefore, BeleniosRF does not allow re-voting and thereby does not provide protection against over-the-shoulder coercion. However, vulnerability to in-person coercion is one of the major objections against remote electronic voting in the first place [10,11,13,14,24,25].

The authors of BeleniosRF argue that changing one's vote is a legally grey area anyway, and most of the countries would need to go through a complicated legal process before they can support it.

While we agree that legislative changes are necessary to support re-voting, we feel that the authors of BeleniosRF over-estimate the complexity of this process.

For example, extensive social and legal debate concerning constitutionality of re-voting took place in Estonia when Internet voting was introduced there. A few months before the first Internet-enabled elections, the President of Estonia brought Internet voting provisions to the Supreme Court for constitutional review, arguing that the possibility to change Internet votes gives advantages to Internet voters in comparison with paper voters. The decision of the Supreme Court did not support this point of view, reaching the conclusion that merely a technical option of casting multiple votes does not put Internet voters into any kind of advantage [23].

While the outcome of a similar legal discussion may be different in other jurisdictions, we feel that re-voting as an easy-to-implement and relatively efficient anti-coercion measure is important enough to review some of the legislative principles. Changing legislation in order to catch up with technological advancements is an unavoidable process anyway.

3.4 Selene

The primary design goal of the Selene scheme proposed by Ryan et al. [31] is achieving a user-friendly end-to-end vote verification protocol. As too strong of a verification mechanism brings along a threat of coercion, the authors of Selene have also paid a lot of attention to mitigating this threat. They propose using cryptographic tracking numbers which are first committed to a bulletin board using trapdoor commitments. After the end of the voting period, clear-text votes with clear-text tracking numbers are displayed on the bulletin board as well. The (voter-controlled) trapdoor can later be used to open the commitment to any tracking number of coercer's liking.

The voter, of course, still needs to somehow identify the real tracking number of her own vote. This is facilitated by sending her the correct decommitment value α. In order to fool the coercer, the voter can produce an alternative decommitment value α' that is cryptographically indistinguishable from α and points to any vote requested by the coercer.

However, cryptographic indistinguishability is not sufficient, as the attacker potentially has a number of side channels available to separate the true α from voter-generated α'-s. The authors of Selene acknowledge this problem and state that α-terms should be transferred over an unauthenticated and private channel.

Unfortunately, implementing such a channel is non-trivial. Note first that in order to mitigate the threat of coercion, it is not sufficient just to drop strong authentication mechanisms like signatures. For example, if α (or its shares coming from the trustees) is sent via regular, otherwise unauthenticated email, it has to carry sender's email address. There are both legal and usability issues that suggest using a fixed official address rather some randomly generated ones. Email is just an example here, similar problems would occur if other taggable delivery channels like instant messaging or web bulletin board would be used.

In principle, the process of preparing a false α' can also include sending it from the official address. In this case there is still the timing side channel that the coercer can use to distinguish the genuine α. In order to counter this, the genuine α-s would need to be sent at randomised moments, and the voter must prepare α' during this period. This is doable and is also proposed by the authors, but it complicates the voter's view of the protocol substantially.

We can also imagine genuine α-s being sent out via regular mail, printed on standard office paper. The voter can print α' out on her home printer, but this assumes using exactly the same kind of paper, printing resolution, etc. In addition, majority of modern colour laser printers mark the printed papers with tracking dots which can be used to identify the printer [30]. We can see that it could be possible to deliver α-s with the help of the postal service, but generating the fake values is not as easy as the authors of Selene probably foresaw. Note also that a vote buyer is typically after a number of votes and he can live with some of the voters being able to fool him as long as their share is not too high.

One can also utilise stronger anonymisation techniques, e.g. mixing or onion routing. These would only help if the full set of messages is larger than just the official α-terms, as otherwise we would have no sender anonymity. One may consider using an existing anonymisation network, say, Tor (as also recommended by Neumann and Volkamer [28]). However, due to significant illegal activity happening over it, utilising Tor for legally binding elections would be questionable.

We argue that this dilemma is at least partially inherent and not specific to Tor. On one hand, too small of an anonymisation set does not fulfil the goal, but fighting doubtful traffic in a large network is practically impossible.

Furthermore, by relying on Tor (let's still use it as a prime example) new problems are introduced. Referring to the objectionable content and general uncontrollable nature, several countries have attempted to block/filter Tor traffic[1]. This makes it hard for expatriates living in those countries to participate in the elections remotely, but supporting expatriate participation is one of the main reasons for introducing remote electronic voting in the first place.

Setting up private channels from the election organiser to all the voters is not a trivial task either. As Selene already relies on a PKI for vote signing, assuming additional access to an authentic public-private key pair for encryption and decryption is probably not a big extra. However, even the α-term encrypted with the voter's public key has to be delivered to her somehow. We conclude that channel privacy does not really help against the soft sender identification problem described above.

In 2019, Distler *et al.* performed an e-voting usability study based on a Selene protocol implementation [9]. Unfortunately, they left the steps related to coercion resistance (including preparing the fake α' and selecting it in the presence of the coercer) out of scope. We also note that their implementation relies only

---

[1] It is hard to get reliable statistics on the extent of Tor filtering, but there exists indirect evidence in the form of the share of users relying on Tor bridges (https://metrics.torproject.org/userstats-bridge-table.html) and observed irregularities (https://metrics.torproject.org/userstats-censorship-events.html).

on a mobile device for both vote casting and verification. This means that verification is inefficient against the malicious device and does not thus fulfil the purpose of verification. We feel that in order to get a more realistic understanding of usability of Selene protocol the authors of [9] should have implemented a complete version, e.g. by using a second channel for verification. Adding extra channels and steps would have likely changed the user perception and feedback.

3.5 Eos

Patachi and Schürmann have proposed the Eos voting scheme based on a specific flavour of ring signatures, namely conditional linkable ring signatures [29]. As each voter can have multiple pseudo-identities in the scheme, conditional linkability allows the signer to choose if the signatures can be linked to the same identity by the verifier.

There are two main anti-coercion measures in Eos. First, the voter can use subliminal hinting (called selecting between "red" and "green" envelopes or alternative pseudo-identities in [29]) while preparing the encrypted vote. In practice, such hinting would be implemented by presenting either a real or pseudo-PIN to a special-hardware voting device or to the coercer who controls the device.

Second, if the actively coerced voter had to cast a vote using a valid PIN, she may later re-vote to update the vote. However, in that case the public bulletin board will contain multiple encrypted votes given by the same pseudo-identity, which may be known to the coercer. In that case, the voter may have to lie to the coercer that the coercer was the last one to cast the vote.

The protocol makes several non-trivial assumptions. First, to get rid of side-channels during submitting the ring-signed votes, one would need to use anonymous channels, but achieving these is quite tricky in practice (see Sect. 3.4).

Second, special hardware tokens would be needed to implement the client-side operations (key management, PIN validation, identity selection, and signature computation). The paper [29] suggests that hardware wallets designed for storing the keys for cryptocurrencies could be used in this role. It might be possible to reprogram such hardware, but distributing the hardware or the private keys to the voters is a non-trivial task.

As the selection between identities would happen by entering a real or pseudo-PIN, we also have all the regular problems of pseudo-PIN management – if the user enters a wrong PIN, the device can not give any feedback (as the coercer might be watching), and would quietly submit a vote that the voter did not intend to (e.g. in the scenario where the voter wanted to use a pseudo-PIN, but accidentally used a real one).

3.6 Selections

A special form of fake credentials called *panic passwords* has been proposed by Clark and Hengartner in 2008 [5]. The essence of panic passwords is what the name says – the user can select a true password together with a set of alternative ones that can be used to covertly alert the system that the user is under abnormal circumstances, e.g. coercion.

The latter is an important threat scenario in case of remote voting, so the same authors have built a coercion-resistant voting scheme called Selections around their core idea [6].

Unfortunately, making human-memorisable passwords to work as fake credentials is even more problematic than in case of cryptographic credentials.

First, a complex registration process is needed. Of course, it has to take place in a controlled, coercion-free environment, but this is a standard assumption. The registration procedure can even be implemented bare-handed (i.e. not requiring the voter to perform computations by heart). An Internet-enabled computer is still required inside the controlled registration booth to print out a voter preparation sheet. This is meant as a countermeasure "... in the event that an adversary ensured she entered the registration process without her sheet" [6].

The only way the coercer can achieve this is to search through the voter's belongings and walk together with her until the door of the registration booth. But if the coercer is prepared to do this much, he can also request the voter to record all her actions with a camera or even send a live stream [3]. As a result, the effect of controlled registration environment will be significantly reduced.

During the registration process, the previously selected and encrypted panic passwords are re-randomised. The voter selects one of the re-randomised encryptions which is posted to a public roster. It is assumed in the protocol that the voter deletes the randomness used for re-randomisation and does not record it. Building security properties on the assumption that some value is deleted is always questionable. There may exist side channels that the coercer forces the voter to use to record or stream the value. If the coercer took part in creating the voter preparation sheet and has access to it, then the re-encrypted panic password on the public roster can be matched with the encrypted panic password on the preparation sheet. Thus, the randomness gives a way to prove the validity of the password given to the coercer.

We also noticed that the registration protocol differs significantly when comparing the full paper (e-print) [7] to the conference paper [6]. In the e-print version, the registration protocol allows the voter to rewind the process back to the re-randomisation phase. In the conference paper, the registration protocol allows the voter to rewind the process back to the beginning, i.e., to selecting new panic passwords. However, the difference is important as some of the coercion protections depend on the rewinding functionality.

Additionally, Selections suffers from the typical problems of password-based systems. Even though [6] proposes measures to increase password memorability, the scenario of voting stretches these boundaries. The idea of [6] was to go through the complex registration process once and then use the credentials over several events. However, elections typically only happen once in a few years, and many voters are likely to forget their passwords over this time, no matter how good of a mnemonic is used. To counter this problem, humans tend to write the passwords down, increasing their coercibility as a result.

4   Other Coercion Properties

In this section, we discuss the extra coercion properties (i.e. forced abstention, casting an invalid vote, and forced surrender of credentials) of the schemes.

A voter can be forced to not take part in the elections if a coercer has a way to check if the voter abstained from voting. As potential attackers, we also consider corrupt election officials and democratically elected politicians who decide to deviate from fair election practices. Such an attacker would be able to to indirectly manipulate a large portion of the electorate.

Forcing the voter to cast an invalid vote can benefit the coercer in (at least) two ways. First, in case the voter is supporting a party opposing the coercer's views, the invalid vote would have no effect and the voter would effectively abstain from the elections. Second, if the invalid vote would be posted to a bulletin board, the attacker could remotely check if the voter behaved according to the instructions. Even if the invalid vote would not be published, it may still be possible that election officials are able to see the value of the vote and thus be able to play the role of a coercer.

In case another person would be able to use the voter's credentials, it would be possible to cast the vote on behalf of the voter. Juels *et al.* [16] refer to this type of an attack as a *simulation attack*.

The rest of this Section is devoted to the discussion of these coercion properties. Table 1 summarises the main assumptions used by different coercion-resistant protocols proposals together with their level of coercion-resistance in respect to the requirements listed in Sect. 2. The only exception is the basic ballot privacy that all the considered schemes trivially satisfy.

4.1   Re-voting Based Schemes / Estonian Scheme

The Estonian voting system provides protection against standard versions of these coercion attacks. More specifically, an outside third party is not able to detect if a voter cast a vote online or abstained as there is no public proof of the vote casting. There is a private bulletin board in the Estonian voting system, which is only accessible to the election officials and auditors. The official voting client software does not support casting an invalid vote. Finally, the signing key of the voter is stored inside of a smart card, hence the coercer would need to have physical access to use the credentials.

However, the situation gets more complicated in case of an attacker who has insider information. The voting system has to verify the ballot signatures to make sure that only the votes of eligible voters are accepted. Thus, insiders could check if a certain voter abstained.

There is also an insider threat when an invalid vote is cast. To cast an invalid vote, either the voter or the coercer would have to create a non-standard voting client. In case the invalid vote would have a correct format and would correspond to a non-existing candidate number of a suitable district, the vote would be decrypted during the tallying process. Writing a voting client that would allow casting such votes is possible as the voting protocol and the communication API

Table 1. Cross-table of assumptions and achieved coercion resistance properties

	Estonia	NV-Civitas	KTV-Helios	BeleniosRF	Selene	Eos	Selections
Special client hardware	●[1]	●	●	○	○	●	○
Anonymous channels	○	●	●	○	●	●	●
PKI / key distribution	●	●[2]	●	●	●[2]	●[2]	○
Subliminal password/PIN hinting	○	●	○	○	○	●	●
Casting a re-vote	●	●	○	●	○[3]	●	●
Non-trivial registration	○	◐[4]	○	○	○	○	●
Receipt-freeness	○	●	●	●	◐[5]	●	◐[6]
Over-the-shoulder coercion resistance	●	●	◐[7]	○	◐[8]	●	●
Resistance to forced abstention	◐[9]	●	◐[10]	○	◐[11]	●	◐[12]
Resistance to casting an invalid vote	◐[9]	●	◐[13]	◐[14]	◐[15]	◐[16]	◐[17]
Resistance to simulation attack	◐[18]	●	◐[19]	○	○[20]	◐[21]	●[22]

● = is assumed / holds   ○ = is not assumed / does not hold   ◐ = may hold
◐ = depends on the implementation

---

[1] Smart card based ID-cards are mandatory in Estonia and widely in use.

[2] PKI is not explicitly mentioned, but its functionality is implicitly described.

[3] Whether re-voting is allowed in Selene depends on the used policy [31].

[4] Information about the registration process of NV-Civitas can be found in [28].

[5] Selene's receipt-freeness depends on the anonymous channel, see Section 3.4.

[6] Whether Selections is receipt free depends on how the re-randomisation randomness is handled during registration. For more information, see Section 3.6.

[7] The property depends on how the coercer prevents re-voting, see Section 4.3.

[8] The property depends on the re-voting policy in the implementation of Selene [31].

[9] The attack can be implemented by an insider, see Section 4.1.

[10] KTV-Helios is susceptible to forced abstention only in the case of an active attacker.

[11] For information about the implementation of Selene, see Section 4.4.

[12] It is not clear whether Selections is resistant to forced abstention, see Section 4.6.

[13] In KTV-Helios invalid votes can be cast, but they will be removed by plaintext equality tests before votes are published in the bulletin board.

[14] See Section 4.3 for information about the coercion properties of BeleniosRF.

[15] Vote casting procedure is not specified in Selene, see Section 4.4 for more details.

[16] Whether it is possible to cast an invalid vote depends on the version of Eos. More information can be found from Section 4.5.

[17] It is not specified how vote is encoded and how votes are tallied in Selections [6].

[18] The coercer might be able to get physical access to the smart card. However, it is possible to re-vote as described in Section 4.1.

[19] The coercer might be able to get physical access to the smart card. However, the voter may be able to re-vote to cancel the coerced vote as described in Section 4.3.

[20] It is not specified how keys are managed in Selene [31]. In case Selene is used as an add-on, then key management may be specified by the underlying voting protocol.

[21] The possibility of casting a valid vote with the voter's HSM depends on the configuration of the HSM. For more information, see Section 4.5.

[22] If the registration process and thus the credentials are remotely monitored then the voter has the option to revoke the registration and vote in person. For more information, see Section 4.6.

is public. Now, if a voter would be able to cast such an invalid vote then either the members of the election committee or the auditor who audits the election result might be able to read the invalid value. Thus, the coercer would have to cooperate with the election officials or the auditor to see the vote value.

In order to get a hold of the signing keys, the coercer would have to take the possession of all of the digital ID-s of the voter along with the corresponding PIN codes. Still, the voter could use a non-digital ID to cast a paper vote in the polling station that overwrites the e-vote. Thus, all non-digital ID-s would also have to be collected by a coercer in case the coercer would like the voter to abstain from participating in the elections. Such an attack could be applied on selected individuals, but this approach does scale.

4.2   NV-Civitas

NV-Civitas was the only one of the protocols that we analysed not susceptible to the three aforementioned coercion attacks. Forced abstention is impossible as the ballots are not signed and are delivered over an anonymous channel. Invalid ballots are either rejected by the smart card or by the voting system after checking the proof of vote well-formedness [28]. It is also impossible to force the voter to surrender the credentials as the voter can give the coercer the smart card with a fake PIN, which would create a ballot with invalid credentials.

4.3   Helios Family

KTV-Helios. While it is possible to cast invalid ballots in KTV-Helios, they do not end up on the bulletin board. Invalid ballots are removed before tallying with the help of plaintext equality tests. Thus, invalid votes are not decrypted.

The authors state that casting an invalid vote can cause the voter to abstain from the elections. The attack would always work in an active scenario where the attacker waits until the end of the voting period to force the voter to cast an invalid vote. In this case the invalid vote would be discarded before the tally and the voter would not have enough time to re-vote. However, if the value of the invalid vote would be known to the voter and there would be time to re-vote, the voter may be able to cancel the previous vote.

As the signing keys are stored on smart cards, it is in principle possible to force the voters to give up the cards, but such an attack would not scale well.

BeleniosRF. BeleniosRF uses a fixed message space for encoding the vote and tallying is done homomorphically. Thus, the possibility of casting an invalid vote depends on the implementation. In case the message space is not used up to encode the candidates, it might be possible to cast an invalid vote that would be published.

The other two coercion attacks could be applied in the case of BeleniosRF. It is possible to force the voter to abstain from voting as there is public proof of participation in the voting event. The signature of the randomised public ballot can be verified by the voter. In case the voter's public key is accessible to the coercer, the latter is able to verify all the ballots on the bulletin board. Also, the voter ID is verified before a ballot is accepted and re-randomised by the bulletin board. Thus, the election officials could coerce voters to abstain.

A coercer might also be able to force the voter to surrender her secret key as no special hardware is used for storing the secret key. However, the voter is only able to give one vote, so the coercer would have to get access to the signing key before the voter casts her vote.

4.4   Selene

Whether Selene is safe from forced abstention attack depends on the implementation of the protocol. The basic scheme is vulnerable as the ballots signed by the voters are published on the bulletin board. However, the optional enhancement of using pseudonymous credentials enables giving signatures without revealing the identity of the voter. Thus, the extended scheme is resistant to forced abstention attack if the coercer can not access the voter's pseudonymous credentials.

Similarly, the ability to cast an invalid vote depends on the implementation of the vote casting procedure and is not fixed on the protocol level. Selene can be used as an add-on on top of another voting system, which may remove invalid votes. E.g., Selene combined with JCJ is resistant to casting an invalid vote [12].

Still, Selene is susceptible to forced surrender of credentials as no hardware token is proposed for storing the secret key. Also, re-voting policy is not fully specified, thus it is not clear if voter's initial choice could be overwritten.

4.5   Eos

Eos is resistant to the forced abstention attack. It uses ring signatures to hide voter identities from the election officials. Also, an anonymous channel is used to cast the vote. Thus, it won't be possible to detect if a specific voter has voted.

The authors of Eos acknowledge that in the basic version of the protocol a coercer could force a voter to cast an invalid vote [29]. As a solution, they propose using a disjunctive zero-knowledge proof protocol, such that the voter could prove that her vote is in the set of valid votes. In that case, invalid votes could be removed before they are tallied and published.

It would be difficult to force a voter to surrender the credentials as that would require getting physical access to the voter HSM. However, the possibility can not be excluded as it is not clear if the correct PIN code could be extracted from the voter or HSM. It might be possible to try out all PIN code combinations in order to give a valid vote. It is also not specified in [29] if the HSM would allow to change the valid PIN codes. A successful change of the PIN would probably reveal the real PIN code. If changing PIN codes is not possible, then the usability aspect of the HSM would come under question. Even if the coercer could use the HSM, the attack would not scale well.

4.6   Selections

It is not clear whether Selections is resistant to the forced abstention attack. While the votes are cast over an anonymous channel and the passwords are re-randomised, there are some questions that can not be answered based on the protocol description. First, the protocol allows to revoke voter registration before pre-tallying, but it is not specified how it could be implemented. The authors of Selections also state that the revocation process might not be covered by coercion resistance. Second, during the registration, the randomised encryption of the password is posted to the roster along with the VoterID. However, it is not stated what the VoterID is or how it is assigned to the voters. Thus, the coercer might be able to use the VoterID to check if the coerced voter registered to use Selections. Third, it is assumed that during the registration process, the voter does not copy or remember the randomisation of the selected password. However, modern technology makes it quite easy to copy and broadcast information. Rewinding some of the registration steps would not help in case the coercer forces the voter to live broadcast the process.

The protocol does not specify the way how the vote is represented or how the votes are tallied. Thus, the possibility of casting an invalid vote depends on the specific implementation of the protocol.

If the coercer would like to get access to the valid credentials, the voter would have to record or broadcast the registration process. However, in that case the voter could revoke the registration before pre-tallying and thus invalidate the credentials given to the coercer together with the vote. After revoking, the voter could go to the polling station to vote in person.

5   Conclusions and Further Work

Developing a voting protocol to meet the requirements of a given jurisdiction is a complex task. On one hand, we would like the protocol to be secure against all critical attacks, but this security comes with a price of increased implementation complexity and technical assumptions that need to be satisfied.

This paper focused on coercion-resistance properties of various voting protocols proposed in academic literature from the practical system developer viewpoint. As academic proposals are not required to include real-life deployments, it is very easy to leave some of the implementation details out of consideration. Unfortunately, there are many devils hidden in these details.

During our research we identified six main (groups of) popular technical assumptions. Some of them (like existence of PKI or ability to cast a re-vote) indeed have readily accessible practical instantiations. At the same time, the requirements to set up anonymous channels or distribute special-purpose client hardware are easy to write down on paper, but quite tricky to implement.

Subliminal hinting using fake credentials is one of the oldest methods to achieve provable coercion-resistance properties, but a recent usability study by Neto et al. [26] found that more than 90% of the test participants did not understand this functionality. This questions the whole idea of using fake credentials.

In general, there is a lack of usability studies that focus on the coercion-resistance aspects of voting protocols. We see this as an important open question that requires further research.

Another general shortcoming of the current proposals is under-specification. On several occasions, it was impossible to determine susceptibility to certain attacks as this would have depended on specific implementation aspects. Sure, a 16-page academic paper can not fit all the details, but we encourage future scholars to accompany their proposals with deployed implementations. This would help identifying potential problems in an earlier stage of academic discussion.

Acknowledgments. The research leading to these results has received funding from the Estonian Research Council under Institutional Research Grant IUT27-1 and the European Regional Development Fund through the Estonian Centre of Excellence in ICT Research (EXCITE) and the grant number EU48684.

References

1. Adida, B.: Helios: Web-based open-audit voting. In: Proceedings of the 17th USENIX Security Symposium, pp. 335–348. USENIX Association (2008)
2. Araújo, R., Ben Rajeb, N., Robbana, R., Traoré, J., Youssfi, S.: Towards practical and secure coercion-resistant electronic elections. In: Heng, S.-H., Wright, R.N., Goi, B.-M. (eds.) CANS 2010. LNCS, vol. 6467, pp. 278–297. Springer, Heidelberg (2010). https://doi.org/10.1007/978-3-642-17619-7_20
3. Benaloh, J.: Rethinking voter coercion: the realities imposed by technology. USENIX J. Elect. Technol. Syst. (JETS) **1**, 82–87 (2013)
4. Chaidos, P., Cortier, V., Fuchsbauer, G., Galindo, D.: BeleniosRF: a non-interactive receipt-free electronic voting scheme. In: Proceedings of 2016 ACM CCS, pp. 1614–1625. ACM, New York (2016)
5. Clark, J., Hengartner, U.: Panic passwords: authenticating under duress. In: HotSec 2008, Proceedings. USENIX Association (2008). http://www.usenix.org/events/hotsec08/tech/full_papers/clark/clark.pdf
6. Clark, J., Hengartner, U.: Selections: internet voting with over-the-shoulder coercion-resistance. In: Danezis, G. (ed.) FC 2011. LNCS, vol. 7035, pp. 47–61. Springer, Heidelberg (2012). https://doi.org/10.1007/978-3-642-27576-0_4
7. Clark, J., Hengartner, U.: Selections: Internet voting with over-the-shoulder coercion-resistance. Cryptology ePrint Archive, Report 2011/166 (2011). https://eprint.iacr.org/2011/166
8. Clarkson, M.R., Chong, S., Myers, A.C.: Civitas: toward a secure voting system. In: 2008 IEEE Symposium on Security and Privacy (S&P 2008), pp. 354–368. IEEE Computer Society (2008)
9. Distler, V., Zollinger, M.L., Lallemand, C., Roenne, P.B., Ryan, P.Y.A., Koenig, V.: Security - visible, yet unseen? In: CHI 2019, pp. 605:1–605:13. ACM, New York (2019)
10. Gerck, E., Neff, C.A., Rivest, R.L., Rubin, A.D., Yung, M.: The business of electronic voting. In: Syverson, P. (ed.) FC 2001. LNCS, vol. 2339, pp. 243–268. Springer, Heidelberg (2002). https://doi.org/10.1007/3-540-46088-8_21
11. Hoffman, L.J., Cranor, L.F.: Internet voting for public officials: introduction. Commun. ACM **44**(1), 69–71 (2001)
12. Iovino, V., Rial, A., Rønne, P.B., Ryan, P.Y.A.: Using selene to verify your vote in JCJ. In: Brenner, M., et al. (eds.) FC 2017. LNCS, vol. 10323, pp. 385–403. Springer, Cham (2017). https://doi.org/10.1007/978-3-319-70278-0_24

13. Jefferson, D.R., Rubin, A.D., Simons, B., Wagner, D.A.: Analyzing internet voting security. Commun. ACM **47**(10), 59–64 (2004)
14. Joaquim, R., Ribeiro, C., Ferreira, P.: Improving remote voting security with code-voting. In: Chaum, D., et al. (eds.) Towards Trustworthy Elections. LNCS, vol. 6000, pp. 310–329. Springer, Heidelberg (2010). https://doi.org/10.1007/978-3-642-12980-3_19
15. Juels, A., Catalano, D., Jakobsson, M.: Coercion-Resistant Electronic Elections. Cryptology ePrint Archive, Report 2002/165 (2002). https://eprint.iacr.org/2002/165
16. Juels, A., Catalano, D., Jakobsson, M.: Coercion-resistant electronic elections. In: Proceedings of WPES 2005, pp. 61–70. ACM (2005)
17. Krips, K., Willemson, J., Värv, S.: Implementing an audio side channel for paper voting. In: Krimmer, R., et al. (eds.) E-Vote-ID 2018. LNCS, vol. 11143, pp. 132–145. Springer, Cham (2018). https://doi.org/10.1007/978-3-030-00419-4_9
18. Krips, K., Willemson, J., Värv, S.: Is your vote overheard? a new scalable side-channel attack against paper voting. In: Proceedings of Euro S&P 2019, pp. 621–634. IEEE (2019)
19. Kulyk, O.: Extending the Helios Internet Voting Scheme Towards New Election Settings. Ph.D. thesis, Technische Universität Darmstadt (2017)
20. Kulyk, O., Teague, V., Volkamer, M.: Extending helios towards private eligibility verifiability. In: Haenni, R., Koenig, R.E., Wikström, D. (eds.) VoteID 2015. LNCS, vol. 9269, pp. 57–73. Springer, Cham (2015). https://doi.org/10.1007/978-3-319-22270-7_4
21. Locher, P., Haenni, R.: Receipt-free remote electronic elections with everlasting privacy. Ann. Telecommun. **71**(7), 323–336 (2016)
22. Madise, Ü., Martens, T.: E-voting in Estonia 2005. The first Practice of Country-wide binding Internet Voting in the World. In: Krimmer, R. (ed.) Electronic Voting 2006. LNI, vol. 86, pp. 15–26. GI (2006)
23. Madise, Ü., Vinkel, P.: Internet voting in Estonia: from constitutional debate to evaluation of experience over six elections. In: Kerikmäe, T. (ed.) Regulating eTechnologies in the European Union, pp. 53–72. Springer, Cham (2014). https://doi.org/10.1007/978-3-319-08117-5_4
24. Mitrou, L., Gritzalis, D., Katsikas, S.: Revisiting legal and regulatory requirements for secure E-voting. In: Ghonaimy, M.A., El-Hadidi, M.T., Aslan, H.K. (eds.) Security in the Information Society. IFIPAICT, vol. 86, pp. 469–480. Springer, Boston, MA (2002). https://doi.org/10.1007/978-0-387-35586-3_37
25. Mohen, J., Glidden, J.: The case for internet voting. Commun. ACM **44**(1), 72–85 (2001)
26. Neto, A.S., Leite, M., Araújo, R., Mota, M.P., Neto, N.C.S., Traoré, J.: Usability considerations for coercion-resistant election systems. In: Proceedings of the 17th Brazilian Symposium on Human Factors in Computing Systems, pp. 40:1–40:10 (2018). IHC 2018
27. Neumann, S., Feier, C., Volkamer, M., Koenig, R.: Towards A Practical JCJ/Civitas Implementation. Cryptology ePrint Archive, Report 2013/464 (2013). https://eprint.iacr.org/2013/464
28. Neumann, S., Volkamer, M.: Civitas and the real world: problems and solutions from a practical point of view. In: ARES 2012, pp. 180–185. IEEE (2012)
29. Patachi, Ş., Schürmann, C.: Eos a universal verifiable and coercion resistant voting protocol. In: Krimmer, R., Volkamer, M., Braun Binder, N., Kersting, N., Pereira, O., Schürmann, C. (eds.) E-Vote-ID 2017. LNCS, vol. 10615, pp. 210–227. Springer, Cham (2017). https://doi.org/10.1007/978-3-319-68687-5_13

30. Richter, T., Escher, S., Schönfeld, D., Strufe, T.: Forensic analysis and anonymisation of printed documents. In: Proceedings of IH&MMSec 2018, pp. 127–138. ACM, New York (2018)
31. Ryan, P.Y.A., Rønne, P.B., Iovino, V.: Selene: voting with transparent verifiability and coercion-mitigation. In: Clark, J., Meiklejohn, S., Ryan, P.Y.A., Wallach, D., Brenner, M., Rohloff, K. (eds.) FC 2016. LNCS, vol. 9604, pp. 176–192. Springer, Heidelberg (2016). https://doi.org/10.1007/978-3-662-53357-4_12
32. Willemson, J.: Bits or paper: which should get to carry your vote? J. Inf. Secur. Appl. **38**, 124–131 (2018)

Author Index

Printed in the United States
By Bookmasters